Retired investment banker Geoff himself using his JSSL Russian forty years later as *The Private Life of Kim Pl y* and *Kitty Ha With Seventeen Names*. He is an Honorary Fe 's College, Oxford, and lives in Bermuda.

Harold Shukman retired recently as university lecturer in Modern Russian History at Oxford and is an Emeritus Fellow of St Antony's College, where he was for a number of years Director of the Russian and East European Centre. His books include studies of the Russian revolution, biographies of Lenin, Stalin and Rasputin, translations of the plays of Evgeny Shvarts and Isaac Babel and novels by Kataev and Rybakov, and the works of Dmitri Volkogonov. He edited *Agents for Change: Intelligence Services in the 21st Century,* and *The Winter War (1939-1940)*.

SECRET CLASSROOMS

A Memoir of the Cold War

Geoffrey Elliott and Harold Shukman

With an Introduction by D. M. Thomas

ST ERMIN'S
PRESS

A *St Ermin's Press* Book

First published in Great Britain in 2002
by St Ermin's Press
In association with Little, Brown

Revised paperback edition first published in 2003

A CIP catalogue record for this book
is available from the British Library.

ISBN 1 903608 13 9

Typeset in Imprint by M Rules
Printed and bound in Great Britain by
Clays Ltd, St Ives plc

. . . Rukoi pristrastnoi
Primi sobran'ye pyostrykh glav . . .
Uma kholodnykh nablyudenii
I serdtsa gorestnykh zamet.

('A showy compilation, maybe,
but look kindly on it as you read.
If nostalgia adds a sad perspective,
Cool reason makes us quite objective.')

Alexander Pushkin,
Dedication to *Evgeny Onegin*

Translated by Geoffrey Elliott

Contents

List of Illustrations

Watercolours by Patrick Procktor
Late for School, a *kursant* scurries across Russell Square 41
The longueurs of a Bodmin summer afternoon 72
Seemly Dancing, at Queensgate Terrace 157

Naky Doniach, the MOD Inspector of JSSL (*Iona Doniach*).
Dame Elizabeth Hill, 'Liza', Professor of Slavonic Studies and Director of the Russian Course at Cambridge, in 1956 (*Jean Stafford-Smith*).
George Bolsover, Director of the School of Slavonic and East European Studies (SSEES).
Ronald Hingley, the first Course Administrator in London (*Ronald Hingley*).
Staff at Crail, 1957 (*Brian Hawkins*).
Bodmin in the early 1950s (*Cornish Studies Library*).
Outdoor lesson with Vladimir Koshevnikoff, Bodmin 1955 (*Tony Divett*).
Patrick Procktor chats with crew members of the Soviet cruiser *Ordzhonikidze*, Portsmouth 1956 (*Patrick Procktor*).

Secret Classrooms

Midshipmen at Bodmin, September 1954 (*Malcolm Brown*).

Choir practice at Bodmin, 1953 (*Cornish Studies Library*).

Card-playing in Russian, Bodmin 1953 (*Cornish Studies Library*).

Crail Harbour, 1947 (*photograph courtesy of St Andrews University Library*).

The last real soldiers leave Crail for Korea, July 1952 (*photograph courtesy of St Andrews University Library*).

Geoffrey Elliott on a recent visit to Crail (*Geoffrey Elliott*).

Mrs Chernysheva (*by permission of the Syndics of Cambridge University Library*).

Liza Hill, George Trapp, Mrs Hackel and Mr Plyushkoff (*by permission of the Syndics of Cambridge University Library*).

Outdoor lesson with Marina Fennell, Cambridge 1952 (*Alan Pattillo*).

Weekly test at Cambridge, 1954 (*Tony Divett*).

'Morning parade' – waiting for the bus at Newmarket, 1954 (*Mike Frewin*).

Cartoon of Dmitri Makaroff (*Samovar*).

Alan Bennett and Michael Frayn, summer 1953 (*Gollancz/Humphrey Carpenter,* That Was Satire That Was).

Finale of *The Tenebrae of St Petroc*, Bodmin 1955 (*Patrick Procktor*).

Curtain call for *The Cherry Orchard*, Cambridge 1952 (*Keith Argent*).

Dennis Potter at Bodmin, 1953 (*Faber and Faber/Humphrey Carpenter,* Dennis Potter).

D. M. Thomas (*by permission of the Syndics of Cambridge University Library*).

Peter Woodthorpe as Boris Godunov, Bodmin 1953 (*Cornish Studies Library*).

A working day in Russell Square, 1951 (*John Roberts*).

Queensgate Terrace, in its earlier days as the South Kensington Hotel (*Tony Blee*).

'Bye 'Bye Baby: Ben Chaplin and other radio-monitors in Jack Rosenthal's TV film (*Channel 4*).

Introduction

Looking back at my childhood now, it seems utterly fated that I should have learned Russian and thereby fallen in love with all things Russian. Why otherwise should my first memory of print and pictures be of a feature on the Russo-Finnish War, in *Picture Post* magazine, when I was barely five? The photo of ghostly white-coated soldiers moving through a snowy birch forest stirred me mysteriously, as I sat in a small working-class Cornish bungalow. Vaguely I gathered that the Red Army were the enemy. But only a year later, they were our brave allies; which suited my father much better because, as a socialist, he admired what he knew of the Soviet system, though he had also spent ten years in California and loved American democracy from first-hand knowledge. Happily, in tune with my father, I followed the advances of Zhukov or Patton, pincering the Nazis, in *News Chronicle* maps. My father didn't have much time for the class-ridden English.

He and I together listened approvingly to Sir Stafford Cripps giving a radio talk about the Soviet Union. Cripps had said to his escort, 'These people look as if they own the streets!', and his escort had replied, 'They do!' We became, for two years, emigrants to Australia; and there, while plastering with a White Russian immigrant labourer, my father heard a very different reality about the Soviet Union. For me too, a different Russia was entering my life – a few haunting bars of Rachmaninov, played every night on a 'Popular Classics' programme.

There were, then, these seemingly fateful early chords, many of them inevitable for a child of the Second World War. They would have lost their special significance in my memory but for an apparent misfortune. My family returning to England when I was sixteen in 1951, I won a place to read English at Oxford, but only *after* two years of National Service.

And so it was that I found myself, one bleak November day, on the windswept parade-ground of the Joint Services School of Linguists, in Bodmin, Cornwall. Still dazed from having escaped half way through the horrors of Basic Training, I was vaguely aware that we were assembled in three distinct groups. When we were summoned to 'Get on parade!', we soldiers advanced with exaggerated arm-swings and boot-thumps; the airmen moved with a nonchalant, easy superiority, as if they were Battle of Britain heroes; and the sailors . . . the sailors trotted a few yards in a rollicking, self-parodying way.

Geoffrey Elliott and Harold Shukman, authors of this history of JSSL, vividly depict the narrowness of our world. 'Shirted by Viyella and Aertex', we were youths 'whose trouser belts had snake-shaped buckles, whose food and sweets had for many years been officially rationed, who collected bus and railway engine numbers with a zeal bordering on the manic . . .' If our parents holidayed at all, it was in Paignton or Margate, 'candyfloss "Kiss Me Quick" resorts . . . Over-indulgence in Guinness, Babycham or Merrydown Cider at 3/6d a bottle presented the biggest risk of substance abuse.'

I remember that first parade because the Regimental Sergeant Major – fearsome like all his kind – bawled me out for some slovenliness and, when I gave my name as 'Thomas', bawled even louder: 'Thomas! I've heard of you! I'm going to be watching you!' I knew I was no soldier, but the thought that I was already *known* as the worst soldier among these hundred or two mostly bespectacled and nerdish lads was pretty terrifying.

I began my Russian course with that ignominy; and ended it with equal ignominy when, through a crass error of vocabulary, I threatened a supposed prisoner of war with castration. His howl of joyous derision echoed around the whole camp. Small wonder I was finally graded 'suitable for low-level interrogation after further training'. I suspect even that was over-generous, and I thank God I was never in a position where I'd have to ask some quaking Red Army private his name, rank and number.

We learn here that the Prime Minister himself, no later than 1950 – so presumably Clement Attlee – had ordered the creation of a school for Russian linguists. The Cold War was under way, and might easily soon turn into a hot war. Too few people could speak Russian. To the immense credit of all involved, the school was created swiftly, was organised intelligently, and staffed by teachers, both Russian and English, who were skilful and enthusiastic. In the ten years of its existence, 5,000 young men with competence in Russian were trained. And it is rare to find a school – especially run with military discipline and intensity – whose Old Boys speak of it with almost universal respect and affection. For many, including the dramatists Alan Bennett and Michael Frayn, the years at this school were indeed some of the best years of their lives. And that is because JSSL achieved far more that what it intended to achieve. It trained potential interpreters and translators – but it also changed people's lives.

I described to the authors one proud moment I experienced. We had to recite a Russian poem. I think I chose a Pushkin, but it might have been Lermontov. Anyway, one of our tutors, Vera Grech, a former actress with Stanislavsky's Art Theatre, had tears in her eyes, and was heard to say that I must have Russian parents. That was a compliment to me – I had a feeling for poetry and also had fairly good Russian pronunciation – but it was much more a compliment to our teachers, Vera Grech included, because they were able to communicate to us their love of Russia and her language. John Drummond, later Director of the Edinburgh Festival and Promenade Concerts, wrote of his time at JSSL: 'I find it difficult even today not to feel deep inside that I am partly Russian . . . As baptisms go it was total immersion.'

Another term for it might be brainwashing, but our brains were being washed not with ideology – there was never any crude anti-Soviet propaganda, which is remarkable – but with the complex beauty of the Russian language. I wasn't aware of it at the time; my attitude was totally pragmatic; I would have opted out of National Service if I could, it was a great nuisance; but since I couldn't, this was as congenial a way of spending it as I could possibly hope for. Especially as, almost uniquely, I was near home and could have some home comforts almost every weekend. And if I worked hard, I might be among those selected to go to a *quasi*-university course at Cambridge.

This I managed to achieve. In Cambridge, we were addressed by the energetic and charismatic director, Elizabeth Hill, who told us we must *rabotat', rabotat', rabotat'* – work, work, work – and if we did we would fall in love with ourselves. And if we didn't – we would find ourselves off the course. By diligently learning word-lists, I clung on week by week. I fell in love, not with myself, and not with Russian, but with the music of Sibelius; for another invaluable aspect of the Russian Course for me was that my roommates, from much more cultured backgrounds, were already connoisseurs of classical music. We bought LPs, just invented then, and wildly conducted symphony after symphony in our room. There was never any class distinction; we seem to have been a remarkably democratic bunch. There were, it is true, one or two who stood out through intellectual distinction. On my Course the obvious leader – older, sophisticated, handsome, already with a Ph.D – a kind of admired Steerforth – was one A. K. Thorlby, later a distinguished academic. One felt he was on easy terms with Liza Hill and other tutors, and I envied him his air of insouciant superiority.

It was not until I had finished National Service and was well under way towards an English degree at Oxford that the full force of Russian struck me. *Doctor Zhivago* had just sensationally appeared in the West. It was my summer vacation; I had a job in my local library. I became so immersed in the wonderful novel that I would read it during my two-mile country walk to work. The weather was balmy; the book was stirring my own juvenile creative juices. I was walking to a library, and reading about Yury Zhivago entering a library and seeing his lost love, Lara, there. It seemed a defining moment. I was reading *Zhivago* in English – I could not have fully understood the Russian text – yet I felt I was reading a ghostly Russian underneath the English, and that I understood the Russian soul. And that the Russian language was my Lara – mysterious, often incomprehensible, maddening, yet forever loved.

As *Secret Classrooms* makes abundantly clear, there were hundreds if not thousands of young men whose lives were similarly enriched, even transformed, by that Russian Course. The numbers applying to the Slavonic departments in universities suddenly multiplied. The JSSL was created for a practical military purpose, to help defend against a Soviet attack that seemed then all too likely. It succeeded in that aim; but ultimately of far greater significance was that it created a generation of young and influential Britons who had generous, respectful and affectionate feelings for Russia – the eternal Russia of Tolstoy, Pushkin and Pasternak.

After reading *Secret Classrooms*, I am left with the regret that I did not work harder and learn more. I would like to do it all again!

D. M. Thomas

Prologue

All of this is in the 1950s.

On an asphalt parade-ground a couple of hundred young men from the three Armed Services, an unusually large number of them bespectacled, are laughing and chatting despite the freezing drizzle as they drift into a semblance of order. Those in Army khaki and RAF blue serge are loosely wrapped in 'capes', waterproof ponchos of a First World War cut. Nothing as utilitarian as capes for the Navy Coders Special, however. They are kitted out in dark-blue double-breasted raincoats which tradition mandates are to be called 'Burberries' – never, ever, 'macs'.

The sense of impending chaos is not helped when the Navy group take it into their heads to march forwards swinging their left arms in time with their left legs, a co-ordinated gawkiness that adds to the sense that this is a shot from 'Monty Python's' 'The Men of the 20th Armoured Division Perform Close Order Swanning About' and compounds the frenzy of the visibly despairing NCOs. Even without minor rebellions of this kind, the parades are always a touch confused since each Service does very much its own thing. The Army and the RAF are trained to

raise their booted feet knee high and then stamp them energeti-
cally down on the asphalt, hence the term 'square bashing', but
the Navy, most of whose commands seem to outsiders to be the
single word 'Ho' uttered with different inflections, is sensibly content to let its Coders slide their comfortably shod feet gently
together.

To make the picture even untidier, within the Army contingent
the men come from many different (and nearly all now long forgotten) regiments and corps, and so have shoulder flashes in a
variety of colours and styles, different cap badges, and berets
ranging from blue through purple to black. These do nothing to
conceal a tendency to hair of a length that on a more military
parade-ground would have led the Sergeant Major to bawl from
an inch behind the hapless soldier's ear: 'Am I hurting you,
sonny?' 'No, Sarn't Major.' 'Well, I bleeding well should be, I'm
standing on your hair . . . take this man's name, Corporal . . .'
One who has found himself conscripted by some quirk of a clerk's
pen into the Military Police attracts unenviable attention from
the NCOs in his red-covered peaked cap, while a myopic
Wykehamist cruelly misplaced in The Rifle Brigade, who by tradition march at a much brisker pace than lesser units, constantly
trips over himself adjusting to the slower tempo.

When things have settled down as much as they are going to,
the Camp Adjutant of the Joint Services School for Linguists
announces plaintively, 'Now some of you may think this is funny,
but I don't. Someone has stolen a hut.'

In a classroom in a Victorian house near Cambridge Station, some
months later, a selection of the young men we saw on the parade-
ground are now behind battered school desks, squirming in
scratchy Service-issue tweed jackets and grey flannels which
might have been clandestinely tailored for the Escape Committee
at Colditz. Under the direction of a courtly old gentleman with a
heavy white moustache and gold-rimmed glasses they are taking
turns to read aloud in Russian passages from *Crime and
Punishment* and translate them extempore into English. The door

opens and frames a short woman dressed in a black suit, an academic gown draped neatly around her shoulders, her dark hair in a severe bun. She exudes energy – an attribute she claims comes from having had a Caucasian wet-nurse – and gazes sharply and possessively around the room. Everything that follows is in Russian. The class stands, bids her 'Good Morning' in chorus, is told to sit down, and the newcomer – Professor Elizaveta Fyodorovna Hill – distributes a stack of essay manuscripts with a volley of critical comments. She unsettles the class (many of whom will distinguish themselves with far greater confidence in British public, academic and literary life in the years ahead) by staying on to ask them what they did at the weekend, what films they saw, punctuating the process with comments on everything from their pronunciation to they way they use the English '. . . Er . . .' to cover a pause rather than the Russian filler word '*znachit*'.

The large creaking lift at Gloucester Road Underground Station, in London, around 8.30 a.m.: a middle-aged man and a red-eyed woman are engaged in a bitter private quarrel. Around them, trying to avoid each others' eyes and not to laugh, are a group of young men much like those we glimpsed in Cambridge. Most are wearing the same sort of Ruritanian approximation of civilian clothes and, clutching their imitation leather attaché cases, they have slightly the air of young RAF officers furtively gathering at a Silesian railway station for the final lap of The Great Escape. The quarrel escalates. Accusations of infidelity, theft, and worse, zing to and fro. It is all conducted in Russian. When the lift stops, the wrangling pair disappear down the tiled corridor unaware that all those around them, the London University counterparts of the Cambridge group, understood every unhappy word.

A few months later, others who have graduated from that windswept parade-ground find themselves in a stuffy room in an anonymous building. Whether it is tucked away on an airfield or at the back of a military base in Germany, Cyprus, Hong Kong, or even middle England, the room is virtually the same. It is stuffy because it is manned twenty-four hours a day, because the windows are shuttered, because nearly everyone is smoking and because it is filled with the heat of electronic gear. There may be up to twenty intercept positions in the room, each with an Eddystone radio receiver, on top of which squats a large battleship-grey Ferrograph reel-to-reel recorder. A Formica desktop runs the length of the array.

An operator sits at each position. Some are idly spinning the receiver's dials looking for traffic; others with a 'carrier up' are crouched forward in concentration. Some may be breaking the rules by listening to jazz on 'The Voice of America', but most of them are scribbling on their multi-leaved logs staccato exchanges between Soviet tank commanders and infantry officers, aircraft and their ground controllers, ships and their bases, and submarines and their home ports.

Former Leading Coder (Special) Arnold Bell remembers an episode at Cuxhaven when someone came up with material nobody had heard before. 'The Regular Navy staff thought they had a coup, only to learn a few days later from GCHQ that they had no interest in the Swedish football results.'

1

Roots and Branches

A 'spy school', Stalin's ventriloquist's dummy Andrei Vyshinsky once alleged at the United Nations. 'Effectively a school for secret agents,' declared *The Times* fifty years later.

Though not quite that glamorous, The Joint Services School for Linguists, or 'JSSL', was a key Cold War initiative in which over 5,000 young men were semi-secretly pushed through intensive training in Russian. Its main purpose was to produce linguists to work in Britain's 'early warning' Signals Intelligence system, Sigint, and also via its university component to create a reserve of interpreters who could be called on by the Armed Forces and the intelligence services if real war came.

Ours is a story told from the memories and memoirs, some published, most private and generously contributed to this project, of a cross-section of its students, among them the two authors, as well as from teachers and public and private archives.

JSSL was a school unlike any other. It had no blazer-and-flannels traditions, no cloistered quads, no elm-fringed playing fields. In its nine-year life from 1951 to 1960 it operated from remote military installations and in special enclaves created at the

Universities of Cambridge and London. Its students were some of the brightest of their generation. They needed to be; in the words of one observer, 'no school or university either before or since has been so exacting on its pupils'. That is certainly true. All the more since unlike more conventional schools where a boy could make his mark by getting Colours for sporting achievements, chairing the Debating Society or becoming Captain of House or even the School for a combination of such splendid achievements plus all-round 'good chapmanship', the only thing that counted in the Darwinian world of JSSL was progress in the classroom as measured by the tests and examinations which came round with the inexorable regularity of Days of Obligation in a mediaeval monastery calendar and had some of the same consequences for failure.

What is also true is that because its pupils were bright and instinctively rebellious, and the authorities could not risk cramping their studies with too much discipline, the atmosphere at JSSL and especially its Cambridge arm was unlike any military institution either before or since. On any given day a supposedly serious parade and many hours of tough lessons and homework could be followed by rehearsals for exotic Russian theatricals and liturgical rituals, or barrack-room cabaret acts by young men who would later become famous performers, the rum flavour of the whole experience compounded by a troupe of émigré teachers, many of whom spoke little English, and a military staff many of whom were straight out of 'Dad's Army'.

JSSL's pupils went on to scale many commanding heights. Professors of Russian, Chinese, Philosophy, Psychology, Economics, German, History, Japanese Politics and Drama at leading universities, British ambassadors to Argentina, China, Italy, Libya and the former Yugoslavia, authors, a member of the Royal Academy, novelists, playwrights, poets, screenwriters, actors, leading members of the Bar, economists, Heads of Oxbridge colleges, public school housemasters, officials of the Royal Household, historians, rare book dealers, journalists, including several Moscow correspondents for Reuters, the BBC and Fleet

Street, churchmen – a bishop among them – diplomats, a Director of Public Prosecutions, Controller of Music at the BBC, the British Government's senior interpreter over many key Cold War and détente years, the current proprietor of the *New Statesman*, the Editor of *New Society*, an authority on mediaeval German manuscripts, officers in the Secret Intelligence Service (SIS), 'perhaps the best Rugby coach Wales ever had', the Coroner of Greater Manchester, the Governor of the Bank of England, a Discalced Carmelite Friar, a professional bridge player, and many officers, including a Director and Deputy Director of Government Communications Headquarters, which, as GCHQ, figures importantly in our story. But it is a measure of JSSL's diversity and the multiplicity of the talents that it fostered that many whose careers remained unsung went on to make important contributions in many areas of British public service and in the business world that might well not have been possible without the stimulus of this remarkable educational, social and organisational achievement.

Since so many young men passed through its guarded gates, its existence could not be kept a secret. But the scale of it, and especially its integral role in the Sigint structure, have hitherto been discreetly understated. Though a small number of men learned Chinese, Polish, Czech and later Hungarian for the same purpose, and there is some evidence that the hub of the Sigint network, GCHQ, trained Russian linguists for its own specialised analysis and code-breaking work, this narrative will concentrate on the Russian programme in its National Service context, of which both authors have personal experience, Harry Shukman on one of the earlier intakes, Geoffrey Elliott one of the last. Between them their experiences happen to cover all five JSSL establishments.

Parallels have been drawn between JSSL and the Middle East Centre for Arabic Studies, or MECAS, at Shemlan in the hills above Beirut. That too acquired unwarranted – and in its case actually dangerous – notoriety as a 'spy school', but the two institutions were significantly different.

JSSL was part of Britain's defensive response to the Cold War. It was run on behalf of the Armed Services by the RAF, and its students were young men from the Navy, Army and RAF, almost all of them conscripts, or 'National Servicemen'. Its sole aim in life was to produce Russian linguists.

In contrast, though its students included many serving officers, MECAS was an essentially civilian institution, operating under the wing and watchful eye of the Foreign Office. While it focused hard on language, using many of the same intensive techniques as JSSL, it also sought to inculcate a sense of regional history, politics and culture, in the wider context of readying its students to make important contributions to Britain's longer-term strategic, business and military interests in the Middle East; for many years British embassies in every country in the Middle East and North Africa were headed by a succession of 'Mecasians'.

However, the biggest difference was in scale. MECAS's Thirteenth Course in 1956/7 had forty-one pupils, while JSSL at the same point was training 550 translators, another forty-five men in the final stage of the Interpreters' Course, and 145 Reservists who had been called back for brief 'refresher' courses. Another hundred or so JSSL men were divided between the two Universities. When MECAS closed in 1978 after thirty-four years, some 1,100 students had passed through its various courses, perhaps one fifth of the number so successfully trained by JSSL over its much shorter lifetime.

JSSL has also been misleadingly compared to Bletchley Park, where so much intellectual firepower was harnessed in the Second World War to crack the German 'Enigma' traffic. But JSSL was not Ultra Mark 2. Despite its place in the Sigint structure it was a school, and a school with only one purpose: to provide 'total immersion' training in Russian. Bletchley Park by contrast was a massive code-breaking station, and though it operated under the teasing cover name of 'The Government Code and Cipher School', teaching was not in its mandate.

JSSL was not the first Service effort to develop Russian linguists. Someone must have taught Major Jarvis, a bright young officer who in 1854 purloined a copy of the Russian General Staff's map of the Crimea. The War Office balked at the expense of

14

having it translated, whereupon the Major seems to have taken a dictionary and managed enough translation and transliteration to be able to hand over an Anglicised version to Whitehall in what a future Commandant General of the Intelligence Corps later termed 'about the only good intelligence action in that mainly disastrous . . . campaign'. Thanks to the research of Harvey Pitcher (academic, author and Cambridge-trained interpreter), we can date what was almost certainly the first organised initiative to train Army and Navy officers all the way back to 1887 when a Captain Rason RN 'studied Russian in St Petersburg and passed his Interpretership Exam there, being one of the first to do so', according to Walter Philip, turn-of-the-century head of the Muir and Mirrielees department store in Moscow (which in its Soviet-era reincarnation became one of those gloomy emporia like the nearby GUM, where the perennial, almost total lack of merchandise for sale shocked even that ardent supporter of the Soviet system, Kim Philby). Rason, who Admiralty records show was actually the first naval Russian interpreter, listed 'languages' as his hobby, and set the tone for future generations of interpreters by having not just linguistic skills – he also spoke Arabic – but a broad range of outside interests, including bringing back to London from one of his later voyages 'the first live specimen of the small orang-utan' for which he was warmly commended by the Royal Society. And like later Regular Officers whose Services sometimes had difficulty finding postings that matched their language abilities, he ended his career as the first British Commissioner of the New Hebrides.

Judging from letters written by Philip to his wife Laura in London about the progress of two later officer students named Fitzwilliam and Carter, by 1907 the programme had shifted to Moscow, took almost a full year and involved 'a batch of officers', all no doubt destined to be players in the last phases of The Great Game of Russian–British imperial rivalry in Central Asia, and post-Revolutionary intervention in the north of Russia and the Caucasus. Fitzwilliam and Carter worked hard – and played hard too. '. . . poor Carter had a nasty gash over his right eye after striking the back of a chair while ragging with Fitzwilliam,' Philip wrote rather Pooterishly. In another distant foretaste of aspects of life at JSSL fifty years later, Carter seems to have been given to 'amateur theatricals with love scenes' and was even billed to appear at the 'English Church bazaar' as a ventriloquist. Both buckled down, however, and passed the Interpreters' Examination within five marks of each other, the pass mark in those days being 80 per cent, and they then would have collected a £200 bonus plus £42 to cover their travelling expenses home. There is no record of how well the programme worked overall though we do know that in the immediate pre-Revolutionary period the British embassy to Russia had only two officials who qualified for the £100 p.a. interpreters' allowance.

The most interesting glimpse of the next phase comes not from British files but from those of the KGB, and involves one of the central figures in our story, the redoubtable Professor (later Dame) Elizabeth Hill, ferociously Slavophile and Sovietophobic daughter of another once prosperous Scots-Russian merchant family in St Petersburg. We shall refer to her with affection and respect, as did all her JSSL students, though never to her face, as 'Liza'. Glen Dudbridge, who later became Professor of Chinese at Oxford, captures the essence of the woman he remembers from his time as a Cambridge RAF student: 'She was one of those super-energetic, positive and dynamic characters that one meets only once or twice in a lifetime.'

Liza's family business Whishaw-Hill & Co. had been trading coal for 200 years. Her Lancing-educated father had married into the Russian nobility, and by the time she was eight Liza (who was christened Bessie May but changed her name by deed poll in later life) was fluent in four languages: 'English and Russian which I spoke with my father and mother and French and German which the Governesses taught us.' Life was good until the Revolution gusted through the mahogany doors of the Hills' sprawling apartment and scored a neat red line across their bank accounts. Her brothers had already made their own lives in England, but Liza, her parents and her two sisters, Desinka (Daisy) and Mamie, started on a spiral that began in high-class London hotels, waiting in vain and in embarrassment for money to turn up, and spun them down via St John's Wood and Putney to two rooms and a gas-ring in Earl's Court. Patrick Hamilton's Hangover Square took over from Pushkin's Hermitage.

Her mother coped. Her father scratched a living winning shillings playing bridge and selling boxes of chocolate door-to-door. Liza's determination and her languages helped her battle her way into a teaching post at a girls' school in North Wales, and then up the splintery academic ladder through English social and sexist barriers to get her Ph.D in 1928. Along the way, she was a fellow student at King's College, London, of Joshua Cooper, who went on to play leading roles at GCCS and GCHQ and may well have been Liza's introduction to that less visible side of the Whitehall world.

A chance encounter at London University in the 1920s had brought her together with Doris Mudie, one of the last descendants of the family which, through its ownership of Mudie's Circulating Library, had helped shape nineteenth-century British reading tastes; Doris was to be her lifelong companion.

When they met, Doris was already spending her life and what was left of her money helping lame dogs over stiles and promoting good, often lost, causes; she had spent time in Russia after the Revolution running soup kitchens for waifs and strays. About all she had left was her large family house in London's Vincent Square, between Victoria Station and the Thames, which she invited Liza to share with the generous and almost certainly true invitation: 'Why don't you come and live with me there and do your studies. Don't worry, I'm not a lesbian.'

After a spell working as private tutors, Liza and Doris collaborated in translating Russian, German and French books and novels including a well-chosen and useful selection of Lenin's published letters, for which Liza was duly lambasted in the Soviet press, and writing under the pseudonym 'J. Penn' 'a book of comic tales' about the more bizarre habitués of the old-style British Museum Reading Room, illustrated by the cartoonist David Low.

In 1936 Liza muscled her way into the first Lectureship in Slavonic Studies in Cambridge, where she was soon joined by

Doris, now almost penniless and recovering from the first in a series of nervous breakdowns.

But the Cambridge segment of our story lies ahead. While still a lecturer at London University's School of Slavonic Studies (SSEES in its present-day expanded acronym) in the 1930s, Liza had been running one of the successors to that pre-Revolutionary Russian programme, in which Regular Army officers spent several months of intensive study first at King's College and later at SSEES followed by a four-month spell with an émigré family in Paris or one of the Baltic states designed to hone oral skills. Small scale though it was, this Army initiative came to the notice of the NKVD's hyperactive London *rezidentura* – already running the 'Cambridge Five' and other key 'assets' in 1935 – when the Soviet 'illegal' *rezident* in London, Alexander Orlov, was told by a university source codenamed, not very subtly, as PROFESSOR, that British SIS officers were also learning Russian at SSEES. Not only was Liza one of the principal instructors but she was a niece of General Miller, the Tsarist officer who had commanded the anti-Bolshevik White Army in northern Russia and now headed the staunchly anti-Soviet 'General Military Union' in Paris. Miller vanished in 1936 after being kidnapped by the NKVD in broad daylight on the steps of a Metro station.

As unearthed in the Moscow files by John Costello and Oleg Tsaryev, all this made the School a particularly tempting target of opportunity for Soviet intelligence – a target given to none other than the raffish Guy Burgess, then busy building his 'cover' as a BBC talks producer and anxious, as agents always are, to impress his Soviet controllers.

Burgess, codenamed MÄDCHEN in NKVD cable traffic (the use of the German word for 'Little Girl' was an attempt to suggest, in case the traffic was being intercepted and broken, that this might be a German operation), 'went to the Institute of Slavonic Studies [*sic*] asking them to recommend a teacher', Orlov cabled his masters at Moscow Centre. 'The University luckily sent him to Hill, who gave him one lesson privately. The next step will be for him to ask her to put him in a group or pair him with other pupils so that he may get a better ear for pronunciation and to make lessons livelier. Thus we count on approaching other pupils since MÄDCHEN knows how to make friends,' Orlov concluded, without evident irony.

Orlov's successor, Arnold Deutsch, reported that Burgess had described the School as having so many SIS officers among its students that it was 'a focal point of the local firm'. He also claimed that Burgess had got on good terms with Liza by suggesting she might be a candidate for one of his broadcasts, and that she 'probably had very good relations with the [SIS] people who work here'. If Moscow had any doubt about Liza's intelligence ties it would have vanished when Burgess told them that, in addition to the General Miller connection, one of her brothers was Brigadier George A. Hill, an intelligence veteran who had not only worked for SIS in Russia but who claimed in his memoirs, perhaps with some exaggeration, to have been a friend of Trotsky, a connection enough in itself to have had Stalin reaching for his blue pencil.

In fact Burgess had the wrong George Hill (Liza later asserted that the Brigadier was no more than a distant relation from a Baltic offshoot of the family, and that her brother was George E.). However, had the Russians checked, which they almost certainly did, they would have found enough 'form' among her real brothers to have added considerable fuel to their suspicions.

Eric Hill had been killed while serving in Russia in the aftermath of the First World War with the Poole Mission, which was charged with a mix of British interventionist, intelligence and imperial agendas in the turmoil that followed Russia's surrender at Brest Litovsk; in the same period George E. had been attached to the British forces supporting, vainly as it turned out, the White Armies of his uncle General Miller. After later service with the Indian Army, George became an infantry intelligence officer and was posted 'missing, believed killed' at Dunkirk.

Her third brother Alfred, whose Scottish roots on his father's side, as Liza remembered, had helped him gain a commission in The Black Watch, had been attached to the Bruce Lockhart

Mission to Russia, a group suspected by the new and nervous Soviet authorities as having the same mix of overt and covert interventionist agendas and an even more suspicious involvement, confusingly also involving George E. Hill, with the adventurer and spy Sydney Reilly. When the Soviets decided enough was enough, Alfred spent some time behind bars with Bruce Lockhart in the Lubyanka. According to Liza, Alfred was later attached to MI5 for a period and was in charge of the British interpreters' team at the post-Second World War Potsdam conference.

At all events, after his flashy start Burgess had been unable to make any headway in cultivating the alleged SIS officers at the School. Not surprising, since most of them, if they existed, were probably in those days brisk military types unlikely to take kindly to a garlic-gnawing Old Etonian who made little secret of the fact that his main extra-curricular activity was cruising public toilets with a well-thumbed copy of *Middlemarch* under his arm to while away the time between close encounters of an ancient kind.

As for his curricular activity, he evidently achieved very little. Even in his sad and vodka-sodden exile in Moscow in the early 1960s, Burgess seems not to have advanced his Russian beyond those early, minimal SSEES forays. Mark Frankland, by then Moscow correspondent of the *Observer* and himself a London University Interpreter from his Navy service, recalls that the defector's Russian was 'primitive and pidgin, so poor in fact that Burgess and his then live-in Russian boyfriend could not even have a satisfactory quarrel'.

Burgess's further claim that Liza herself had worked for SIS and might soon resume an active role by travelling to Moscow, and to that end was 'ingratiating herself with left-wing university students sympathetic to the Soviet Union', is unsubstantiated.

Burgess also told Moscow around the same time that the SSEES Director was a former MI6 officer who was planning to return to Moscow 'with the intention of renewing his work', while in rather odd contrast the Director's secretary 'was known to be a Communist'. Until 1939 the Director of SSEES was Liza's mentor at King's College, the late Sir Bernard Pares, a pioneer of

Russian Studies in the UK and a man who had spent much time in Russia before and after the Revolution, first as what seems to have been a set of unofficial eyes and ears for the Foreign Office, with contacts official diplomats could not reach, and later as a representative of the *Daily Telegraph*. There is no reason whatever to suggest that he was attached formally to SIS though something, presumably his movements in and around Russia, had earned Pares an entry in the Gestapo's '*Sonderfahndungsliste*' identifying the prominent UK personalities whom they planned to arrest following a German invasion of Britain.

Other pieces of the early Russian studies mosaic are a recollection by Liza later in life of running a Course for twenty Army officers, 'among them the [then] Duke of Wellington', in 1936 and a fragmentary reference to a 1939 'refresher course' of two weeks run by Liza for Army officers whose names had been pulled from the files as having trained as Russian interpreters at some point in the inter-war period, a series of Second World War Service courses at London and Cambridge in Japanese, Russian and other Slavonic languages and the Inter-Services Russian Course run by Liza, now at Cambridge, in 1945–6 with what the file notes as 'conspicuous success'. It had been set up under the auspices of the Inter-Services Language Committee chaired by an RAF Arabist, Basil Reay.

(Around this time she also had an unofficial enquiry from GCHQ asking if she could accommodate twenty American officers for advanced Russian training, their commanding general apparently being unhappy about whatever scheme the US Army was then operating in Europe. Characteristically she replied positively, but nothing seems to have come of this.)

Although the record is again not clear, by Liza's account the Cambridge Course began when she heard that a search was underway in Canada for Ukrainian émigrés who could serve as interpreters for the post-war British Control Commission in Germany. She promptly bustled round to the War Office asserting that she could train British officers who would be far more reliable than any émigrés. Twenty-six weeks of intensive tuition would take a student to the point of speaking slow but grammatical Russian with immediate recall of 400 words of vocabulary and another 4,000 in reserve via 'recognition or deductive value'.

The Course drew in a mix of commissioned and non-commissioned officers including a 'glum and bewildered' Guards Sergeant, who claimed that he was totally out of his depth since he had volunteered for a 'Rations Course'. Liza encouraged him to persevere and, according to her, he finished with flying colours.

Another account of this early Course describes Liza's students as being – unlike later Service intakes from JSSL – 'fully integrated into the life of the university'; they were housed in Colleges rather than, as later, a central Mess, wore gowns, and followed the Slavonic Studies Faculty curriculum. Its author is the traitor George Blake, who arrived at Downing College in late 1946, sent by the Secret Intelligence Service, not long after he had joined its permanent staff after earlier service in Holland and Germany.

Though they can hardly avoid the whiff of a self-serving attempt to justify why he did what he did, Blake's memoirs match those of many others in later generations in highlighting Liza's gift for inspiring all her students, 'myself included, with a love for all things Russian. I must stress here "Russian" and not "Soviet" for she had little time for the Soviet regime . . . I look back upon my time in Cambridge as one of the watersheds in my life. It opened up new horizons to me. I acquired a key to the rich storehouse of Russian literature. I began to get a better understanding of the Russian people and develop an interest and liking for their customs and traditions.'

Facts such as that in Soviet as in Tsarist times these traditions included a secret police of unsurpassed reach and power, the Siberian exile system, later brutally refined by Stalin into the Gulag, visceral anti-Semitism, and a cowed and impoverished population, are aspects of *la vie en Russe* on which Blake perhaps understandably does not dwell.

Blake claims to have finished the Course 'with top marks'. Regrettably the otherwise comprehensive Hill Archive at Cambridge has no record of his result; someone who worked with him in a later incarnation recalls Blake's Russian as being in fact 'about GCSE' level. Since the Second World War had put the Baltic states 'off limits', and government foreign exchange to fund stays in Paris was in short supply, Blake's variant of the usual follow-up spell with an émigré household saw him posted to a small village outside Dublin to lodge with a mushroom-farming Tsarist prince and his wife, daughter of the last Russian Viceroy of Poland, who 'tried against all odds to maintain an air of bygone splendour', though her sofas were vegetable crates covered with chintz.

By coincidence, towards the accelerated end of his career Blake was sent to MECAS; it was from Shemlan in the hills above Beirut that he was summoned home for interrogation and arrest.

Other alumni of that early Cambridge phase included Sir John Harvey Jones, later the dynamic Chairman of ICI, who had enlisted in the Navy at sixteen and was torpedoed twice during the Second World War. He was sent up to Cambridge in 1945 aged twenty-one, where he qualified as a German and Russian interpreter. In 1952 he was awarded the MBE for services to naval intelligence after a tour of duty commanding an E-boat engaged in what was blandly termed 'fishery protection duties in the Baltic'.

Another was the late Gervase Cowell MBE, who later joined SIS. He is deservedly noted in the history books for his role, supported by his wife Pamela, in running the British agent Oleg Penkovsky in Moscow in the exceptionally tricky last phase of the operation when the KGB were closing in. (One of Cowell's contemporaries on the Course, Roderick Chisholm, was his predecessor at the Moscow SIS Station. We can only speculate whether any sharp-eyed KGB counter-intelligence analyst would have spotted their two names juxtaposed in the cast list of a 1949 production of *Boris Godunov* at the ADC Theatre.) But as one of his many friends reminisces, 'Gervase, who was a fine artist and sculptor, would probably be just as happy to be remembered as the only SIS officer who had a set of verses in Japanese haiku format published in *The Jerusalem Post*.'

Those early students were drawn from all levels across the three Services in what seems to have been a rather unsystematic process, hence the bemused Guards Sergeant. For instance, in later years the much larger and more organised JSSL would ensure that all its university students would be of broadly equal rank as officer cadet or midshipman, whereas in the immediate post-war period expediency demanded less stress on rank and something closer to a meritocracy. There may have been less stress, but in the Services there was never total disregard; Paul Foote, who joined the course from the Army as an Other Rank in the period just before the Colleges began to be used as accommodation, remembers that officers messed comfortably at a nearby camp while he and others were billeted 'in the house of an old slattern (a struck-off nurse, it was reckoned)'.

But what was it that, so to speak, kick-started these smaller scale, 'preparatory school' efforts into what was to become the vast and efficient 'comprehensive' of JSSL? The answer was the Cold War.

2

A Negative Peace

The Second World War ended in a confusing mix of jubilation and new worries. Overnight Russia resigned from its often uncomfortable position as the West's wartime ally and went back to the more familiar adversarial role it had played for much of the nineteenth century and the 1920s and 1930s. The Iron Curtain rattled down. Germany was defeated and divided but half of Europe was dominated by a new and aggressive superpower that, as the years went by, seemed to be overtaking the West's space and building nuclear weapons and the bombers to deliver them. In Europe itself, the Soviet blockade of Berlin in the winter of 1948–9, their takeover of Czechoslovakia in 1948 and Hungary in 1949, the expulsion of the Chinese Nationalists to Taiwan and the proclamation of the People's Republic of China, the Sino–Soviet pact, the Korean War, the Soviet crushing of the popular uprisings in 1953 in East Germany and Hungary, and year after year of sabre-rattling over German reunification and rearmament and the status of Berlin, all ratcheted up the tension, the sense that a new and possibly terrible conflagration lurked ahead. In the wider world, almost wherever one looked uprisings, insurgencies and quests for independence piously predicated on an anti-colonialism encouraged from Washington and believed in by the Labour Government in the UK, but whose flames were assiduously fanned by Moscow – all added to the unease.

Spending money it could ill afford on an Empire-scale defence budget was part of the British policy response. Another was conscription, National Service, or 'the call-up', which in the period we are reviewing required young men to spend two years in one of the Armed Forces with a further three years' liability for recall as a Reservist.

However, the defence planners soon highlighted a major weakness. Probably as a consequence of an Empire- and Euro-centric educational system that reflected centuries of national preoccupations and priorities, Britain found that it had nowhere near the number of Russian speakers it might need if its worst fears were realised and there was a war with the Soviet Union.

If this happened, the three Armed Services needed to have men, and many of them, who could speak the enemy's language, interrogate prisoners and refugees, understand captured documents, administer occupied territory, run propaganda and psychological warfare operations, and listen in to battlefield and higher level radio and telephone conversations; early planning files refer to the prospective students as 'War Interpreters'. These linguists simply did not exist in any meaningful numbers.

Even short of war, the lack of linguists was, if anything, even more acute when it came to meeting intelligence needs. 'Know your enemy' is the cardinal principle of defence, but Russia was a formidable intelligence target. In the 1950s most of it was effectively closed to Westerners. Trade and cultural links were almost non-existent. The few Western businessmen allowed to visit were kept under tight surveillance and were regular targets for entrapment and blackmail attempts.

Collection of 'human intelligence' on the ground thus presented major problems; running agents 'in place' was a matter of chance and high risk, and border-crossing efforts to infiltrate agents or collect intelligence were almost always doomed to failure, betrayed by NKVD agents inside émigré organisations in Germany or by Kim Philby, sitting at the heart of SIS. One of the many misperceptions in East–West relations at the time was Stalin's conviction that British intelligence penetration of the Soviet Union was pervasive. When Philby and others consistently reported that in reality it was almost non-existent, Soviet paranoia led the NKVD to conclude for a while that the Cambridge Five must be double agents themselves.

So if the West was to get not just operational and order-of-battle intelligence but, at the most basic level, early warning of any Soviet surprise move or threat such as the massing of troops or aircraft, it was essential for it to rely again on the battery of Sigint techniques which had proved so valuable operationally in the First World War, diplomatically in the inter-war period and strategically in the Second World War – intercepting and interpreting voice and Morse communications, telegrams, telephone and teleprinter traffic, and in later years collecting electronic data from radar and the telemetry signals emitted from missile test sites and space vehicle launch pads.

However, to mount a year-round, 24-hour Soviet-targeted Sigint collection initiative required an equally sizeable pool of Russian speakers. National Servicemen who were coming fresh from school or university were the natural reservoir from which young men with a flair for languages could be tapped. What was needed was a system that would pick out and then train a large number of them to become quickly proficient in Russian.

Whitehall had been wrestling with the language problem since 1945 via the time-honoured formula of a Royal Commission, whose remit was to look at the wider picture of how all languages – Oriental, Slavonic, East European and African – might be better taught in what was still in every sense an insular country where difficult languages were not widely admired and thus not widely taught, even though only a century or two earlier its polyglot educated classes had been the envy of Europe. Sir James Newton, director of London University's School of Oriental and African Studies, made an important contribution to the work. Oleg

Gordievsky, whose perceptions on these issues are always interesting in view of his KGB background, has recently suggested that the gullibility of the Cambridge Five and other young men and women who fell under the Communist spell in their undergraduate years in the 1930s was due in part to the insularity of British academic life at that period but also to their poor command of foreign languages, since the truth about the USSR in those years was being written mostly in Polish, Finnish and German.

Under the Commission's umbrella the Foreign Office set up a Committee on Russian Studies, whose members included representatives from the British Council, the Royal Institute of International Affairs at Chatham House, Liza Hill, now at Cambridge, and her counterpart at London University, George Bolsover, a blunt Lancastrian and Russian scholar who had just finished a spell attached to the British embassy in Moscow.

While it was deliberating, the archives show that the Admiralty was already operating a Russian course at Benet House, Mount Pleasant, in London, and there is also a reference to an Army course in Camberley, but what can be seen as the first building block in the larger JSSL structure was put in place in 1949 when the RAF set up a Russian-language school at Kidbrooke, in south-east London. Thirty regular RAF officers and ten Army Other Ranks and NCOs had been labouring since the beginning of January to learn the Russian alphabet when after three weeks Pilot Officer Gordon Jones, a twenty-two-year-old National Serviceman recently graduated from Liverpool University with a First in Russian, arrived as CO and Chief Instructor, to the immense relief of Squadron Leader Gibson, who had been taken out of retirement to do the job.

Jones found himself running the course with 'a few copies of the Semeonova Grammar, three huts and three instructors: Nikolai Smirnov, a dandy in spats who claimed he'd been the Tsar's official photographer; Boris Ranevsky, a former actor (who reappears later in this account); and Count Mikhail Lubienski, a Pole with superb Russian. Later that year they were joined by Grigory Tlatov, who had been evacuated from revolutionary

Russia to the Far East and spoke Japanese, and a Colonel F. de Ramer.' Furniture, books, a Russian typewriter and other necessities were acquired by Jones from the Air Ministry Educational Services, and he proceeded to devise a curriculum, with weekly tests, conversation groups, wordlists and other features that figure in our story of the National Service courses to come.

Liza paid Kidbrooke a visit at the end of February and startled the students, all forty, by announcing that they were going to write a letter to a Russian friend with assistance from her. 'With her magical and persuasive personality,' Jones recalls, 'she credibly persuaded everyone that they had achieved a miracle after about seven weeks' study. It gave the Course a big boost.' (Surviving reports by Liza on a couple of her inspection visits typically found plenty to criticise.) Each course lasted twelve months, at the end of which they took the Civil Service Interpreters' Exam in London. Some officers were then sent to Russian families in Paris, others to work in an earlier version of the Signals Intelligence world which will loom large in our story. Two RAF senior NCOs went to Moscow to work in the Air Attaché's office. Jones stayed on after demob until September 1950, when he was replaced by Flt Lt J.D. Wood, who had completed the Cambridge Course followed by Paris, and would go on to Bodmin as Deputy CO.

The RAF move was prompted by the fear that if a Soviet attack came, it would almost certainly be in the air, using weapons of mass destruction. 'The ability to hit back at the outset . . . and take the [air] offensive at the start' was a central plank of the planned British response.

Speaking for all three Services in 1947, the British Chiefs of Staff worried that 'within the Soviet Union the high level of security achieved makes our collection of intelligence difficult and makes it all the more likely the Russians will have the advantage of surprise at the outset . . . it is of the greatest importance that the intelligence organisations should be able to provide us with adequate and timely warning . . .'

Not surprisingly, the planners soon concluded that Kidbrooke was not enough. Given the risk of war, a much larger effort was needed, which could not be mounted there for reasons of space. This view was reinforced by the Admiralty and adopted by the Joint Intelligence Committee (JIC) in 1949.

By 1950 the first outlines of the JSSL scheme, whose basic structure was to remain in place throughout its life, though emphasis and scale changed along the way, were being debated and documented by a Ministry of Defence Working Party on Russian Linguists. There would be schools to train linguists for 'monitoring, translating and other intelligence work', combined with university schemes where a top tranche of students would train even more intensively; they would then get a further final several months' booster course to turn them into practically bilingual interpreters to handle 'conference work, important interrogations and the handling of important documents'. It recommended that two schools be set up, sited close together and ideally near the universities where the interpreters would be trained. Using as points of reference 'the American school in Germany', which ran a six-months' Russian course, Kidbrooke, the 1:12 ratio of the 'average English public school' and the far from average Eton (1:9), the Working Party recommended that JSSL should have a staff/pupil ratio of 1:10.

Cambridge was to 'be pressed to take as many as possible of the interpreter "language cadets" [as they were then being styled; the Russian equivalent is *kursant* or in the plural *kursanty* and is used often below], perhaps as many as 300 per year'. The balance of 150 would go to London. Even though they also recommended that 'an English teacher is definitely to be preferred to a foreigner who has not a wide command of English' (*sic*), a view Liza seems to have accepted for the teaching of grammar, her belief that the spoken language was best taught as far as possible in Russian by Russians prevailed. Though Liza was obsessed with the need for proper Russian pronunciation, she stressed to the Air Ministry that, 'it's far more important to us that these officer-cadets should come up [to Cambridge] with a solid training in the Anna H. Semeonoff Grammar [usually referred to as 'The Semyonova' and one of JSSL's standard textbooks] . . . rather than that we

30

should be sent officer-cadets with perfect Russian pronunciation and slovenly grammar'.

All of this was a tall order, but it worked. The Working Party's 'secret' memorandum regretted that siphoning off so many talented men to learn Russian would 'make serious inroads into the numbers of potential officers and NCOs among National Servicemen', but this was a price that had to be paid.

Though it had originally been the view that Britain had five years in which to build up these linguistic resources, 'the international situation makes it imperative to plan for a three-year programme'.

The Working Party cited an extract from a 1949 paper by the Defence (Transition) Committee, which explicitly referred to the numbers of translators that would be needed 'at the outbreak of war'. Admiralty papers the following year are sprinkled with references to the need for linguists 'on D day' and 'within twelve months of war'. To meet a projected need within those first twelve months for 833 first- and second-class linguists, at the time the Navy had only twenty interpreters and first-class translators. The Admiralty estimated the aggregate requirement for all three Services combined was 912 first-class and 2,872 second-class translators; the bureaucratic precision of the figures does not detract from the seriousness of the gaping shortfall.

Though deeply traditional in so many respects, the Navy was nicely ahead of its time in considering whether women could be used in these roles. They concluded that they could not be relied on to 'assist in meeting the main commitment', not for any chauvinistic reason but simply because WRNS' terms of engagement did not include any Reserve service liability. That meant that 'there can be no certainty they would be available for recall in the event of war' and the major investment in training would thus be wasted. But it was suggested that the 'good offices' of the women's colleges be sought 'to enlist the support and interest of individuals' and some thought was also given to offering women Short Service Commissions as an inducement to serve for longer.

When the Interpreters' Course was first discussed, Liza and others thought the final few booster months could follow the pattern established for Regular officers who had worked on their spoken Russian through a spell with an émigré household in Paris. The rumour circulated among members of the first Course, in London as well as Cambridge, as John Roberts recalls, that Liza 'was working on the government' to bring this about. But this was felt unworkable for interpreters coming out of the JSSL system. This was principally a matter of numbers, but there is also an implication in the file that, unlike their grizzled professional counterparts who were officers and thus knew how to behave, young National Servicemen might be too easily distracted in an ambience of Gauloises and Juliette Greco. According to a 'secret' memorandum of November 1951, 'Though the officers are given schemes of work and are required to do regular exercises, the training is largely informal', hardly a strenuous regime in which to spend time in Paris at taxpayers' expense, even though, as the memorandum notes, periodic visits were made from London 'to inspect arrangements and assess progress'.

The inspection visits themselves were no doubt a much sought-after Whitehall perk.

The Paris scheme seems to have been, or to have become, rather laxer than Liza had originally envisaged it – her first outline called for daily translation exercises, a weekly 1,000-word essay and monthly tests to be taken at the embassy or some other official site. Another idea of hers which fell on deaf ears was that, if Paris was off limits, interpreters should spend six months in a country house where only Russian was spoken until 9 p.m. and where even the domestic staff would be Russian.

Instead, to her unconcealed chagrin, it was decreed that after university interpreters would simply be sent back where they started, to the basic language schools for a final six months for a combination of oral practice and learning the Russian terminology of their respective Services. Historian (Sir) Martin Gilbert seems to have had the unique experience of being the only JSSL student to have enjoyed Paris at the Army's expense, even if it was only for a fortnight, a diversion probably brought about by the fact that illness had caused him to mark time between two Courses.

Cambridge (where Liza's Department was approvingly noted as an 'up-to-date institution . . . using highly developed methods') and London were chosen largely for their track records in this type of training, but also because not many other universities had adequate facilities and 'at others the Slavonic Faculties would be unsuitable because of their Communist sympathies'. A 'Moderating Committee' was set up to make sure that there was a proper balance in the various curriculum components between academic standards and the specific needs of the Services and 'user departments', the point having been made that the Universities would need delicate handling and perhaps 'approaches at the highest level' to allay any concern that they were being asked to compromise their standards. Its members included George Bolsover, Liza, and Wing Commander (later Group Captain) Edgar Harrington (an Education Officer and subsequently JSSL's first Principal). Another member was the late Naky Doniach of GCHQ, who, as one of the planners and later as 'Inspector' of JSSL on behalf of the Air Ministry, played a key background role throughout the life of the scheme.

Doniach was born in London in 1907 into a family of recently arrived Russian-Jewish refugees, his father a Hebrew scholar and his mother a political Zionist. Naky – or to give him his full name, Nakdimon – started his studies at King's College, London, in 1923, in Hebrew, Greek and Latin; at the same time he was learning Arabic at the School of Oriental Studies. Two years later he won a scholarship to read Hebrew and Arabic at Wadham College, Oxford, the first of a number of scholarships and prizes which helped him to continue his studies. He then embarked on the life of a private scholar, bibliophile and bookseller, a career that was brought to an abrupt and violent end when his entire stock of Judaica and Orientalia was destroyed in the Blitz.

He joined the RAF in 1940 and became a squadron leader in an intelligence unit at Bletchley Park. After the war he worked at what had now been translated from GCCS to GCHQ at Eastcote and as Director of the Joint Technical Language Service when GCHQ moved to Cheltenham in 1952. His flair for languages and administration – he had taught himself Russian, gone on to teach it to GCHQ staff for a while, and was also responsible for supervising the Services' teaching of Chinese – made him GCHQ's clear choice as their representative.

Doniach later recalled a meeting in the Treasury in Great George Street in November 1950 when he was told by the Air Commodore in the Chair that the order to go ahead with the JSSL project had come directly from 10 Downing Street. The Working Party toured Whitehall, finding that in addition to the sizeable Service needs already identified virtually every Ministry and Department from the War Office to the Board of Trade badly wanted Russian speakers for their own work. Some already employed a handful of émigrés but these were woefully lacking in the technical and commercial language skills even non-military Whitehall needed.

The Home Office set to work trying to identify potential teachers from among the Russian émigré community. Liza had considerable input, and the files show that she was sent many lists of names (not a few from among her large circle of friends and acquaintances) for assessment. She often sat in on the interviews at the Air Ministry, when candidates were evaluated for their potential teaching skills.

A 'secret' letter to her from a now indecipherable Whitehall box number submitted seventy-three reports on 'aliens who seem to have a useful knowledge of Russian'. The author regretted that, while 'we have been trying to follow up your suggestion that we should pick out real Russians from the USSR, there are a number of difficulties about it. First, because many of these persons did not register as Russians and only disclosed their nationality in the course of the present interrogations . . . Second, because many of the people we find to be Russians are unsuitable on personal grounds, illiterate or would be security risks . . .' Some 5,000 personal files were scrutinised but only about 100 candidates were regarded as possibly suitable. These were screened by the Security

Service – perhaps not always with unremitting diligence, according to allegations in the House of Commons some forty years later.

Liza was central to the planning effort in many ways. The official files show her as the author of a cogent paper reviewed by the Working Party making a strong case for Cambridge as the focal point, with herself as Director, and rather imaginatively suggesting vacant hangars at the partly unused Short's Aircraft Factory on Madingley Road as the Course's home – a suggestion that future members of her Courses who enjoyed their creature comforts must be thankful was not pursued. Those with more of a yearning for adventure in the Richard Hannay style might have been intrigued had they known of a suggestion made to Liza in 1951 by Robin Fyfe, the owner of Craignish Castle in Argyllshire who was anxious to rescue it from a 'state of financial precariousness'. In a letter capitalising on some wartime connection with Liza, he suggested that he and a partner, a retired RN commander whose mother, like Liza's, came from Russian aristocratic stock, would run the Castle as a language school under War Office auspices, concentrating mainly on Russian. Fyfe claimed that his idea, which he asked her to support in Whitehall, had the backing of 'Major Strickland of Military Intelligence'. There is no record of Liza's reply or any further examination of this idea, though it may have had a bearing on her suggestion that interpreters should be trained in a country house where only Russian was spoken and all the domestic help was Russian too.

She also had an eye to the future and capitalised on the defence priorities to add to the discussion her thoughts on society's broader needs. She pointed out that a large pool of trained interpreters and translators would create a reservoir of men who could be encouraged to go on to take degrees in Russian and even offered full grants, with the aim of creating future teachers and university lecturers in Russian, thus bringing the language into the mainstream of British secondary and higher education. Even though the use of grants as she envisaged it did not materialise, this as we shall see was far-sighted and its contribution to Russian studies in the UK proved one of the JSSL scheme's major legacies.

For someone as profoundly anti-Soviet as Liza, her memorandum strikes one slightly odd note when, ignoring the Cold War theme completely, she suggested that the UK needed Russian speakers because it found itself at 'a time when so many of Britain's interests are contiguous with those of the USSR'.

Liza's personal archive also contains a 1954 letter to the University's General Board in which she laid out in detail the contribution she felt she had made: 'before this series . . . was launched as a national initiative, as the recognised authority on intensive Russian language training I acted as adviser to Service departments on Russian-language training, advised on syllabuses and standards, visited the Army and RAF centres where Russian was being taught, went through hundreds of official records to discover the potential teaching personnel in this country and sat as the Russian-language expert on Selection Boards for the Principals and Instructors of the Service Russian Language Schools for Translators and preliminary and post-university training of officer-cadet interpreters; compiled material for use at the instruction bases; explained to the native instructors selected the methods I had devised at Cambridge during the Inter Services Russian Course 1945/6 . . .'

On top of all that, she did not fail to point out that she had scoured Fenland auction rooms and the second-hand furniture stores on the Newmarket Road for used classroom furniture so as to keep down costs!

George Bolsover told the Foreign Office that London University would be agreeable to taking on interpreter training 'providing his Governing Body were satisfied that the normal work of the University would not be adversely affected'.

By March 1951 the papers had become 'Top Secret' and had gone via the JIC to the Chiefs of Staff. Though the numbers of men had been trimmed somewhat, the need was still regarded as pressing and for what appears to be the first time 'Signals Intelligence' was identified as the major customer for these language skills.

The JIC concluded that of the Russian speakers needed in the years ahead, Sigint requirements accounted for 1,678 and 'special services' 242, which together would absorb 72 per cent of the total. Responding to an earlier Chiefs of Staff query why more of the need for linguists could not be met by employing English-speaking Russians or other Slav-speaking foreigners (with no language training cost), the JIC noted:

a) No foreigners can be employed on Signals Intelligence duties;
b) Vetting [of foreigners] must be regarded as a less certain means of weeding out undesirables because the information available on them is limited;
c) An alien whether naturalised or not working for a country at war with his own would have unpredictable reactions;
d) Public criticism in war might force the Government to intern aliens of an enemy country however reliable they might be;
e) Aliens employed on interrogating compatriots would be ineffective as they would be regarded as traitors by the POW [prisoners of war];
f) Their employment would make the planting of agents more easy [*sic*];
g) Those with relations or friends in war areas might be subject to coercion by enemy agents in this country.

The Sigint Board has ruled, the JIC added, 'that only third generation or earlier naturalised subjects may be employed on Sigint duties'. Had this latter instruction been followed to the letter, Naky Doniach and one or two others who appear in these pages would have had to find other employment. The matter of how much all this was going to cost had begun to raise its head early on, but Ministers were firmly advised that 'the requirement is unanimously described by the Intelligence Departments of the Services as essential [so] the solution is inevitably expensive'. After some effort to trim the figures, the JIC told the Chiefs of Staff bluntly:

If the Intelligence Organisation is to fulfil its function in war, then its requirements of linguists should be met. These

requirements have now been cut to the minimum. If for financial
or manpower reasons these requirements are [further] cut, then
the intelligence available will be proportionally reduced.

Monetary comparisons with values fifty years ago can be misleading, but it is fair to conclude that – though to soften the blow,
ignoring capital and probably many other costs, the financial staff
seemed to have convinced their seniors that the average cost to
produce a translator from the system was a seemingly modest
£398 per capita and an interpreter £839 when all its aspects were
taken into account, from accommodation to the cost of the various
Service technical language and signals-training schools outside,
but a key part of, the teaching framework – the JSSL scheme was
in today's terms a multi-million pound commitment.

In November 1951 the Treasury sanctioned £200,000 as initial
expenditure by the three Service departments. Cambridge was to
receive £38,500 p.a. for its services, a figure which the Cambridge
Treasurer admitted to Liza in 1954 had yielded 'a fairly handsome
profit . . . of about £17,000' (bearing out suspicions voiced at the
Ministry of Defence in 1952 that the University was taking
advantage of the situation and seeking 'unacceptable' terms for
the rental of teaching premises of which they had the monopoly).

Other than the estimate which will not surprise London *kursanty* that they could be adequately fed on a princely five shillings
per head per day, specific figures for London are hard to find.

After approval by the Chiefs of Staff and Ministers, the project
then moved into the hands of a 'Progressing Committee', whose
members again included Doniach. Bridling at an early suggestion – no doubt some Whitehall in-fighting ploy – that his
organisation might not need to be involved further, he is minuted
as retorting that GCHQ 'as a substantial user of those to be trained
would wish to continue to be associated with the direction of the
scheme'. The machinery began to move ahead. It was proposed
that the RAF's success in running Kidbrooke made it the best
choice for administering the new arrangements. The Air Ministry
agreed, but called on the help of the other two Services to find

accommodation and administrative staff. The choice of the RAF to spearhead the effort may also have been related to the critical importance of the air element of Sigint – described by one historian as 'one of the growth areas of the early intelligence Cold War'.

That it was all a scramble is indicated by an Admiralty memorandum of April 1951, which notes that 'Training is to begin in September or October this year. But when I tell you that suitable National Servicemen have yet to be selected, the universities approached and a site for the Service schools to be found, you will see the scheme has not got far in matters of practical detail . . .' As we shall see, University Course A was launched even before the schools were put in place. Even by January 1952 the Admiralty was admitting difficulty in making up the numbers for its quota of JSSL places, though the Army and RAF were confident that they had enough applicants to take up the shortfall.

The haste may explain why when the JSSL sites were eventually selected, the choice flew in the face of the planners' recommendation that the schools should be located close to one another and also to the two Universities, since the first two 'Joint Services Schools for Linguists' were set up in September 1951 in Cornwall and Coulsdon, on the edge of the Downs south of Croydon, meeting neither criterion.

The Walker Lines Barracks, just off the Bodmin bypass and run by the Army in response to the Air Ministry's call for burden-sharing, was a poorly built hutted camp thrown up in a hurry at the start of the Second World War and most recently the depot of the Education Corps. The files note that £1,000 (perhaps £20–50,000 today) had to be spent on refurbishment, a sum all of those who passed through it in the next few years would agree was woefully inadequate. Commander Barham, whose previous experience as a naval interpreter in Japanese must have qualified him in the eyes of his superiors, became Principal of Bodmin, while Flight Lieutenant Wood, who had run Kidbrooke, became his deputy.

Although those who were posted there would have disagreed (one described it as 'the awful remnants of WW2 prefabs'), Coulsdon was viewed by the parsimonious planners as being in what estate agents might call 'move-in condition' without any further expense required. In a part of Coulsdon shown on early maps as 'Tin Town', because of the rows of huts with corrugated iron roofs hastily thrown up in the First World War to house the newly recruited militia, the agglomeration of spare buildings for JSSL was an appendage of the Brigade of Guards Depot in Caterham in the Surrey hills. As they drifted across to some of the canteen and other facilities they shared, JSSL's unmilitary, bottle-eyed 'swots' in their baggy uniforms must have been a bizarre contrast to their shaved-scalp, razor-creased and shiny-booted neighbours, and it did not take long for the Guards Sergeants to adopt as a new charge to hurl at their victims: 'You look like a bunch of effing Russian linguists.' From the linguists' side of the barbed-wire fence the demonic discipline of the Guards was invoked by their RSM, who at moments of maximum frustration would threaten to march his charges across for a taste of 'the machine'. Coulsdon closed in 1954, and Bodmin in 1956, replaced by Crail (also an Army responsibility though housed on a former Royal Naval Air Service station) in Scotland.

Space also had to be found for the interpreters. 'Cecil Lodge' and 'The Grove' overlooking the gallops in Newmarket were the first residential units for the Cambridge Course, though such was the urgency to get the scheme going that the students on the first two Interpreters' Courses were temporarily housed on RAF Stations at Waterbeach and Oakington. Despite bleating from the Beaverbrook press about giving the military priority over mums, £42,000 was then paid for a ninety-three-year lease on the former 'Stella Maris' Maternity Home, soon renamed Douglas House by some bureaucrat anxious to pay homage to the Air Marshal, a short bicycle-ride up the Trumpington Road from the centre of Cambridge. Another £14,000 was paid for a fourteen-year lease on another residence known (appropriately for a building housing Russian students) as The Hermitage, an elegant eighteenth-century house in Silver Street which had an annexe round the corner at Newnham Terrace with a skiff moored at the bottom of the garden.

The RAF, which had supervisory responsibility for Cambridge, soon leased Foxton Hall, a featureless Victorian pile on the site of

49 Russell Square

Patrick Proctor

what had been the Manor House of the eponymous village, on the A10 some twelve miles south of Cambridge. The other properties were relinquished and Foxton remained 'The Officer Cadets' Mess' for Cambridge until the programme ended.

London's first students lived in a five-storey building at 5 Sussex Square, uneasily poised between the grand façades of Hyde Park Gardens and the seedy lodging houses, Army surplus stores, and truss and rubber goods emporia in the mean streets around Paddington Station. It had been used in 1945 to house servicemen learning Japanese and Chinese. Later Courses were accommodated at 46 Queensgate Terrace, a double-width street running between Gloucester Road and Queensgate, built in a high, pillared-portico, nineteenth-century City paterfamilias style that would have appealed to John Galsworthy. By coincidence, as the writer Michael Smith has recently recorded, the British pre-war code-breaking effort, once housed in the Admiralty and later in the Strand, had for a time been located just a stone's throw away, at 178 Queensgate itself.

Before it fell into Admiralty hands, the houses in the Queensgate block used for JSSL had been knocked together and had spent many genteel years as a hotel where lavender-scented maiden aunts withered quietly away behind the aspidistras. Though known to the Post Office as 'Furze House', by a process of Navy alchemy worthy of Gilbert and Sullivan it had technically become a ship, with the rather democratic name of HMS *President*.

The Cambridge classrooms were in a Victorian house rented from Jesus College at 5 Salisbury Villas, in Station Road, while London *kursanty* initially studied in Georgian-façaded buildings owned by the British Museum at 38 and 47 Russell Square.

The buildings were ready, the curriculum had been worked out, the blackboards and sticks of white chalk were in place, and the textbooks and exercise books were neatly stacked. The search was on for staff. The world heard of wars and the rumours of wars. All that remained was to find the pupils to man the electronic battlements.

3

Fellows of Infinite Tongue

Most school stories focus on individual heroes and villains among the pupils. Here we have no Tom Brown, no Flashman, no Stalky. Instead, we arguably have upwards of 5,000 central figures, children of the Second World War and teenagers of the Cold War, shirted by Viyella and Aertex, clothed at various stages of childhood and adolescence by school outfitters up and down the country, Montague Burton, The Fifty Shilling Tailor and Cecil Gee, whose trouser belts had snake-shaped buckles, whose food and sweets had for many years been officially rationed, who collected bus and railway engine numbers with a zeal bordering on the manic, and for whom bananas were almost as much a novelty as Bulgarians.

Physically their generation tended to be on the puny side, even though not a few wasted their teenage pocket money trying to build muscles and deter bullies via a 'Charles Atlas' correspondence course – 'You too', the sketch of a steroid-stuffed Hungarian promised them, 'can have a body like mine.'

They grew up in a landscape smudged grey by the coal fires that still heated most homes, over which the first high-rise blocks of flats were beginning to loom like tombstones. London *kursant* Brian Verity recalls being ushered down from the balcony of the Empire, Leicester Square, to the stalls in the middle of Chaplin's *Limelight* because the screen was half obscured by the smog that had seeped indoors. As they grew into adolescence, the cloying aroma of 'Old Spice' aftershave replaced the vapours of Vick and Wright's Coal Tar Soap that had lingered in the crevices of their childhood. It was a Britain in which radio and its catchphrases still dominated the popular mind and imagination over television. Their mothers and several million other housewives tuned in at 4.15 p.m. each day, many surreptitiously sipping a glass of Sanatogen tonic wine, 'fortified for the over 40s', as the pages of 'Mrs Dale's Diary' transported them into the tranquil middle-class life of a doctor's household.

The 1950s were years in which at various points and in no particular order Bill Haley and his Comets, 'The Goons', Elvis Presley, James Dean, Marlon Brando, Harry Lime, 'Dick Barton – Special Agent', *Look Back in Anger*, Buddy Holly, Humphrey Lyttleton, Holden Caulfield and *Lucky Jim* figured in the pantheon of cultural icons, with Tommy Steele and the long-lasting Cliff Richard coming up fast on the outside.

The secret world itself took on a new sheen in the person of James Bond, whose dry Martinis 'shaken not stirred' and Savile Row tailored tropical-weight worsted were a long way from the mugs of sweet tea and horse-blanket serge uniforms many JSSL graduates would find in the neon-lit, windowless twenty-four-hour world of Sigint. Back then, football heroes parted their hair in the middle, took out their dentures and took a last puff on an Extra Strength Craven A cigarette before the big game, and had strictly non-trophy wives. Cricketers remained sharply divided between amateur Gentlemen and professional Players. It was a decade in which, nearly fifty years before Starbucks was even thought of, the high-street espresso coffee bar became the young people's rendezvous of choice.

Britain was an inward-looking country; a contemporary newspaper boosted Paignton, Morecambe, Prestatyn and Margate, among many other similar candyfloss 'Kiss Me Quick' resorts, as family holiday destinations. Scooter-proud Mods tussled with Rockers on rain-swept seaside promenades while other young people dressed up and went ballroom dancing; over-indulgence in Guinness, Babycham or Merrydown Cider at 3/6d a bottle presented the biggest risk of substance abuse.

It was a time when an editor could be fired for running a mildly satirical poem about the choice of a preparatory school for Prince Charles.

It was a country which was inward-looking, well drawn in the opening pages of Humphrey Carpenter's book *That Was Satire That Was*, on the birth of the new phase in British comedy in the 1960s. In one sense his book is also part of the sequel to this history, since several key characters were JSSL *kursanty* who had begun to develop their styles and even some of their later scripts in Bodmin, Crail and Cambridge. It was a country where the remedy promoted for marital stress ('. . . Jean and Jimmy's marriage seemed to be breaking up. Once gay, lively and popular with their friends . . .') was not counselling or Viagra, but Horlicks in warm milk at bedtime.

It was a Britain whose Festival in 1951 to celebrate rather prematurely the dawn of a new Elizabethan age anticipated the Millennium fiasco by almost half a century by sporting a plastic dome – its designer Russian-born – as the centrepiece of its London site.

JSSL is a school whose old boys' memories, as these pages will show, are still vivid almost half a century later, but which are woven from very varied strands, depending on when they served, whether they came straight out of school or from university, which arm of the Forces they were in, whether they went on to the University Interpreters' Course and if so where, and whether they later worked in Sigint. The loom of memory also creaks a bit under the weight of time, and its cloth, though mostly the genuine article, is sometimes selectively woven; to quote one cynic, 'I am of an age where autobiography is the only kind of fiction I can handle.'

However, there is at least one common denominator: 99.9 per cent of the students were conscripts. Boys of eighteen accepted National Service grudgingly, often resentfully, but at the end of the day inevitably as part of the response to the Cold War threat and the need to maintain the Empire, part of the price of being British, like warm beer, arbitrary pub closing hours and terrible food. Between 1947 and 1961 some two million young men went through National Service in the Army and just over 433,000 in the RAF. The figure for the Navy was much less.

The Empire was still alive, though, like *The Cherry Orchard*, soon to be broken up and put into the hands of new owners. Writer, actor and satirist John Wells, who would probably have fitted comfortably into the JSSL 'culture' but who was commissioned into the Royal Sussex Regiment and sent to Korea in 1956, told Humphrey Carpenter that his Regiment '. . . stopped at Gibraltar with the Union Jack flying. We then went across the Mediterranean . . . and the next stop was Aden, with the Union Jack flying. Then we went to Colombo with the Union Jack flying . . . then Singapore with the Union Jack flying. Hong Kong the same and we just didn't stop anywhere where there wasn't a British presence. And it just seemed perfectly natural. There was no sense of colonial shame.'

Those who could not get medical exemptions for flat feet or bad eyes, or deferrals for further education, reported for duty, had their heads cropped and underwent the ritual humiliation of Basic Training; as so many have characterised it in almost identical words, it was 'the most miserable time of my life'.

It was an experience which universally for the Army, and generally for the RAF, would make induction into HM Prison Belmarsh seem like the first day at a Boy Scout camp. Shock and unreason, lunatic routines, harsh penalties, a sense of being in a totally alien world were all played out to the background of savage yells from bullying NCOs with a mental age of ten but a highly sophisticated line in sadism. Everyone who went through it remembers it, as no doubt they were meant to.

Boys who had been at schools with a 'Combined Cadet Force',

with Army, Navy and RAF sections, had a slight edge since such war-winning skills as how to polish boots and belt-brasses to a mirror gloss and stamp in foot-tingling cadence through an elegant 'about turn' were already familiar, but even they found those first shrieking twenty-four-hour days hard to take. One linguist remembers the Tannoy system in his Basic Training unit: 'While we stood in childish terror through our first inspection, the swaggering, snarling performance played to a soft accompaniment from the loudspeaker – a sickly orchestration of Debussy's *Clair de Lune*.'

In contrast the Navy, already becoming far more of a technically oriented Service with less need for conscripts, and efficiency a greater concern than bullying young men into conformity or discipline, treated its National Servicemen far less brutally. A Service whose opening indoctrination sessions for recruits incorporated, as it did for several *kursanty*, a showing of Noël Coward's Second World War Navy-boosting film *In Which We Serve* has to be given credit for a sense of style, all the more so since one of its more powerful messages was the 'class-levelling' effect of officers and men sharing the perils of warfare.

Many conscripts saw active service in the world's trouble-spots, and not a few were killed. Many enjoyed their time and looked back on it with pride as enjoyable and worthwhile. Many learned useful skills, even if only to lead and command. But for others, once Basic Training was behind them the saddest part of the mainstream National Service experience was the utter waste of time of it all, two years of largely mindless duties pushing paper, driving trucks or counting blankets interspersed with the burlesque of Service rituals.

By comparison, the Russian Course had obvious attractions. It would be hard to deny the charge made then and today that in terms of lifestyle it was a 'cushy number', especially at the university level. But it was far more than that. It was hard work. 'Much harder certainly than university proper or anywhere else since,' one *kursant* remembers. Substituting 'language' for 'military' and 'arms', in Gibbon's description of how Roman legions were trained, 'language exercises were the important and unremitting object of their discipline. The recruits were constantly trained both in the morning and the evening, nor was age or knowledge allowed to excuse veterans from relearning what they had completely learned. Large sheds were erected in the winter quarters lest their useful labours might receive any interruption from the most tempestuous weather and it was carefully observed that the language [learned] should be double the weight of what was required in real action . . .'

An early draft of the qualities needed for selection for JSSL was almost certainly written by Liza since its cardinal and capitalised point was that above all a candidate had to have the 'The WILL to learn the language'. Those who knew her can almost hear her saying it. Next came powers of concentration, good memory, accuracy, good health, age not over twenty-five ('and the younger the better'), a background of grammatical terminology (knowing what gerunds, infinitives and declensions actually were), and a School Certificate in Latin or another foreign language. In what again sounds classical Liza style, the note asserts that 'a slight knowledge of French or German is no criterion'; a Higher School Certificate in Science was a better alternative since it suggested that a boy was well trained in accurate working. Selection of unsuitable candidates would be a 'cruelty' to them and a waste of public money. A footnote to another version of the paper added delicately, if inconsistently, as we shall see, that candidates should also be of British parentage.

The memories of most of the students suggest that the selections were generally perceptively made even if a few inevitably fell by the academic wayside. But it must at times have been too much of a temptation for a regimental commanding officer, or his naval and air-force counterparts, to fob off on JSSL anyone who looked or indeed was odd, or likely to be an unmilitary nuisance, and as a result most intakes initially contained a small handful of men who were decidedly several pages short of a full dictionary. Men who did not wash, country boys escaping the shackles of their Wee Free upbringing by drinking themselves into a nightly bucket-filling stupor, men who let their Russian slide because they were learning Hausa as a hobby, gays who regaled their wide-eyed colleagues with accounts of their dreams about encounters with the late, ramrod straight, Queen Mary, a man who disappeared to London claiming on his return that he had performed at the London Palladium with the 'skiffle' artist Lonnie Donegan. They did not stay long.

In a profile drawn very early in the history of JSSL, 65 per cent of entrants were already graduates and another 35 per cent had places waiting for them at university after National Service; this balance varied markedly Course by Course but as the years passed and the Courses grew smaller, those proportions were more than reversed, with far more young men coming to JSSL from school, armed with university places and scholarships but encouraged by their Colleges to get National Service out of the way so that the obligation would not cloud their time at university and that after graduation they could pursue their careers without interruption. This is borne out by one recollection that most of a mid-1950s' JSSL entry were boys straight from school with university places ahead, and only 'a sprinkling of self-consciously senior citizens'. The twelve men on Cambridge Course M – the smallest of them all – included just one graduate.

Intellectual qualities were the key determinant but to complicate matters Army interviewers were instructed to exclude from the linguist category any men who appeared to have the capability to be technical and combat officers. The RAF did the same in respect of potential aircrew. A Ministry of Defence official, obviously steeped in the spirit of G. A. Henty, took the view that *a priori* men with officer qualities would not 'be interested in language training'. Those most suited to it would be men 'who would wish to enter the Educational or Intelligence Branches'. Had the word been in currency then, one can almost hear him curling his lip and calling them 'nerds'. In many cases though, his instinct may have been right. A young man with the prospect of a commission in a good regiment, Mess nights, High Cockalorum, flags and flummery, tartan trews and a paternalistic relationship with 'my Jocks' all overlaid with a whiff of cordite might well not have been tempted by the thought of effectively going back to a classroom to do something difficult.

No study of a British institution of this period – or indeed of any period – seems to be able to avoid issues of class. Otherwise objective interviewers probe for it, and from some of the reminiscences we have seen it was in the front of several young men's mind as they traversed JSSL. In the US by stark contrast a weighty and until recent years classified Second World War study by the US Office of Strategic Services of how men were evaluated and selected for clandestine work describes batteries of written and oral tests, profiles of the candidates by every conceivable parameter, but makes no mention of social background. And race is referred to only to make the point that in selecting men to work behind the lines in the Pacific islands, men of an appropriate ethnic background might blend in better.

Contrary to a claim in the *Sunday Express* of December 1953 that 'Eton, Harrow and other famous public schools provide half the students . . . of the school for eggheads', most in fact came from good grammar and the less headline-grabbing public schools. Based on distant impressions, the Army students were generally drawn from middle to upper-middle class and professional families, living in London and the south, while the RAF students tended to include a larger proportion of men from the north. Looking back on his contemporaries, Michael Frayn commented, 'I would think the overwhelming tone of the course was probably lower middle class and hard-working grammar school; that was the basic intellectual and emotional and social set of people.'

As always the Navy was something of an exception. Several factors seem to have combined to give the JSSL naval contingent, in memory at least, rather a Home Counties flavour. First the Navy needed fewer National Servicemen than its junior Services, and could be more selective in its initial choice of conscripts. Second, its rule that even if a candidate was academically qualified for the Interpreters' Course, he had to pass a

Commissioning Board before being admitted, introduced another element of pre-selectivity in its identification of candidates for JSSL. Though the idea was later dropped, the Admiralty originally wanted to go further, feeling that linguists wishing to serve in the Navy should not even be enlisted in its ranks at the outset, but simply 'earmarked' and trained with Army and RAF contingents and 'only transferred to the RN when they have qualified'.

The naval groups always had a certain sense of a breed apart, accentuated by their quaint if functional dress and their Nelsonian language and customs. When in the early days of the Second World War a small team of RN officers arrived to commandeer a massive country mansion as the Navy's new Signals school, where many RN linguists had their technical training in later years, instead of making for the master bedrooms they upturned the mediaeval-scale pine tables in the kitchens and 'slung our hammocks between the legs'.

We shall look in more detail later at the JSSL 'school magazine' but one of its anonymous correspondents, who may well have been reading Nancy Mitford's *Noblesse Oblige*, sought to catch some of the Service distinctions in spoof JSSL letters home. The Navy Coder Special complains from Bodmin to an aunt in Hampshire about his canteen neighbour's 'pathetic repetition' of 'serviette' and his request for 'not too much greens, please,' during the 'one-course travesty of dinner at 7 p.m. Quelle vie!' He asks Aunty to send him 'another bottle of our sherry'.

The RAF man begins his letter with a polite 'thank you' to Mum for the food parcel, asks nostalgically what films are showing at the local Troxy and tells her 'that Bill what was in the same form as me at grammar school, was in the last intake'. He closes 'with love to Dad, Ethel and Harold'. There is no matching Army letter, the correspondent sniggers, 'as we have no evidence that the Army can write at all'.

However, by most accounts the most perceptible divide was neither schooling nor Service but age. Though perhaps only three or four years separated those arriving from school and those who had been to university, the gulf in worldliness and learning discipline was far larger. As Marcus Wheeler, then a Classics graduate, later a Professor of Russian, recalls: 'Those of us who had graduated from university were inclined to be laid back and disparaging of the idealism of the younger *kursanty* . . .' Patrick Procktor, whose National Service with the Navy took him from work in a builders' merchants in Holloway where he had ended up when his family could no longer afford to pay to keep two boys at Highgate School, through Bodmin, London University and Crail, drew a distinction between the 'more carefree, insouciant, if you like, attitude' of some public school boys and the 'intensity' of many of those from grammar school.

As David Marquand, until recently Principal of Mansfield College, Oxford, remembers, 'the atmosphere was intense, a little precious, and beneath a skin-deep veneer of effortless nonchalance it was desperately competitive, not only or even mainly in respect of linguistic prowess. It had obvious affinities with life at university but our noses were kept much closer to the grindstone and we were thrown much closer together.' One of the reasons, along with the grim rewards of failure, that competitiveness was so much a feature of life was that JSSL students had just come from an environment at school or college where results were the key to the future and the regular scanning of the JSSL test scores as they were posted each week and month was an accepted, if 'nail-biting', feature of life.

John Field, who was later to become British High Commissioner in Colombo, and who had joined the Cambridge Course after school, Basic Training and Bodmin, was struck by the 'exhaustive and compelling knowledge of the cultural world' displayed by the *kursanty* who were already graduates. 'Thanks to them I came across the twentieth century, discovering Prokofiev and Britten, Alfred Deller and Fischer-Dieskau, Sartre and Gide, T. S. Eliot and Edward Thomas, abstract art and the theatre.'

One day perhaps a psychologist might collect enough JSSL data to determine whether the real key, the skill spotted shrewdly or intuitively by many of the front-line JSSL selectors, was less being 'good at languages' than a more general 'way with words', a feel for language as a tool. So many ended up in professions in which verbal dexterity, a deeper than usual vocabulary and fluency, all mattered. Writers, actors, barristers, churchmen, diplomats, journalists, even academics, have to put on a performance at lectures, and to 'publish or perish'. Peter Woodthorpe felt his success with Russian came from being an instinctive imitator, a skill which he put to good use on the stage, and Alan Bennett's flair for the nuances and rhythms of contemporary English is almost unsurpassed.

Jokers suggested that while the selectors pricked up their ears if a candidate had been to, or had a place waiting at, university, the acid test for entry to JSSL was glasses; the thicker the lenses, the better one's chances.

JSSL challenged its students and in many cases obviously or subtly changed their lives. As a National Serviceman and later a Reservist, Alan Bennett saw all three JSSL locations as well as the Cambridge Course, remembering it some thirty years later as, 'in a way it was the most enjoyable period of my life . . . there are only one or two periods I'm nostalgic about and that's one of them', a view endorsed by Michael Frayn, who trod the same path and relished 'the delight of it'. He found himself with 'very congenial people . . . I have to say I enjoyed it very much.'

'An education like no other I have known or can imagine,' in the words of Myles Burnyeat, later Fellow of All Souls and Professor of Ancient Philosophy at Oxford. John Drummond (then, like Professor Burnyeat, in the Navy and later Sir John Drummond CBE who went on to do so much for British music at the BBC and to direct the Edinburgh Festival and the Promenade Concerts) wrote in his memoirs: '. . . so pervasive was the experience that I find it difficult even today not to feel deep inside that I am in some way partly Russian . . . as baptisms go it was a total immersion.'

D. M. Thomas, who has contributed our introduction, was impatient to get to Oxford to read English, and hated having to do National Service. 'Even on the Russian Course I longed for it to be over, so that I could resume my real life . . . Every weekend in Cambridge I'd buy books to increase my knowledge of English literature; yet almost without my knowing it I was beginning to love Russian literature . . . and then later realised that this annoying interruption was actually one of the richest and most seminal experiences of my life. Not for the only time, I found that providence seemed to know better than I what was good for me!' The legacy of JSSL was to be felt in his transla-tions of Akhmatova and Pushkin, and his biography of Solzhenitsyn. 'But,' as he now reflects, 'much more than that, my novels, including *The White Hotel*, are impregnated with a sense of Russia.'

John Massey Stewart felt the Course directed him 'after a few years into becoming a "Russianist", in my case journalist, writer, lecturer, photographer, environmentalist and latterly consultant: it was a lifetime bitten by the Russian bug.'

For Jim Reed, Professor of German at Oxford, 'Russian remains a great and marking experience, a lasting love and source of pleasure and some pride. There is nothing quite like the relish of reading Russian aloud – a poem of Pushkin, a page of Tolstoy – with no audience, behind closed doors alone with the mouth-filling and heart-warming sounds of that wonderful lan-guage.' Reed was unconsciously echoing the proud claim of the eighteenth-century scientist and scholar Lomonosov – whose name has adorned Moscow University since its foundation in 1755 to the present day – that Russian 'has the majesty of Spanish, the vivacity of French, the delicacy of Italian, and the richness and concise imagery of Greek and Latin'. Lomonosov might have been surprised to see that English, which he stu-diously ignores in his comparisons, seems on its way to becoming the lingua franca of twenty-first century Europe.

Another contemporary wrote of an experience 'something like an intense pre-university course . . . my university days would have been impoverished without it.' And an RAF translator recalls his Bodmin and Crail contemporaries as 'all in all a more impressive group' than those he encountered when he went up to university after National Service. 'Many were avid music listeners and were keen and sometimes very good performers . . .'

The antiquarian bookseller, Eric Korn, for many years a *Times Literary Supplement* columnist and long-term panellist on the erudite radio programme 'Round Britain Quiz', is remembered by Michael Frayn as having produced while still a student at Bodmin an 'absolutely wonderful' translation of the last poem written by Mayakovsky before he committed suicide. He sees his fellow *kursanty* as 'corpuscles of vodka along the aorta of British cultural life . . . blown permanently off track by a wind from the birch woods'.

But a fair question from a non-linguist reader before we go too much further would be, 'Why the big deal? What's so hard about learning Russian?' Without getting into comparative philological league tables, the alphabet for one major thing, a daunting glacis which had to be overcome in the first few days to allow access to the language in the castle within.

There were times when frustrated JSSL students felt the alphabet's inventors, St Cyril and his brother St Methodius, had much to answer for. Their names destined to be forever twinned like Laurel and Hardy or Swan & Edgar, they were sent out from Byzantium as missionaries around 900 AD, mastered the Slav dialect then spoken in Moravia and conceived the Glagolitic alphabet to record it. What we now call Cyrillic is a later, simpler form. Cyril moved on to Bulgaria, where he won over Khan Boris and his people to the true Church and developed another alphabet, Cyrillic, to record the liturgy and Scriptures, deliberately rooted in Greek to underscore the closeness of the Slavonic Church to the Greek Christian tradition.

Among many other difficulties for English speakers, there was also an entirely unfamiliar pronunciation and diction that required novel lip and tongue placement, and at least for non-Classical scholars the fact that the nouns had different genders and declined through six cases according to complex and often irrational rules, while verbs had a variety of tenses, moods, prefixes and patterns

Naky Doniach, the MOD
Inspector of JSSL

Dame Elizabeth Hill, 'Liza',
Professor of Slavonic
Studies and Director of the
Russian Course at
Cambridge, in 1956.

George Bolsover,
Director of the School
of Slavonic and East
European Studies
(SSEES).

Ronald Hingley, the
first Course
Administrator in
London.

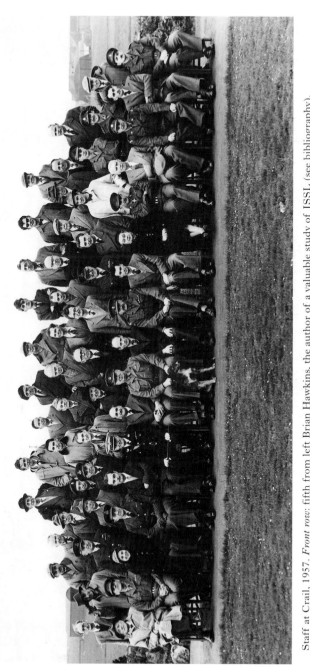

Staff at Crail, 1957. *Front row:* fifth from left Brian Hawkins, the author of a valuable study of JSSL (see bibliography).

Bodmin in the early 1950s.

Outdoor lesson with Vladimir Koshevnikoff, Bodmin 1955.

Patrick Procktor chats with crew members of the Soviet cruiser *Ordzhonikidze* at Portsmouth during the official visit to the UK of First Secretary Khrushchev in April-May 1956.

Midshipmen at Bodmin, September 1954. *Second row*: extreme left in dark glasses Jeremy Wolfenden; *front row*: first left Malcolm Brown, *second left* Jeremy Wolfenden's close friend Robin Hope; also present *back row*: centre David Callender, Oxford Blue and Olympic oarsman, and right Keith Morris, future Ambassador to Colombia.

Choir practice at Bodmin, 1953.

Card-playing in Russian, Bodmin 1953.

Crail Harbour, 1947.

The last real soldiers leave Crail for Korea, July 1952.

Geoffrey Elliott on a recent visit to Crail.

of conjugation. Other than for the handful who may have studied philology, the vocabulary had very few obvious affinities with Anglo-Saxon or Romance languages.

Every word had its own, often mobile, and not logically predictable, stressed syllable and in some positions the letter 'g' was pronounced as 'v' for no obvious reason. Beginners could easily be reduced to sobs by such arcane features as the absence of a definite or indefinite article or the present tense of the verb 'to be', or rules such as the one which mandated that to describe a single object called for the nominative case, two to four required the object to be in the genitive singular but five or more took the speaker down the lawless roads of the genitive plural. So even students who had some knowledge of French or German found it hard going, and for a time the further they went the harder it seemed to get and the more they had to learn. Paraphrasing Mark Twain, many early-stage JSSL students would sooner have declined an evening of free drinks than decline one of the more aberrant Russian nouns.

But for some, probably the majority, the challenge was fascinating and the treasure found in the castle made the effort worthwhile. It included insights into a rich often bloody history not taught in Imperial and Continental-centred English schools, access to the sweep of Russian literature, once described by Herzen as 'an uninterrupted indictment of Russian reality', and a window into the minds of a people. In the process they formed impressions about the Soviet system. Since their teachers had chosen or been forced to flee it, those impressions may have been one-sided, but political indoctrination *per se* was not a part of the JSSL curriculum. Nor was spying, though in the early University Course years potential interpreters were given some practice in interrogation, though only of a formal, Geneva Convention kind.

But even with so much talent to draw on, and the criteria clear, getting the selection system to function properly was a challenge and the paths actually taken to JSSL were many and varied.

4

Uncommon Entrances

The sense of national urgency was such that men were tapped for the first Interpreters' Course at Cambridge before JSSL was even in place and, in the case of Marcus Wheeler, soon after he had graduated and even before he had begun his RAF service. He, John Waine (later Bishop of Chelmsford) and others by-passed Basic Training and were shipped swiftly to Cambridge to be greeted by a harangue from Liza about the importance of the work they were to do.

If they did well, at some future point they might find themselves conveying the truth about life in the 'free world' to meetings in Russian towns and villages. But if they did badly, she warned, bringing out the stick that was used very effectively for the rest of JSSL's existence, they were liable to be 'returned to unit' (RTU'd in Service parlance) or, even worse, posted to Korea. Others summoned there in such haste that they were not paid for three weeks and found their Course A did not have a title for a while included Keith Argent, whisked from counting Army blankets in a storeroom on the eve of a posting to the Middle East, and John Goodliffe, clutching his recent degree in French.

As the system settled down, JSSL filled its classrooms more and more by 'word of mouth', augmented by some sharp talent-spotting in Basic Training units across the country as careers officers tried to find slots for their new charges and by direct lobbying; between 1951and 1958 Liza's files show that she had 167 letters from 'schoolmasters, college tutors and commanding officers'.

As the existence of the Courses became more widely known, candidates being interviewed at the start of their Service may have read a circular or heard gossip in the NAAFI – that 'community centre' of hissing tea urns, sausages and baked beans, mid-morning buns, table-tennis, darts and popular melodies warbled by Lita Rosa over the wireless. Luckily unaware of the Service maxim that one should never, ever, volunteer for anything, they put their names forward for it in the perfectly reasonable belief that hard work in a classroom was preferable to clipping papers together in an orderly room, operating a teleprinter or trying to steer a tank across Salisbury Plain, and a whole lot better than being sent to hotspots like Korea, Cyprus or Malaya, where malevolent foreigners wanted to shoot you. Peter Wilmshurst was moodily trimming his Commanding Officer's lawn with his own razor when he got the message that he was to escape to JSSL.

In many cases conscripts had heard about the Course while in their last days at school wondering what the next two years would bring. Glen Dudbridge was told about it by a friend who had returned to his school in full uniform. He was thus primed to ask about it, and in his first weeks of Service in 1957 an interviewer offered him the choice of Chinese, Russian, Polish, Czech or German-language studies; he opted for Russian.

The selection offered is in itself an interesting indication of the Sigint priorities at the time; a 1953 file shows that the RAF was already classifying its 'radio telephony DF operators' (DF standing for Direction Finding and the term itself a synonym for 'Monitors') as 'A' if they had Russian training, 'B' Cantonese and 'C' Mandarin, and were in the process of adding 'D' for German.

Ron Truman, a tutor in Spanish at Oxford, was at school in

Devon when he went for his National Service medical. He had read a piece in the *Daily Telegraph* about the Russian Course – which suggests that it was not that much of an 'official secret' – and told his interviewer that he wanted to join the Navy and do Russian, an option new to his interviewer, who had to rummage through his papers to find the appropriate information.

Eric Korn's reluctance to take up the opportunity to become an Air Traffic Controller, telling the interviewer he wanted to learn Russian, brought the rejoinder: 'This is the RAF, not bloody Berlitz. What makes you think we are in the business of giving you lessons?' The next day Korn reappeared with the by now well-used cutting from the *Daily Telegraph* and a week later found himself at Bodmin 'lighting fires and learning locatives'.

This approach evidently caught on, and more and more recruits were turning up at Basic Training with their papers marked 'R.L.', meaning that they were destined for the Russian Course. It is probably a safe assumption that this became the norm though the paths were always haphazard. Despite having no evidence of foreign-language skills, Alan Bennett was simply told by an education sergeant at the Yorks and Lancaster Regiment in Pontefract one day that the names of all boys who had School Certificate – there were three in his squad – were going to be put forward for the Russian Course. In fact Bennett, who once remarked that as a late developer it was touch and go whether puberty or National Service got him first, was already armed not just with his School Certificate but a place at Sydney Sussex College, Cambridge.

He went despite some concern that the Regiment might keep him back for active service since he was, *mirabile dictu*, a crack shot with the Bren machine-gun. When Peter Woodthorpe was called up, with a science background at school and a place waiting at Magdalene College, Cambridge, to read biochemistry, he decided for no special reason that he wanted to join the Navy. He was told by a Royal Marines senior NCO that he could 'if you sign up for this 'ere Roossian Course'.

Parents also played a role. The acme of parental lobbying,

reported by the *Yorkshire Post*, came when a mother complained to the Queen that her son had been refused a place on the Course. The outcome is unknown.

Jeffrey Gray, Emeritus Professor of Psychology at The Institute of Psychiatry in London, was on Salisbury Plain, his spirits sinking fast, when he heard that some fellow basic trainees had been sent off to learn Russian while he was left behind applying his Classical education to peeling mountains of potatoes. After his commanding officer turned him down flat, he asked his mother to approach the War Office. The redoubtable Mrs Gray at once told Whitehall that her brilliant son was being wasted in the Army, and one week later Jeffrey was posted to the Russian Course first at Coulsdon, then London, followed by Bodmin, where his Malvolio in a 1954 JSSL production of *Twelfth Night* in Russian was reportedly memorable and no doubt confirmed Mrs Gray's judgement. Terry Wade, a German graduate who returned as an instructor after passing through JSSL and Cambridge, might not have heard about the Course at all had his mother not drawn it to his attention when his post-graduate research was proving frustrating. It also took discreet parental nudging, as well as personal initiative by studying Russian, for Arthur Stockwin, Professor of Japanese Politics at Oxford, to get his place in 1955.

There were less obvious routes too, in one case even a harmless form of simony. When Kevin Ruane applied from the Royal Artillery in 1954, he met a blank wall: it was claimed that the Course had finished. He persisted and was marched in to his commanding officer.

'Stand easy, Ruane. I gather you have a request to make.'

'Yes, sir.'

'Well I have one to make of you. I've discovered you are the only Catholic [pronouncing it Cartholic] on the strength . . . my daughter is a member of the Children of Mary and with Christmas approaching she's asked me to try to sell some of their raffle tickets in the barracks. I was wondering if you could help . . .'

Ruane promptly bought several books of tickets, whereupon his CO revealed that the brigadier responsible for postings to JSSL 'is an old chum of mine', and Ruane was promptly set on a path that led via Bodmin, Cambridge, GCHQ and the BBC Monitoring Service to a distinguished career as a BBC correspondent in Moscow and Warsaw.

Michael Frayn applied for the Course because of a schoolboy fixation with Russia's politics and language, which he had begun to teach himself. Interviewed at his Basic Training camp, he was given a warning with echoes of Liza's earlier apocalyptic vision: 'I suppose you think it's some sort of skive. Well, I can tell you it's far from being a skive – at any point you might be dropped behind enemy lines.'

Tony Divett's passport to Bodmin was his passion for butterfly collecting, discovered by his interviewing officer, an equally obsessed lepidopterist, who promptly endorsed his application to JSSL.

D. M. Thomas was in despair in Basic Training on the Isle of Wight. 'I used to gaze up at Parkhurst Prison and almost wish I was there rather than in our uncouth barracks. I was being bawled out by a sergeant – "Thomas, I'll make a soldier out of you if it's the last thing I do!" – when a runner came up to us: "Gunner Thomas to report tomorrow to JSSL Bodmin, for the Russian Course." This, for me, proved the existence of God.'

The left hands and right hands of the Services being notoriously oblivious of each other, interviewing officers seem often to have been unaware of the planners' warning to keep anyone with a Soviet or East European connection at bay. Peter Tegel had arrived in England in 1939, a seven-year-old refugee from Nazi-occupied Czechoslovakia. In 1948 he became a naturalised British citizen, was duly called up for National Service and during Basic Training at Aldershot was told by his CO that, as he was doing National Service, he would be granted British nationality and put on the Russian Course.

That Harry Shukman had a place on the course was even more exceptional. His parents had emigrated from Russia to the UK in

1913 but never took British citizenship. Shukman left Hendon Junior Technical School at sixteen and was working as a trainee radio and radar engineer in London. He had registered for the RAF in 1949 at the age of eighteen and was given deferment to continue his technical studies at evening school. Two years later he was jolted by an Air Ministry letter stating that he 'may possess dual nationality, British and Soviet'. If he continued his studies and deferred National Service until after his twenty-first birthday, he would have to formally relinquish his claim to Soviet citizenship, a process fraught with hazard. But if he joined the RAF before then, he would relinquish any claim on Soviet status and automatically remain solely British.

The bombshell gave him precisely the excuse he needed to escape from an uncongenial and schizoid mix of technical study, boring factory work, art galleries, playing trumpet in a local jazz band and discovering, in preparation for his first trip abroad – to France – that learning a foreign language was a pleasure. He joined the RAF in 1951 and, after a few weeks mainly spent playing trumpet in the camp band, he was told he could choose between becoming a radar fitter or a Russian interpreter. 'If you choose radar fitter, we'll send you to train for forty-four weeks and you'll end up a junior technician. If you want to be a Russian interpreter, we'll make you a flight lieutenant on £1,000 a year, and send you Paris to live with a Russian family for a year.' This was not a hard choice even if it turned out to be a false prospectus.

Shukman was unaware that to qualify for the Course he was supposed to have at least two 'A' Levels, nor that the authorities had warned against the risks involved in having anyone with a Soviet connection anywhere near JSSL. He thought of the Russian lullabies his mother had sung to him, and the Russian rhyming slang she used and which he had never properly understood. But he also knew that his parents were only Russian by nationality, not by ethnic culture. Russian Jews, with Yiddish as their native tongue, did not necessarily speak good Russian, as the authorities rightly pointed out when commenting on the need for good instructors.

His case leaves questions unanswered. The fact that he had lacked qualifications and proven language ability, and that only a few months earlier his citizenship had been an issue for the Air Ministry, suggests that at this early stage the authorities were in fact encouraging the Services to seek out candidates by intuition, as much as qualification, and not discouraging them from allowing in men who might later be employable in other areas. One clue to this appears in a letter from Liza to the Air Ministry, requesting that a *kursant* who had been RTU'd for an undisclosed misdemeanour be sent back to Cambridge, as 'a man with a partly Russian background is usually an asset'.

Ivor Samuels also came from an immigrant family and though his father had taken British citizenship in 1948, National Service was the key to resolution of the same tricky dual nationality issue, in his case British and Polish. The enlightened Mr Stirrup, headmaster of his grammar school in Walthamstow, to which returning pupils had brought news of the Course, took the remarkable initiative of hiring an elderly émigrée teacher, Miss Alexander, to give weekly Russian lessons to his senior boys to improve their chances. Samuels duly got to Bodmin, went on to the Interpreters' Course and, after some bureaucratic wheeling and dealing over the length of his Service commitment, managed to take up his place at Cambridge in good time.

Another student, who had best be called Alex Smith, appeared at Crail, blond-haired, ruddy-cheeked, the epitome of an overachieving tractor driver on a Soviet propaganda poster. He spoke absolutely fluent Russian but accented and slightly less than fluent English. His parents were émigrés who lived in the Middle East but who had along the way acquired and passed to Alex the gift of British citizenship, the price of which was that he had to do National Service. He spent only a few weeks at JSSL. There was clearly no need for him to learn any Russian and he vanished overnight, probably into some other back pocket of the British intelligence system.

Though he had three 'A' Levels from Highgate School, Patrick Procktor could offer no evidence of language skills. He had heard about the Course from a friend. 'It was rather an attractive idea and also attractive to someone like myself who was rather idle.'

Geoffrey Elliott came to the course from Basic Training in the Intelligence Corps. 'I went straight into the Intelligence Corps Depot in Maresfield in deepest Sussex, as my father had been in that line of work in Yugoslavia and Hungary. I trained in Field Security, which didn't do much for me. When we paraded in the mornings, there was this great style divide between the military way in which we pseudo-policemen stamped about, and the "this is all more than a bit beneath us" air of the contingent from "Ling Wing", men serving out their time after the Russian Course or on a military "refresher" in the middle of it.

'They ambled rather than marched and were always a fraction late getting on parade. Their uniforms didn't fit and they wore their berets jutting straight out at the side like a blueberry pancake, not neatly shrunk and tugged down over the ear like the Field Security hard men. The Russian Course intrigued me because there were Siberian roots on my mother's side though we spoke not a word of the language, but the admin people claimed to have no idea how you went about signing up. But one day there was a notice telling you how to apply to study Arabic. This seemed the next best thing and I put my name in. A few weeks later I was told to report to "Hut 8 behind the Ablutions" for an interview, which turned out to be for the Russian Course after all.

'There was this soft-spoken major, the "War Office Language Tester". When he heard my French, he raised his eyebrows and winced like John le Mesurier, and when we switched to German, his face clouded. I was sure I had failed.

'Maresfield folklore said that if you wanted to know what was going on the best source was Connie, who ran the local pub, The Chequers. Back then it wasn't much more than a couple of smoky bars where the admin NCOs would booze and "Piltdown Pam", "Dirty Betty" and the other Maresfield camp followers hung out. True enough, when I had heard nothing more about the Russian

Course for a while and asked Connie, she assured me that I had a place.'

A probably apocryphal Second World War story records that one Intelligence Corps recruit told an interviewer that he knew 'Arabic, and Modern and Classical Greek. I can also read cuneiform and hieroglyphics.'

'What are hieroglyphics?'

'The language of the Pharaohs, sir.'

He was duly posted to No. 319 Field Security Section in the Faroe Islands.

When Gerry Smith, now Professor of Russian at Oxford, went into the RAF, he had one ambition – to become a professional jazz musician. Persuaded or perhaps deceived by an interviewing officer that while the Russian Course was an interesting alternative to being a bandsman, he had to enlist for three years in order to qualify, he did so, in the process meeting for the first time in his life boys from south of the Mersey and 'the first public schoolboy I ever talked to'.

Although another official file note from the planning period comments that some aspects of the programme would require the attention of the Security Service, very few if any National Service entrants to JSSL seem to have undergone much in the way of vetting to check their backgrounds.

This is not surprising given the numbers involved, and it was probably also concluded pragmatically that the time to take a close look at potential political or other sensitivities would be as and when a student went into a Sigint unit, or to other areas of the intelligence system, and were as the jargon had it 'indoctrinated'.

Nevertheless someone seems to have taken a look at the late Bernard Corry, who later became Professor of Economic History at Queen Mary College, London. Already a graduate of the London School of Economics, Corry was notable in his RAF Basic Training as the sole recruit to enter 'Atheist' under 'religious affiliation'; mysteriously dubbed 'the Baron' by the NCOs, he would be left standing alone on the parade-ground after the Anglicans, Catholics and Jews had marched off to their various spiritual exercises. (Harry Shukman had thought of entering Rotary Converter or Cathode Follower, but chickened out at the last minute and wrote 'Jewish' as the path of least resistance.)

Corry was accepted for the Russian Course but a last-minute Air Ministry letter told him that he was to be posted to Northolt instead as a pay clerk. The only explanation he could think of was that he had signed a statement that he had never been a Communist, when in fact he had.

No other *kursanty* has mentioned having to make declarations about political affiliations although one National Serviceman did claim in a letter to Geoffrey Elliott that he had been turned down because his parents were active Communists and another believed he failed a Navy Selection Board for the Interpreters' Course because his interviewers had been suspicious of his pacifist Quaker education. On the other side of the coin, one of Elliott's fellow *kursanty*, David Paisey (in later life a curator of early German printed books at the British Library), wrote: 'Little did [the authorities] know (or did they?) that familiarity with that wonderful language would make most of us incredibly sympathetic to Russian people and their culture, including modern developments. It is odd given the whole purpose of the Course that there wasn't more in the way of political indoctrination. I was always a crypto-leftie and if they knew, they didn't show it in any way.' Michael Frayn had been half of a 'two-man' Communist cell at his school, which had led him to be interested in Russian, and even though he soon left the politics behind he does not remember ever being asked about his views.

Robin Milner-Gulland remembers how the Cold War atmosphere of the time was so generally accepted that his class in London was taken aback when their instructor Michael Futrell handed out their marked essays on the theme of Soviet politics with the caustic comment, 'Unless you've understood its attraction you've got no right to go dismissing their system!' Futrell, no softie on the Soviets, would one day produce one of the most original books on the financing of the Bolsheviks before the revolution.

Eric Korn, whose father had been born in Poland, remembers being unsure before his National Service which side he was on in the Cold War and reminisces tongue in cheek that he 'reflected that a smattering of the language would be useful if I decided to defect. Others may have thought so too.' Fortunately for all, Khrushchev's denunciation of Stalin's crimes in 1956 settled the issue for him. When another *kursant* told his uncle, a Communist stalwart, that he was going to be trained as a Russian interpreter, he was rebuked for agreeing 'to spy on the working class'.

Patrick Procktor remembered that when he finished the Interpreters' Course, he regarded himself 'as a sort of Communist'. Interviewed in 1994, he could not recall his politics ever having been an issue during his Service; he could not remember the word 'Communism' ever being mentioned in the Navy.

Even without such a difficult task, and such a hybrid mix of pupils, getting large organisations to work from scratch is always hard. For the Armed Forces to embark on a new venture of this scale and with its combustible mix of so many unusual and distinctly 'unmilitary' factors, overlaid by the need for extreme confidentiality if not secrecy, was a major challenge. They did a good job.

5

Exiles from our Father's Land

The administrative and logistical infrastructure of JSSL was substantial. In the front line were the teaching staff, which in one set of Bodmin statistics – it does not seem to have changed greatly in later years – comprised eight Service officers, eight British civilian teachers, twenty-two of Russian or Soviet origin, fifteen Poles, six Latvians, two Ukrainians, one Estonian, one Lithuanian, one Czech and one 'stateless' – with only three women among them. We shall take a look later at some of the characters and at the University Course staff, who were just as much '57 varieties' and in some ways an even more eclectic mix.

Supervising the JSSL instructors were a Principal and Assistant Principal (both British), whose responsibilities and success were prodigious and largely unsung especially in setting and co-ordinating the syllabus and timetable, and juggling parallel and successive courses in and out of the various time-slots and classrooms. Tests had to be set and marked, student assessments made and non-British staff recruited, evaluated and sympathetically but firmly managed. This would have been quite a task in itself in an ordinary, established school, but JSSL, as we have demonstrated, was neither. Its non-British staff were Slavs, moody and volatile by nature, to whom internecine squabbling was a way of life, here exacerbated by differences in background and by national rivalries, not least Polish detestation of all things Russian, and by the edgy precariousness of being refugees. This included the way Russian was to be spoken, which they handled with a clarity and accent so different to that of Soviet émigrés that it was said to be easy to spot the students who had been taught predominantly by the Poles from the way they spoke.

Perhaps the only thing the Principals and their teams could be thankful for is that, unlike a large conventional school, at least they did not have to contend with parent-teacher evenings and Speech Days.

But the schools also had to have appropriate military underpinnings. The same Bodmin statistics – as with the teaching staff, the numbers did not change much in later years – show a commandant, an adjutant, a quartermaster and eighteen 'various', plus another 120 'various' – presumably cooks, cleaners and so on – under the officer commanding the admin wing.

The Services had to select, move around, kit out, pay, feed, house, monitor and discipline their people, and run the conveyor belt that carried them first into the 'training units' and from there to the world of Sigint. They also had to get the balance right, an issue identified in a brief note on the progamme for the final passing out parade in Coulsdon. 'These young language students academically representing some of the best material in the Services' required 'controlling in a manner that was intelligent and firm without undue severity, the object being that the maximum amount of effort might be devoted to the study of languages as was compatible with Service obligations . . .' Though as we shall see the scales tended to tip a little from time to time, on the whole it will be our conclusion that in this as in other respects JSSL succeeded in its aims.

Four groups of National Servicemen – known as 'Translator Entries' and drawn in roughly equal proportions from the three Services – were posted to the Schools each year, in February, May,

August and November. The original plan was that for the first entry of the year the Army students would be sent to Coulsdon and the RAF and Navy men to Bodmin. Similarly for the third, with the venues reversed for the second and fourth intakes. However this arrangement seems not to have lasted very long and most memories are of all three Services at the same School.

By the time they reached JSSL all the students had been exposed to the belly of the Service beast through Basic Training. When they arrived, it was made clear that while they were now in a different kind of institution, they had to work to stay there.

The opening headmasterly homily from the Commandant of Crail summed it up with the well-practised punch line, 'You play ball with me and I'll play ball with you, but remember, it's my ball.'

The JSSL teaching system evolved over the years, but as it was producing the desired results its basic components and methods do not seem to have changed much over its life or with the different locations. Translator students – officer cadets lived a less regimented life – would shamble out of their frowsty huts to breakfast. At 8.30 a.m. they would form up on the parade-ground – at Coulsdon against a background of the 'Slaves' Chorus' from the Guards Depot next door; at Bodmin, if they could see through the rain, a lunar vista of the disused clay workings; and at Crail on a clear day a magnificent panorama, for those not too bleary-eyed to appreciate it, over the Firth of Forth to the Isle of May.

The Service groups then marched – a verb which probably merits quotation marks – down the hill for the start of the academic day at 8.30 a.m., textbooks stuffed in the Services equivalent of the school satchel, the regulation webbing haversack.

There would be a well-thumbed Semyonova grammar, Pears and Wissotsky's *Passages for Translation*, and always those tattered and ticked vocabulary lists. In their early days many students would carry another JSSL staple, the reading primer *Obyknovennye Lyudi* ('Ordinary People') and many can even now recite its less than memorable opening line: '*Dzhon Piters i evo zhena Meri zhivut v nebol'shom novom dome nedaleko ot Londona'* ('John Peters and his wife Mary live in a small new house near London'). The story ended with Mary having a son whom his father wants to call 'Spitfire'. Luckily for the lad's future in the rough and tumble of the school playground, Mary does not agree.

There was recurrent speculation at JSSL that Liza Hill herself had written 'John and Mary' under the pseudonym 'Elizaveta Fen'. This was based on a deductive linguistic leap to do with a perceived coincidence between Liza's three initials in English, EFH, and the Cyrillic characters spelling out E. FEN, plus the link between the latter word and Cambridge, all in all a theory that might once have had a spindle-shanked professor leaping from his Bletchley bathtub shouting 'Eureka'. It was simply incorrect. As they moved on to another JSSL staple, *Crime and Punishment*, the more literary *kursanty* wondered whether the title of Fen's primer was actually a sly allusion to Dostoyevsky's division of the world into 'ordinary' and 'extraordinary' people; the former who 'must lead a life of strict obedience and have no right to transgress the law, because . . . they are ordinary'.

Guidance notes for the teaching staff stressed that 'wherever possible Russian should be the medium of instruction. Particular stress should be laid on the oral phase of each lesson, since hearing the language spoken is an indispensable element in developing *Sprachgefühl*, i.e. the ability to assess instinctively the correctness of what one hears.'

Julian Andrews vividly recalls the application of this approach at Coulsdon on his very first day. 'We were assembled in a large hall with a stage, on which stood an easel and board on to which had been pinned a huge map of the Soviet Union. A neatly dressed man with a military moustache strode on to the stage, greeting us with a smile and a bow. We later learned that he was a former pilot in the Polish Air Force called Shatunovsky (spelling optional), who had apparently been a prisoner of the Russians and had served in a punishment battalion, including mine-clearance. (Shatunovsky would be encountered by RAF *kursanty* at Bodmin later on when he lectured on aerodynamics and aircraft parts.)

Gesturing at the map he began speaking in Russian, using short sentences, often repeated several times, with considerable use of sign language and facial expressions. We began to realise, almost with disbelief, that although we knew none of the words he was using, we were understanding the sense of what he was saying. He kept the performance up for one hour, at the end of which we realised that we now knew quite a lot about the geography and physical characteristics of the Soviet Union. It was our first experience of what became known as the "Direct Method" of language learning, and this full-length lecture, gradually expanding the subject but always integrating part of the text from the previous one, was repeated each week. As a means of introducing us to, and making us familiar with, the sounds and rhythms of the Russian language this weekly lecture, contrasting as it did with the much heavier hours spent on grammatical exercises and translations, gave us right from the start a sense of the musical qualities of the language which are part of its beauty and richness. Shatunovsky was like an alchemist, working with the base metal of a mass of National Servicemen to create people who would become deeply receptive to the golden nuances of a language they had never encountered before.'

Recognising, however, that most of the students were confronting not just another language but the runic mysteries of the Cyrillic alphabet, instructors were also urged that 'the idea should . . . be consistently conveyed that the learning of Russian is not as difficult as it appears to be'.

A sample timetable for the early part of the Translators' Course showed that each class of thirty or so would begin their day divided into small groups for an hour of grammar drill (reading phrases and exercises in chorus), another hour of grammar instruction, forty-five minutes of Russian reading and oral practice, again in small groups, and, after a brief break for tea and sticky buns, another forty-five minutes translating from English into Russian. In this segment a passage in English was read out by the instructor and translated by the class into Russian, first orally and then in writing; during the Course the class worked through some sixty such texts of escalating difficulty. Another three-quarters of an hour doing the reverse – from Russian into English – rounded off a busy morning.

The small groups, or 'syndicates', were a key part of the system, allowing *kursanty* to be switched easily from one group to another depending on their progress, creating in the process groups of broadly equal proficiency.

Towards the end of the Course there were also sessions where the *kursanty* were closeted one on one with an instructor for an hour of oral practice. Terry Wade remembers there were some stormy winter days in Bodmin when one or two *kursanty* couldn't face getting up and let others go in their place, though the instructors either didn't notice or didn't mind. 'If they had been reported, there would have been hell to pay.'

On Mondays, Tuesdays and Thursday afternoons – Wednesday afternoons were free, though there are some memories of a chilly spell of compulsory physical training being involved – lunch would be digested with thirty minutes of Russian dictation, followed by a thirty-minute lecture in Russian, with students sometimes being asked to interpret, ninety minutes of translation from Russian into English, the day then being capped by a session learning thirty new words from vocabulary lists, the instructor repeating each word at least five times with the class parroting behind him in chorus.

JSSL students at Bodmin had their own Clockwork Orange style neologism, devised by Malcolm Brown, to rate their lecturers. Based on the Russian word for boredom, it was called the *skukometr* or 'boredom meter'; the content of a lesson graded in 'skuks', 'megaskuks' and 'killerskuks', the latter deemed to be 'near fatal' in its soporific effects.

Friday afternoons were a time for revision, reading out again all the passages covered during the week, a new passage for comprehension, and tests in dictation and grammar. Saturday mornings were allocated to private study, working with Linguaphone records, revision of the words one was supposed to have absorbed during the week plus ten new ones, and preparation for the week ahead.

The not so subtle presence of both carrot and stick hung over those first few months. The carrot was a chance of a place for a few on the University Course: a civilian existence in a congenial location, learning Russian to a higher, quasi-degree level, higher pay and the knowledge that by the time the process was over the National Serviceman's 'chuff factor' – the period of Service divided by the days left to serve – would show that the risk of a return to real Service life for any length of time was small. The stick was of failing and being sent back whence one came, a fate few cared to contemplate. Both induced much extra 'swotting', a certain amount of showing-off and nervous scrutiny of each new set of test results.

Tony Blee (who went on to make important contributions in UK Health Service management) recalls that at Crail he 'sometimes heard people muttering in Russian in their sleep, they were so worried about failing the next test'.

Papers for the 1957 First and Second Major Progress tests, the latter the watershed for university, with a score of not less than 75 per cent the hurdle rate, show just how far students were expected to come in a few short weeks. In the First, one paper gave them seventy-five minutes to put into Russian tense- and case-testing sentences such as 'Yesterday I bought my mother two red carpets and green and brown curtains. I had to ask whether I could put them on the instalment plan. Fortunately they agreed', and 'The trains from Edinburgh to Crail usually stop at all the small stations. If I travel on the fast train which leaves the capital early in the morning, we pass several stations without stopping.' The two passages for translation from Russian into English, for which an hour was allowed, would have been at least 'O' Level standard.

By the time of the Second Major Test, passages for translation into English had escalated to extracts from a science-fiction story by H. G. Wells and the autobiography of the mountaineer Sherpa Tensing, with a potted biography of Albert Einstein selected for translation into Russian. The grammar questions had become much trickier and the five sentences to be put into Russian had been notched up to the level of 'The little village which was surrounded on all sides by the advancing Soviet units underwent many heavy air raids', and 'You would be very surprised if you knew how much I had paid for the unbreakable glass'!

It would be flattering to think that Frederick Forsyth's portrayal of JSSL Bodmin in *The Devil's Alternative* as 'Little Russia', where his hero was 'virtually able to pass for Russian after six months', was generally accurate. The reality was not quite that, but impressive nonetheless. Comparison with a GCE or university degree curriculum is somewhat misleading, given the Service bias of some of the course instruction and the very heavy emphasis on oral and listening skills. It was common ground among those who followed the Courses in detail that, starting from scratch, the translators in the seven to nine months of language and technical training reached somewhere between Advanced Level and university entry standard in the Russian they spoke and understood, and that in their further twelve months at London or Cambridge the Interpreter candidates covered, in Naky Doniach's view, the equivalent in language terms of a three-year degree course.

Forsyth may still have had a point. Doniach brought back to mind thirty years later a visit to Cambridge when he and one of the senior Russian instructors listened to two *kursanty* talking in flawless Russian: 'It was as though they had swallowed all four volumes of the dictionary.' Doniach speculated to his colleague that the men could actually pass as Russian. The instructor pondered but concluded, 'No, even a well-educated Russian allows himself to make mistakes.'

A school can attract, as JSSL did, the best and the brightest pupils, but to be effective it also needs teachers who can inspire and enthuse, who know their subject, and who can maintain order. Conventional schools had tried and tested recruiting methods and though the occasional sadist, misanthrope or Captain Grimes crept through the net, for them, by and large, staffing was not a major headache. Staffing JSSL was of a very different order.

Whether at Coulsdon, Bodmin or Crail, or, as we shall see later, Cambridge and London, the non-British teaching staff were the essence of the JSSL experience, sometimes gently mocked for eccentricity, sometimes admired for their panache, sometimes objects of sympathy, but never condescension, though there was much misery – the 'sadness of homelessness', as Peter Woodthorpe described it thirty years later – in most of their backgrounds. 'They tried to live and get back to cooking a bit of borscht for lunch and driving these words into us and hearing their language mutilated. And not being treated with great respect.'

This is not to diminish the vital contribution of the young British instructors, themselves brilliant linguists, who were key to the enterprise administratively as well as academically. The first academic head at Bodmin and Crail, until he left to teach at Madras College, St Andrews, and a pioneer of the Interpreter and Translator courses, was Norval Lunan, whose style is remembered as 'minimalist, restrained and tightly focused'. George Bird, the 'Chief Instructor Higher Grade', Brian Hawkins, Owen Lewis, Terry Wade and Peter Meades were probably more like the conventional schoolteachers to whom the *kursanty* had been exposed for the past ten years of their lives, or the younger dons they had encountered at university. They thus did not become – for which they are probably grateful – the subject of anecdotes or *Samovar* articles. But the JSSL initiative would not have worked without them.

For many *kursanty* these refugee Slavs and Balts represented their first substantive contact with 'foreigners', and their memories and adventures were glimpses of a harsh, alien world beyond most British middle-class comprehension. Looking back thirty years later, Naky Doniach felt that JSSL's students were 'carried away by the élan and magic of the teachers, and the whole set up'.

In David Marquand's words, 'the instructors made a bigger and more lasting impression on me than anything else'. He remembers with particular clarity the story of Mr Dudariv at Bodmin whose life had been 'one long tragedy', beginning after the Russian Revolution in the war between the Ukraine and Poland in which he was captured and held in a prison camp for several years, only to be imprisoned again, this time in Czechoslovakia, by the Germans. He was then swept into a British-run displaced persons' camp in Germany, from which he was shipped to England to work as a farm labourer until 'the mysterious workings of Providence intervened and sent him to Bodmin to teach Russian to pimply British adolescents. I shall never forget his plaintive mantra: "If you fail your examinations they will send me back to the fields and the factories."'

Future *Observer* correspondent and, for a short while, SIS officer, Mark Frankland, remembers that, 'Life was dominated by our Russian teachers, clever, slightly crazy émigrés who fought off the boredom of life in Nissen huts on the edge of Bodmin Moor by talking to us about their passions and drilling us in complex Russian swear words.'

Brian Hawkins, whose career as a senior teacher of Russian to Service and diplomatic students continued long after Crail itself closed, wrote of his émigré colleagues as 'highly qualified people in their own right'. The fact that many were, as someone else commented gently, 'rather lacking in English' was actually an advantage, given the stress on giving all instruction in Russian wherever possible.

The foreign staff did not have a monopoly on odd English – a War Office sign outside the gates of Walker Lines read: 'Joint Services School For Linguists – Please Drive Slow.'

Hawkins remembered: 'Many of them were landed gentry, diplomats, officers and lawyers; they included a prince, a baron, a couple of Counts and a senator.' There were also those 'of whom little was ever discovered or revealed'. One had served in the Foreign Legion after escaping from Hungary.

Martin Gilbert recalls that a Latvian instructor told the class he had been taken by the German occupation forces to Katyn, the site of the murder of thousands of Polish Army officers, to show that it was a Soviet, not a Nazi, atrocity. He also remembers *kursanty* repeatedly and provocatively asking one of the Russians the Russian word for 'slavery', only to watch the poor man exploding. 'You don't know what slavery is until you have lived in the Soviet

Union!' Other stories – that an instructor had seen the bodies of the dead Tsar's family, including Anastasia, at Yekaterinburg, or that another had resorted to cannibalism to survive the siege of Leningrad – suggest that some instructors themselves got a kick from seeing their naïve students grow ever more goggle-eyed as the amazing Siberian Nights' Tales unfolded.

One corner of the Officers' Mess where the instructors gathered in the evenings 'resembled nothing so much as a session of the Polish Government in exile . . . In addition there were those who had fought for the Russians against the Germans and those who had fought for the Germans against the Russians and had the Iron Crosses to prove it.' This theme surfaced in the House of Commons in 1990 in a debate about alleged Ukrainian war criminals to whose post-war entry into Britain the authorities had turned a blind eye; some of them, it was claimed, ended up as instructors at JSSL. No names were given and the allegations confused Crail and Bodmin.

These allegations aside, it has to be said that many of the staff had great charm, although others had rather rough edges. One pre-Revolutionary instructor was heard to dismiss a new Soviet-era arrival as '*gorilla sapiens*', and when Terry Wade joined the staff at Bodmin in 1955, his émigré colleagues were up in arms that the Officers' Mess provided Soviet newspapers. 'The dispute was eventually transferred to the Mess Suggestions Book, with comments such as [in Russian], "I would advise officers and gentlemen to learn Russian using the Russian classics." After some time, all the pages of suggestions were found to have been neatly cut out, and the Soviet newspapers remained.'

All the émigrés, whatever their background, were unsettled and *déraciné* in a way most of their students, insensitive and English, quite failed to understand. Though landing a secure post at JSSL must have been a godsend, the isolation of Bodmin and Crail must have seemed another manifestation of the exile experience.

The results of JSSL at every level are a credit to the staff selection process, to the structure of the syllabus but above all to the instructors themselves. However old, eccentric or gruff, they all had something, whether a natural ability to teach, charm, authority or style, that caught the imagination of their pupils, made them want to learn and moved them along so rapidly and successfully.

They had training. They were given *The Teaching of Modern Languages* issued by the Incorporated Society of Assistant Masters, and Charles Duff's *How to Learn a Foreign Language*. They were told to make lessons 'lively and practical' and to develop them based on familiar situations. But many spoke little English. They were not professionals. How many English speakers forcibly translated from Chipping Sodbury to Chelyabinsk via some cold and confusing refugee centre in Munich, at the age of fifty or more and speaking only broken Russian at best, could cope with teaching English as a foreign language? Maybe some could handle conversation, but grammar and literature? And not just picking up errors but offering constructive criticism, evaluating the students class by class, spotting the weaknesses and working on them?

One thing that stands out is that slightly less than half the non-British instructors were actually listed as Russians, the others being variously Polish, Latvian, Ukrainian, Estonian and Czech. But a straightforward interpretation of this may not be correct. In the wake of the Second World War, many Russians were not keen to declare themselves as such to the refugee authorities in Europe for fear of deportation. The Russian element was also carefully differentiated on the list, as the staff were bitterly keen to do among themselves, between 'Russian' and 'Russian (ex-Soviet)'. What a world lay between the prosaic entry for 'Mr Volkonsky, V., age 58, Russian' and the poetic memory of what that tall, courtly gentleman had once been as the noble Prince Volkonsky – who seems to have been entitled also to style himself 'His Serene Highness' and one branch of whose family traced its roots back to the medieval Saint Michael of Chernigov – now stripped of his former rank and social position but left with impeccable manners, a gold-topped cane and a St Petersburg accent.

Wherever they came from, they had a history of dislocation,

threat, dispossession, families left behind and general alienation that was personal and painful. So many JSSL pupils have memories of the staff that to distil them for the general reader is not easy. Many of the instructors served in at least two of the Schools (and in some case beyond, as the system took a new turn in the 1960s), and it is easier to combine some of the more noteworthy images from all three Schools in one chapter.

What is the right criterion? A man or woman with style might be memorable but might not have been a good teacher. Geoffrey Elliott recalls that the distinctly unstylish sixty-year-old Mr Krohin had a constant cold, and the appalling habit of carefully spreading his rebarbative handkerchiefs over the radiator to dry during class, which in that steam-heated atmosphere had the lethal effects of a Sarin attack in the Tokyo subway. So no points for style. But he was somehow a marvellous teacher at the most basic level of the alphabet and the 'this is a pencil' routines, which now sound like child's play but which were the essential entry point into the language.

Do we remember Madame Levitskaya because the JSSL *kursanty*, as quick as schoolchildren everywhere to stick teachers with nicknames like 'Black Dan' or 'Loudspeaker', tagged her as 'The Black Widow', or 'Keep Death Off the Roads', echoing a poignant road safety poster of the time. Or because never having quite mastered the English definite and indefinite articles, she once asked the commandant at lunch, 'Excuse me, Colonel, will you please pass water.'

And what's in a name? Many remember Mr Wassiljew, a tall and distinguished man already then approaching seventy, as much for his baffled rage about the way the British pronounced his name as for his teaching. When he left Soviet Russia, he had been given naturalisation papers in Munich, which meant that the Russian spelling of his name, Vasilyev, was transliterated into German as 'Wassiljew'. He felt – quite rightly – that of all people his students should know how to pronounce it properly rather than in the literal English way. Another name to whom it is difficult to put a face but which seems to leap from the pages of

William Gerhardie is the gentle Estonian Mr Mandre-Methusalem.

There was Mr Ross, a young philosopher who enthralled his classes with the matter-of-fact account of his capture by the Germans in the siege of Leningrad and his subsequent escape to Denmark.

Nor were a colourful background or eccentricity the only factors that made an impression. These were young men and it is hardly surprising that of all the teachers at Coulsdon the one who comes gratifyingly to mind fifty years later was a pale, young woman with bee-sting lips, slightly prominent cheekbones and huge, sad blue eyes. In the cold damp winter of 1952, which must have reminded her of her native Leningrad, she always wore a new navy-blue coat and 'halo' hat, for all the world an English Sunday-school teacher. But when she spoke, it was not Bible stories that were evoked in the minds of her imaginative young pupils.

Two of the most memorable stars in a JSSL firmament that had more than its fair share of remarkable people were Dmitri Makaroff and Vladimir Koshevnikoff. (Though pedants will disagree with the 'ff', this is the orthography used in the Staff List.) Makaroff was born in 1927, in the international melting pot of Shanghai teeming with desperate refugees, its business run largely by British *taipans*, but its real economy by an underworld of Chinese gangsters and warlords. His Russian émigré parents moved on to settle in Australia. His father had studied wig-making at the Paris Opéra before 1914, returning to Russia at the outbreak of war, and it was from him that Dmitri would learn to make beards, straighten crêpe hair and build up a theatrical beard. But, he says, his mother's great love of music was a more fundamental influence than his father's beard-making. She had studied in Moscow under the composer Mikhail Ippolitov-Ivanov and, in Dmitri's view, might have become a celebrity had she not accompanied his father on their flight from revolutionary Russia. He recalls that, despite their impoverished émigré life in Sydney, his parents took him as a small child to see all the celebrities who visited Sydney in the early 1930s. 'My first opera was *The Flying*

Dutchman. Was this, alas, prophetic? I fear so. I am still of no fixed abode. The mountain of books, papers and *objects* gets ever higher.'

He read Classics at Sydney and set off on his eclectic version of the Gap Year. This included a spell in a Benedictine monastery in Belgium, and after eighteen months employed in several 'dismal office jobs' in London he came to rest (in a manner of speaking since he was incurably restless) as an instructor at JSSL, where he was entered in the Staff List as 'Stateless (ex Russian)', which was a gross but far from unfamiliar bureaucratic error. Like many thousands of other Russian refugees, the Makaroffs had indeed been 'Stateless' until 1937, when they became 'British Subjects, Australian Citizens by Naturalisation'. Dmitri himself switched to 'British Subject, Citizen of UK and Colonies' in 1954, after more than two years at JSSL.

The youngest of the 'non-British staff', he was unmistakable even at 100 yards, his shabby duffel coat billowing in the wind, his dark hair tousled, an ivory cigarette holder jutting jauntily upwards in a style reminiscent of Franklin D. Roosevelt, and shouting in Russian at his adoring one-eyed pug dog 'Mamai' if it pulled away on its lead. Mamai (named after a havoc-wreaking – but ultimately defeated – Tatar Khan) at its painstaking toilette was a diverting feature of his classrooms. (Cigarette-holders, by the way, became *de rigueur* for many smoking *kursanty*, and some even aped the frugality of their Russian role models by cutting cigarettes in half and keeping them in a tin.) Makaroff was fondly remembered by Peter Woodthorpe as an 'intelligent, flighty, bespectacled, moustached, irreverent, extraordinary man who loved the theatre', though the moustache does not seem to have been there when a JSSL cartoonist sketched him.

The more outgoing of the two and visibly the more eccentric, Koshevnikoff, then in his forties, was the son of a Moscow merchant who had gone into exile in Berlin. (His name, in common with most Russians who had lived outside their homeland, had been slightly distorted and in the UK of today would be spelt Kozhevnikov.) He claimed to have auditioned for the Ballets Russes, but was turned down by Diaghilev as too tall. The great impressario's loss was JSSL's gain. Koshevnikoff, known to his students as 'Kosh', was the nearest most *kursanty* had yet come to a 'mad Russian', running classes while prone on the floor or, once on a hot day, teaching from outside the room, the only sign of him cigarette-smoke curling through the window. He once sent David G. Jones and his class out to forage for every kind of mushroom which he then cooked on a Primus stove in the classroom, while giving a relaxed lecture on the different species.

Koshevnikoff is remembered today as much for his considerable efforts to awaken his students' interest in the whole rich spectrum of Russian poetry as for his theatricality. Weather permitting – a major caveat in Bodmin – on Wednesday afternoons, which were set aside for sports and cultural activities, a poetry-reading group of about half a dozen would meet at a secluded spot and sit in a circle on the grass. Koshevnikoff would throw down a couple of packets of cigarettes and open two bottles of white wine. With the deep-seated Russian conviction that 'one drinks to free the soul', he would then insist that everyone drank at least two glasses before reading a poem of his choice. He was regularly perplexed to find that the young aesthetes in the group saw no necessary connection between drinking wine and loosening their tongues, let alone their souls. His love of the sound of Russian is still treasured by Patrick Andrews, who remembers the day, at RAF Tangmere, when the Russian for 'emerald' occurred, and 'Kosh' beamed: '"It is a beautiful word", he said . . . "Unfortunately, for the purposes of this course it is not an important word." He then picked up a piece of chalk and an eraser, slowly and lovingly wrote *izumrud* on the blackboard with his right hand, and immediately wiped it out with his left.'

The relative penury in which he and most of the staff existed did not seem to stop him treating students to suppers at the Judge's Lodgings of Bodmin's Royal Hotel to educate them in discriminating between four or five brands of champagne, a skill he regarded as essential for any real gentleman. While in exile in Berlin, where among other diversions he had been a tennis partner of Vladimir Nabokov, Koshevnikoff had once spent an entire month's wages to treat himself to the luxury of a box to see the Bolshoi perform *Boris Godunov*. But as he had only wanted to see the first and third acts, he had stayed outside for the second. 'So extravagantly Russian,' Patrick Procktor, to whom he told the story, remembers fondly. Procktor also recalls 'Kosh' reliving his time as a ballet dancer by practising his *attitudes* and *balance en air* 'while we midshipmen conscripts scratched over the Pushkin construe'.

Looking back with nostalgia on his time at JSSL, Makaroff says: 'One's age willy-nilly is a vital ingredient in life's cookery course. Koshevnikoff was old enough to be my father and he stood in the same age ratio to the older members of the staff. Was this wide age-bracket intended by the masterminds who planned JSSL? What an extraordinary multifaceted microcosm we instructors turned out to be, a veritable cauldron of creativity. Wouldn't have missed it for the world!'

Koshevnikoff's view of how life should be lived was shared, as Philip Ivory remembers, by Colonel Godlewski, a former Polish officer in his sixties 'with a large cavalry moustache and the air of many acres and stables in the background'. The Colonel (who, like all his colleagues, princes, senators, ministers and generals, had to put up with being entered in the Staff List simply as 'Mr') would wax nostalgic about midnight balls and drinking champagne from ballerinas' slippers, and taught his young men Tsarist drinking songs. 'My dears, you have no idea . . .'

In a later chapter we will pull back the theatre curtains on the important contribution that Makaroff and Koshevnikoff made to the JSSL legacy outside the classroom, and will also bring on stage later some of the equally eccentric characters who populated the staff rooms of the University Courses. But first we have seen what the students were supposed to master, and have had glimpses of some of the characters who taught them. If these made up the choir, what about the places where they sang?

6

Surrey Hills and Cornish Pasties

When JSSL opened there, Coulsdon was already far less the small country town in the Surrey Downs, which rated a mention in the Domesday Book, than an outer suburb of London; the last squire of Coulsdon Manor, Edmund Byron, died in 1921. The entrance to JSSL's hutted ghetto was located behind The Fox public house amid the surrounding downs and Coulsdon Common, one stretch of which was nicely known as Happy Valley. In an early example of the knife-edge between the military and the intellectual on which JSSL always balanced rather awkwardly, J. D. H. Cullingham remembers a halt on a regular Sunday route march over the hills, when his squad was ordered to go and look at the mediaeval wall painting in Chaldon Church.

The camp squatted uncomfortably and unloved on the backside of the Guards Depot of Caterham, much as though a leper colony had been summarily erected by the City council outside the walls of Oxford's Radcliffe Infirmary. Its NAAFI overlooked the Guards' drill square, itself overshadowed by William Butterfield's 1886 Gothic chapel.

The linguists thus had a ringside seat as the Guardsmen were being drilled and humiliated, like animals in a circus or prisoners in another era desperate to believe that '*Arbeit Macht Frei*'. It sent chills up their spines. 'Only Alsatian dogs were missing.' It was clear that Coulsdon could be the first stage of a very comfortable way to spend one's two years' National Service. On the other hand, the sights and even more the sounds of the Guards' ferocious discipline next door and the recent scars of their own Basic Training were a powerful reminder of the savage state to which one might revert if noses were not kept to the academic grindstone.

Another part of JSSL folklore was that one manic element of the Guards' regime arose from an edict by Queen Victoria herself after her beady eye had lighted on a slovenly soldier at Windsor Castle. This prescribed the inspection at 6.30 every morning of one item of kit – burnished boots, brasses, a pipe-clayed belt, a bearskin Busby brushed to glossy perfection – specified only very late the night before, which had to be in impeccable parade-ground condition. If it did not pass muster, it would be hurled out of the window and have to be redone. By comparison with this sort of treatment, which legend had it the Queen had decreed was to last 100 years and curiously enough came to an end in the 1950s, hours spent huddled in a blanket swotting up word lists and verbs was Nirvana.

The main drawback with Coulsdon, as with Bodmin, was the cold, or rather that when winter came the shoddy barrack huts were just not up to the job of keeping out the cold and wind, and fuel supplies were scarce. Michael Frayn remembers being sent with a group of fellow students to scavenge in the snow along the clinker-surfaced paths of the Guards Depot next door looking for recyclable lumps of coke. It was Frayn who recalled the adjutant's peevish complaint about a stolen hut, which had been dismembered to feed the students' stoves. The officers may have been competing to see which of them could make the stupidest announcement of the year, since a few days later the students were admonished for using too much toilet paper. It was during that near-Siberian winter that the Regimental Sergeant Major appeared on the parade-ground one freezing morning to find his usual place usurped by a lifelike replica snowman, complete with a pace stick under its arm. That was as nothing to his fury when, on another of the many mornings that fog blanketed the camp, growing ever thicker as the morning parade went on, a curious silence in response to a set of barked commands and a swirl of breeze that cleared the fog for a moment revealed that the entire school had slipped silently back to their huts as a joke.

The Coulsdon programme was virtually indistinguishable from the pattern already described: the three Services parading in the morning and then splitting up for classes in elementary Russian, and doing little else. For the overwhelming majority of *kursanty*, unless they had already done Russian at school – and they were precious few – it was at Coulsdon that they first heard Russian spoken, and even more likely that it was here that they first saw a real live Russian. On the social front, Coulsdon itself offered little or nothing beyond the NAAFI, a couple of pubs and 'The Orchid Ballroom', a 1930s' Palais de Danse on the Brighton Road in Purley from which an enterprising *kursant* once borrowed a commissionaire's uniform complete with peaked cap, gold braid and tassels, and appeared at a JSSL dance to score a great hit with the local girls by pretending to be a senior officer from the Soviet Embassy, whose English was limited to a few key but effective phrases.

Croydon had the illusion at least of a little more life, with its pubs, coffee bars and cinemas, including the cavernous Davis Cinema where a sixpenny seat way up in the highest tiers offered a view of the screen no larger than a postage stamp, and a 'vaudeville theatre'; playbills of the period announced Phyllis Dixey, 'The Girl The Lord Chamberlain Banned', Vera and Goldie the Wonder Horse, Issy Bonn and his sketches of the Finklefeffer Family, and the 'American harpist' Robert Maxwell (surely no relation), all company in which Archie Rice would have felt much at home. There was even a rather louche bar discreetly tucked away up a flight of stairs near the Town Hall. London itself was not far away. However, since Sunday was the only day students were allowed to leave the Coulsdon area, and they were still only on basic National Service pay, the opportunities for frolicking in the Great Wen were limited (though one entrepreneurial soul bought a disused hearse in which he would give fellow *kursanty* rides up to London at weekends); it was only if they moved to university that *kursanty* were given the rank of officer cadet (or midshipmen in the Navy's case) and paid on a sergeant's scale, £5 a week in the early days and a little more on later Courses.

The surrounding Downs and Coulsdon Common offered some attractive walks and country pubs, though the paths sometimes ran uncomfortably close to the various grim Victorian lunatic asylums, as they were then uncompromisingly termed, that back then were a sad feature of the Surrey landscape. Caterham itself had housed a large institution for many years and it was only in the late nineteenth century that some pricking of political correctness saw the 'Asylum Arms' more neutrally re-labelled. Not so at least one of the institutions which continued for some years to advertise baldly its accommodation 'for idiots and imbeciles'. Those who could pay had the extra benefit of 'all the comforts of a private home as well as instruction and amusement'.

Predictably, the status of the camp was such an open 'secret' that, as Coder Special Gerald Seaman recalls, local bus conductors on duty on the routes between Purley, Coulsdon and Coulsdon Common used to delight in shouting on arrival at The Old Fox by the camp entrance: 'Moscow Corner! All change!'

Coulsdon was closed in February 1954, its final parade taken by the Director of Military Intelligence, and JSSL's mantle was taken over by Bodmin, then so cut off from the world that locals travelling into Devon talked of 'going to England'.

JSSL students' contemporary comments about their life there 'Amid the Alien Cornwall', some of them actually written in Russian, often unconsciously echoed the nineteenth-century lamentations of the languid young ensigns in stories by Lermontov or Pushkin, whose regiments found themselves posted to some benighted provincial town thousands of *versts* from the bright lights and ballrooms, where time hung heavy, local society was introverted and parochial, and mothers did their best to keep their daughters at a safe distance.

Unlike Russia, Bodmin gambling was generally limited to

bridge played for intellectual satisfaction rather than estate-threatening stakes, although Alan Bennett recalls a mania for low-stakes poker sweeping the camp for a brief period, and competition in the weekly tests was an intense but harmless substitute for duelling pistols at dawn in the birch groves.

In those distant days before motorways and regional airports, Bodmin, halfway between Exeter and Land's End, must have seemed quite unusually isolated. It was not even on the main Great Western Railway, a proposed station having been rejected, so local legend claimed, because the mayor at the time the railway came through was a carter who wanted to monopolise the carriage of goods from the nearby junction into the town. The branch line into Bodmin, it is also claimed, was eventually laid at the insistence of the War Office when the town became the headquarters of the Duke of Cornwall's Light Infantry (DCLI). For some time new arrivals pulling their kit together and getting ready to alight as the train slowed past Walker Lines and puffed into the station would see the word 'YAITSY' in large Russian letters whitewashed on the roof of one of the JSSL huts as a farewell message to a retiring commandant. They would soon find out it meant 'BALLS', and also that the writers had their grammar wrong since the plural of *yaitso* is *yaitsa*!

Memories of life at Bodmin, or any of the JSSL camps, are inevitably affected by the weather at the time. Cold and rain are recurrent themes. Ivor Samuels recalls that John Westwood, a former *Manchester Guardian* journalist writing on naval subjects, wrapped himself against the cold at night in sheets of the newspaper for which he wrote. It brought to Malcolm Brown's mind Alun Lewis's line, from his poem describing an army camp on a wet Sunday, about finding 'no refuge from the skirmishing fine rain'.

Brown's verbal snapshot of Bodmin is probably as close to the collective memory as we can come. It was, he remembers, 'no beauty but it had no pretensions either. It was earthy, ordinary but individualistic. It was its own place, take it or leave it. From the camp we could see to the south . . . the so-called Bugle Mountains, mini peaks and cliffs of spoil left by the English China Clay mines, dour in grey weather, gleaming white when caught by the sun . . . Beyond the station sturdy late nineteenth-century and early twentieth-century villas lined the road down into the town, where the main street turned sharply westward between a mix of shops, building societies and two distinctive chapels, the more modest one a sanctuary of the Countess of Huntingdon's Connection, the sturdier one distinctively Victorian, a substantial Methodist Tabernacle further up the hill. The Anglican church stood apart on the eastward side, a handsome traditionally Gothic building in its own grounds.'

Walker Lines was a wartime camp, built as an extension to the barracks of the DCLI just in time to harbour men evacuated from Dunkirk. Named after the DCLI's long-time Colonel-in-Chief Sir Bridgwood Walker, they also housed US forces assembling for the D-day landings. These were the last 'real' soldiers to pass through.

A recurring memory of Bodmin's wet and often very cold winters was the Cannon stove. Each block there had its own temperamental, smoky black beast in the centre of the passage, and each week one of the students took turns as 'stove orderly' with the task of pandering to its insatiable appetite for fuel, some of it stolen from the generous stock available to the Sergeants' Mess, and trying to encourage it to stay alight. The water supply often froze, and Alan Bennett recollects waking to find his blankets covered with frost. Fourteen men shared a hut and, when reveille sounded at 6.30 a.m., 100 pyjama-clad figures jostled for fifty washbasins. Quite often water for shaving had to be boiled in mugs on the hut stoves, and for several days one winter when the entire water supply froze solid *kursanty* gave up any attempts to shave and paraded with growths of stubble that probably reminded their more paranoid instructors of other, more distant camps.

It was at times like these that the students quoted the camp wisdom that 'God created Bodmin because Purgatory was full up'. One wrote that there was an uneasy parallel between the laconic clerical entry in a JSSL linguist's official Service record, 'Posted to Bodmin', and the nineteenth-century Cornish euphemisms for going to jail – 'being took to Bodmin' – and being confined to the local asylum – 'he was put to Bodmin'.

New arrivals like Philip Ivory might have wondered whether Walker Lines was some extension of the asylum when in their very first introduction to the language the entire intake filled the camp hall to hear a 'tubby and seedy old Russian' take them on an imaginary guided tour of the Russian capital. 'You are in park. *V parkye*. In bloody Moscow. You see woman with big breasts, *s bol'shimi grudinkami*.' They were asked to repeat and 200 young voices chorused '*s bol'shimi grudinkami*'.

The summer of 1953 was remembered by one *kursant* as wonderful. It rained only once, he believes, perhaps unrealistically, when to mark the Coronation the entire camp was paraded for inspection by an ancient Air Vice Marshal, wizened and bent and now soaked to the skin like everyone else – it was perhaps his last outing. Alan Pattillo opted to spend his leave in Cambridge, rather than trek hundreds of miles to Scotland, and remembers watching the Coronation on Liza's TV in Cambridge. 'When she sprang to attention at the first notes of "God Save The Queen", we all shuffled to our feet.'

Baffled wrath over food that even by military standards was poor – at one stage macaroni cheese was served several times a week – was resolved one memorable evening when a guard on the gate took a close look at the small plump passenger slumped in the sidecar of a motorbike driven by a member of the admin staff. It turned out to be a side of bacon wrapped in Army uniform, part of a black market initiative that had been running profitably for many months.

Some *kursanty* who either had money of their own, or had managed to save something, spent £10 on ten driving lessons, pooled their resources and bought cars for a few pounds. Some of these would be collectors' items today, like the 1936 wooden-framed, canvas-covered Riley whose doors flew open as it was driven too fast along the high-hedged, narrow lanes of deepest Cornwall, or the enormous 1930 Austin 24 which only those versed in double-declutching could drive. Some were real lemons, given to expiring in a hiss of steam and a puddle of oil in the middle of the night on Bodmin Moor.

Weekends in the summer were usually spent on the coast, at Newquay or Fowey, or with an occasional pilgrimage to the midnight matinée at the open-air Minack Theatre at Porthcurnow. A comfortable, free bed was to be had in the first-class compartments of the trains parked for the night at Penzance, where a guard would come round with a friendly wake-up call and the sojourners would set off, after a hot-water shave in the toilets, for early bacon and eggs at a local drivers' pull-up.

Though Bodmin's thirteen pubs were said to give it one of the highest urban ratios of licensed premises per acre in the UK, one attempt by a JSSL team to 'crawl' through all of them in a single evening ended in incoherent ignominy. Mixing draught Guinness with draught cider in a poor man's version of 'Black Velvet' was a recipe for disaster and David Birt remembers the aftermath of one heavy session as 'the only time in my life I have been overtaken by someone crawling. I was resting in a hedge at the time.' There was not much else to do, to the point where, when a Billy Graham rally came to town, it was lugubriously described by one doleful *kursant* as 'the only cheap entertainment to be had in this blasted hole'.

The Palace Cinema – remembered as 'grubby and uncomfortable' – offered limited distractions, though Walker Lines had its own makeshift cinema where admission was free, understandably since the programmes were usually restricted to Soviet propaganda films, such as *Meeting on the Elbe* about the end of the Second World War, a film that would have won hands down at Cannes had there been a prize for bare-faced mendacity. It was some consolation for those who missed the Everyman Theatre in Hampstead that the organisers were also able from time to time to get their hands on such highbrow gems as Cocteau's *Le Sang d'un Poête* or Buñuel's *Un Chien Andalou*.

The atmospherics at the Bistro Bar of the 'Members Only' St Petroc's Club were by some accounts a touch too close to 'feasting with panthers' to suit a broader taste, though looking back one Bodmin *kursant*, who later went on to marriage and distinction, described it as 'a very nice gay club. The only nice one I ever knew.' As we have noted, those were innocent, not to say naïve, days and other *kursanty* who dropped in for a drink, like Paul Barker, the distinguished social commentator who edited *New Society* for some twenty years, came from backgrounds so sheltered that they had no idea of the club's orientation. The proprietor was the boyfriend of the actor Eric Portman, a new insight for the many naïve souls whose adolescent picture of him had been formed by his roles as the imperturbable silver-haired Senior British Officer in *The Colditz Story* or an equally stiff-upper-lipped performance in *One of Our Aircraft Is Missing*. It would not have come as a surprise to Portman's valet, who told Kenneth Tynan years later that 'every time we go to the cottage in Cornwall he gets tight and the first thing he does is smash every mirror in the house. I have to replace everything every Monday morning.'

The St Petroc's decor, recalled as 'very vulgar . . . cellophane butterflies on coloured poles and slithering, multi-coloured bead curtains', is said to have been designed by another club habitué, Oliver Messel, while the background music consisted of the soundtrack of *Kismet* – 'Take my hand, I'm a stranger in paradise . . .' – on endless repeat.

By contrast the rubicundly Pickwickian actor, James Hayter, whom some JSSL students ran across one day in a Mousehole pub, proved staunchly butch. He signed his autograph on a cheque made out to one of them: 'Please pay John Steen Sweet Fuck All.'

In a waspish spoof of how to pass a free evening in Bodmin, a JSSL wag wrote at the time: 'What more innocent way to end the day than in the Tremarrow Palais de Danse. As we stride in, a quartet of apple-cheeked natives approaches us and we are forced to drink a quart of cider each. With sloe-orbed girls we discuss the local chapels and we perform the heart-wringing West Cornwall Schottische. Then we are beaten up and thrown out.

'It is near midnight. From a fishloft come the strains of the Tremarrow Mothers' Hymn-Singing Society at their evening session. Down on the beach the men huddle around their beacons and wait for the pleasure-steamers to pile up on the rocks. The cry of a Customs man being pushed over the cliff wafts faintly to us. Pixies appear and start to fool around on the grass . . .'

Another wit observed that a fellow student, whose car bore a window sticker announcing 'Keep your distance – Your daughter may be in the back seat', was an incorrigible optimist: Cornish girls could only rarely be lured even to venture apprehensively into the front. Though some relationships certainly did flourish, in one case to the point where a JSSL student not only married a local girl but returned to Bodmin and served twice as its mayor.

Whether or not they actually locked up their daughters to protect them from the brutal and licentious soldiery, the tradesmen and workforce of Bodmin, whose population in the 1950s was just over 6,000, must have benefited considerably from the presence of JSSL; and not just commercially.

Though one wonders quite what the mythical ladies of the Hymn-Singing Society would have made of some of the more outré manifestations, JSSL made considerable cultural ripples here and later in Scotland. Bodmin, 'Abode of the Monks', had seen a variety of forms of worship dating back to pre-Christian times, and had been much visited by Welsh missionary prelates, one of whom, Petroc, claimed by some to be synonymous with St Patrick, was the town's patron saint. Still, two days of Russian Orthodox services in 1955 must have raised some eyebrows. An iconostasis was installed in the Chapel and a choir mustered to chant the Church Slavonic rituals under the direction of a Serbian priest, who did at least deliver his sermon in English.

It is not clear from the chronology surviving today whether this was a trailer for, or a sequel to, the first of two religious and many classical performances put on at JSSL and conceived, written and produced by the two instructors we singled out earlier, Dmitri Makaroff and Vladimir Koshevnikoff.

The first of their religious pieces, *The Tenebrae of Petroc*, was put on in the impressive Bodmin Parish Church. The action took place in front of the altar while the Gregorian chant of the Office of Tenebrae (the offices of Matins and Lauds for the last three days of Holy Week) was sung in the background. Edward Morgan, who played the Devil, remembers that the church was freezing and the audience mystified.

On the classical front, a production in Russian of *Boris Godunov* in the summer of 1953, with costumes Makaroff had borrowed from Covent Garden and background music from Musorgsky's *Pictures from an Exhibition*, and Respighi's *Fountains of Rome*, literally transferred to the West End – a week's run at the School of Slavonic Studies. Dragooned with his fellow *kursanty* to attend a performance, Malcolm Brown remembers the occasion well: 'Unfortunately it was a very hot afternoon and the play was extremely long and the language extraordinarily difficult so that we did not make the most enthusiastic of audiences.' Later, as a Cambridge undergraduate, Peter Woodthorpe, who played Boris, and who thirty years later could still recite in perfect Russian the opening speech, took the title role in the Marlowe Society's version of *King Lear* directed by Shakespearean scholar 'Dadie' Rylands – a don of beauty and a joy if not for ever, at least for very many years – and who was one of the two leads in the West End première of Beckett's *Waiting for Godot* and moved seamlessly into a stage career.

In 1954 JSSL Bodmin's 'Players of the Muse of Fire' presented the first performance in England of *Hamlet* in Russian, designed and staged by Makaroff and adapted by Koshevnikoff from Pasternak's translation. Jeffrey Wickham, later to make his career as a stage, TV and screen actor, played Hamlet and the cast was all-male with the tantalizingly unidentified exception of The Player Queen. A contemporary review records a production that might be thought just a touch avant-garde by 1950s' Cornish standards:

'The setting of the play was eighteenth-century Russia after the death of Peter The Great, when Russia was ruled by a series of matriarchs; heavy rococo background and atmosphere of court intrigue. The soliloquy "To be or not to be" was spoken during a minuet, the play within a play given as an operetta sung in Italian, the players in chinoiserie costumes.'

Other Bodmin productions by the pair included the first English performance of *Twelfth Night* in Russian. 'An all-male cast. A modern dress representation, Illyria as England and the play a fantastic representation of contemporary manners,' the *Shakespeare*

Quarterly noted, though it did not mention the 'sensual music' by Richard Strauss or the choreography after Petipas and Fokine. In 1967 London's Royal Court staged the play in a production designed by Patrick Procktor, with Makaroff's precepts much in mind. Reviewer Benedict Nightingale certainly caught the Bodminesque echoes, complaining about its 'extraordinary confusion of late nineteenth-century Italian soap opera, twentieth-century British baroque and sheer mystification . . . something from The Black and White Minstrels . . . a bit of *The Gondoliers*, a Red Indian Squaw and Belch as a Balkan brigand . . .'

Makaroff also produced *Othello* in Russian with bewildering costume switches between masks, Dorian Gray smoking-jackets and full Army battledress. A JSSL reviewer described the linguist who took the part of Desdemona as 'gentle, anguished and never for a moment breaking the illusion of this very difficult impersonation', a gift which probably stood the actor in good stead when later in life he became a British ambassador. But while liking Act 1, the same reviewer panned Act 2, with the producer 'cutting the play's throat before our eyes'. Cocteau's *Orphée* in French was remembered by a spectator as 'darkly sinister'.

The team's farewell to Bodmin, again in the Parish Church, was *The Vespers of Petroc* done as 'a liturgical ballet' of the Journey of the Magi to a background of music by Monteverdi. After the Magnificat, a local reviewer wrote, '. . . the whole company swept out in procession against the Gothic pillars of the nave . . . leaving the Church in darkness and silence until the Church bells rang out'. Makaroff himself played Petroc, and the *dramatis personae* also included three bishops, a king, a queen, 'Attendants, Demons, Clerics', a Taxiarch, and a 'Madame Bibi' (who seems to have strayed in from some other plot). *Kursant* Reg Sheppard recalls his own contribution as 'fourth incense-swinger'.

Since the main responsibility for translation, adaptation and scripting of these productions seems to have been Koshevnikoff's, while his alter ago orchestrated the production, the verse on their attribution written by some starry-eyed Makaroff fan at JSSL may be slightly unfair, if neat. He proclaimed:

> 'They're gravely mistaken
> When they say it was Bacon
> Or Marlowe or Essex
> Or one of the less sex
> And Shakespeare's as far off.
> The answer? Dmitri Makaroff.'

It is easy to tease the effort. Asked years later about what his interviewer called this 'teaching by drama, in a rather advanced fashion', Patrick Procktor described it as, 'Well, camping, really.' The St Petroc's productions were 'a series of *tableaux vivants* in costumes and we had enthusiastic costume designers from the ladies, who were all mad about Dmitri'.

However, these productions and plays were much more than *Carry On up the Clay Pits*. They were at what would now be called 'the cutting edge'. We have to admire the exuberance of their creators and the verve of the actors, and though some of it may have been 'camping', to wonder what part the efforts of Makaroff and Koshevnikoff may have played in the development of individual careers and longer term in the broadening of British theatrical horizons, let alone what they did in helping those involved to drill deeper into the rich seams of the Russian language and its literature.

The latter point was picked up by the astute observer Naky Doniach, who thought that the students were 'emotionally captivated' by the plays. He felt all students learned better when they were at an 'emotional peak' and that absorption in the classical aspects of a difficult language created what he termed 'self-mesmerism' through which the language became a cultural reality. He suggested that the JSSL theatre programme was not a spontaneous development by its two prime movers but actually conceived and encouraged by the administration with these factors in mind. He regarded Makaroff and Koshevnikoff not just as men of verve, drama and poetry but excellent all-round teachers, whose skills were of particular value in the conference simulation and interrogation classes that were more a feature of JSSL's early days.

We wrote earlier about the many diverse strands of memory JSSL has produced. The theatre is one of them. Many involved remember these productions as exciting and challenging, the highpoint of their JSSL experience. Others have commented unkindly that at least to act in the plays was far better than the boredom of being part of the press-ganged audience having to spend an evening watching a performance one could barely understand. For yet others the theatre went almost completely unremarked. (Part of Bodmin folkore is that Kenneth Tynan travelled down from London to review one of the productions for the *Observer*. No record of a review has come to light.)

Certainly many, especially from the Bodmin era, went on to write and act; the 1957 and 1958 listings of productions by the Cambridge Footlights Club show JSSL Bodmin *kursanty* to have been well represented – Michael Frayn, Joe Melia, already distinguished for his fine imitation of the American entertainer Danny Kaye, John Drummond, Michael Collings (described by Drummond as 'Cambridge's answer to Kenneth Williams, and quite as funny'), and David Gillmore, subsequently Permanent Under-Secretary at the Foreign Office, among them. Many others also made notable contributions to the theatre, the screen and TV.

Though it is hard now to assess, it seems clear that the aesthetic side only absorbed a minority of the students. Others got on with their work, ogled the local girls, usually in vain, drank, played cards, did crosswords, went through minimalist military motions to keep boots polished and trousers more or less pressed, and wrote home dutifully to mothers and girlfriends. Some for whom the religious diet was too rich even cycled over to the village of Nanstallon to attend the Methodist chapel there.

A Bodmin boy who, had he lived to see them, might have looked askance at the arty goings on around JSSL was the robust author Lt Colonel Herman – later Hector – McNeile, an Army officer who had a 'good', i.e. highly unpleasant, First World War with the Royal Engineers, hence his pseudonym of 'Sapper'.

Born in the jail hospital while his father was warden of its naval section, 'Sapper' created the upper-crust, upper-cutting hero,

'Bulldog Drummond', who would nowadays be beyond the pale of political correctness but whose derring-do delighted large numbers of 1930s' readers and filmgoers. The epitome of the xenophobic mindset, the good Bulldog, his cigarette-case loaded with 'Turkish this side, Virginia that', was always ready to black the eye of a 'vile Red hound' or 'Dago blackguard' in defence of the realm and the English way of life. The goings on at the Church would have struck him as decidedly rum. It is claimed that one unspecified production raised the eyebrows of the Bishop of Truro as potentially heretical. On the other hand, the pro-gramme for the Vespers specifically states that it is being performed in the Parish Church 'with the authorisation of the Bishop of the Diocese'.

It was probably in the nastier days of winter that yet another seam of JSSL cultural life – the Music, Debating, Film and even Philosophical Societies and the Camera Club – came into their own. The bleak weather sweeping across the moors may also have seemed rather homely to a group of Norwegian air-force officers who were posted there in 1954 as part of the close collaboration between the UK and Norway at the time in Sigint work. They went home proudly clutching Service Translators' certificates and boasting that they had been taught Russian 'by Polish teach-ers . . . from 7 in the morning to 6 at night'.

When it became clear that Bodmin was to close, the orotund Canon Harmer of the Parish Church, a great supporter of the Players, appealed to local MP Douglas Marshall, who in turn wrote to the renowned Great Game player Fitzroy Maclean, then Parliamentary Under Secretary of State for War. But there was to be no reprieve; Marshall was told that Walker Lines was 'not really a suitable camp for the School' and that some £17,000 would have to be spent to get it into shape, but that it was more a matter of administrative necessity than financial expenditure since Walker Lines might be needed if 'mobilisation were to take place which would mean uprooting the staff and students . . . at the worst possible time'.

Recent reports that in 1955 the Government built a hidden

underground complex in East Fife to serve as a command and control centre for Scotland in the event of a Russian nuclear attack have led some to speculate that the move of JSSL and its cadre of Russian speakers to the same area may not have been unrelated. We have seen no evidence whatever to suggest this, and gladly leave any possible linkage to the researches of future generations of historians and conspiracy theorists.

In a valedictory note in the JSSL magazine, a feature of camp life which we will review in more detail below, a *kursant* quoted the editor of the *Bodmin Gazette* as writing that the students would be much missed. 'It seems they love us for our charming selves and our culture and not, O Thou Cynic, for our money.' The *Gazette*'s editor would also be relieved since his house shared the same erratic water supply as the camp and often ran dry. Another writer speculated that sales of the *Sunday Times*, the *Observer* and vodka would slump. What would become of the unsold stocks of maps of Eastern Scotland cannily laid in by the Bodmin newsagents? 'And will the pretty girls of Bodmin return eagerly or wistfully to the stolid blandishments of Bodmin's youth who stand and eye us so glassily as we emerge blinking from the Palace Cinema?'

The *Cornish Guardian* took a less whimsical view, pointing out that JSSL had employed 100 local civilians. The loss of their earnings, as well as the salaries of JSSL officers and instructors and the pay of the students themselves, would leave a shortfall in local income of more than £100,000 (perhaps £1,000,000 or more in today's values).

Twilight descended. The ageing, discreetly rouged roués of the St Petroc's Club stared moodily into their Crème de Menthe puffing at their multi-coloured Sobranie 'Cocktail' cigarettes. 'Little Russia' and its lissom Lermontovs were lost and gone, and the club itself would soon follow suit. If any whiffs of incense lingered in the arches of the Parish Church, the next Cornish gale blew them away forever.

7

The High Road to Scotland

Like Bertram Mills' Circus moving to winter quarters all JSSL, its people and paraphernalia, blackboards, dictionaries, typewriters and desks, were crammed into one special train, with urns of tea and sandwiches provided by the Catering Corps, and headed north via Crewe to Crail in what is ringingly known as the 'East Neuk of the Kingdom of Fife', thirteen miles or so south-east of St Andrews. A *kursant* doing a take-off of Boswell on his tour of the Highlands wrote, 'the military has established on that promontory a school of languages for the relief of the sons of gentlefolk reduced to penury, that they might acquire the rudimentary elements of erudition'.

For the refugee staff it must have had overtones of yet another exile, another move into an uncertain future, even echoes of the Trans-Siberian Railway. As it chugged through East Wemyss, Largo, Elie, Pittenweem and Anstruther (pronounced 'Ainster' as if to prove Russia had no monopoly on quirks of language), some of the smaller students dozing in the luggage racks, one older gentleman was heard to murmur dolefully as he peered out of the window, '*Prostory, prostory*' ('nothing but empty space').

But all went off well and Lieutenant Colonel Rose, the Commandant, Spoonerishly congratulated everyone on the move: 'When we got here there wasn't a drop of furniture or a stitch of water . . . jolly good, carry on chaps.'

Today's Crail has been made over for the tourist trade, with its own Heritage Centre, the broad sweep of Marketgate (said to have once been one of the largest mediaeval marketplaces in Europe) and boasting boutiques, comfortable hotels and a picturesque harbour. It is hard for JSSL men from the 1950s to reconcile it with their memories of an unpretentious, salty fishing community, far more a village than a town, weatherworn working boats moored against its curved sixteenth-century jetty, its 1,200 population imperturbable and incurious, and also very grateful to the Sassenach civil servants who had brought 600 or 700 people to the camp up the road, with the prospect of jobs for many of the villagers as cooks, cleaners and handymen. One student recalls that the Crail men were referred to as 'the sypsies', in much the same unconsciously condescending way that JSSL men in Bodmin had called the Cornish locals 'grockles'. In fact the Crail term comes from the name of the local farm which provided some of the JSSL workforce. At the time the *Sunday Express* claimed that the Crail locals referred to JSSL as 'that there interrupters school'.

As with Bodmin, the 'trickle-down' effect on a small community of the wages, rents and other spending must have been considerable, though the Servicemen did not have that much disposable income and even by 1950s' standards there was, Heaven knows, little enough to spend money on. The single instructors lived on the site. Those with families rented what they could around the village, odd pockets of Mother Russia or the Pripet Marshes in among the 'two up, two down' slate cottages. In one of them the much loved Koshevnikoff lived with his mother and sister, who also taught on the Course, again usually so short of cash that their lighting consisted of a single candle on a soapbox.

In its wartime heyday JSSL Crail had been HMS *Jackdaw*, a naval air service station used predominantly for torpedo training.

Last used as a staging-post for units of the Black Watch en route to Korea, it straddled the purpose-built road that ran arrow-like out of the village to the rocky shoreline.

To the north of the road, up on the hill, were the dormitories, the Mess hall, the Officers' and Officer Cadets' Messes, the parade-ground and the theatre – a rather grand term for a small-ish building with a stage which doubled as the gym. To the south across the road lay the administration buildings and the single-storey classroom blocks, framed by disused aircraft hangars behind which lay the original tarmac airstrip, used from time to time by visiting Service brass-hats and less officially by mem-bers of staff wanting to try out their high-speed driving skills. Compared to its predecessor camps Crail had the inestimable advantage of having inherited from the Fleet Air Arm a reason-ably efficient central-heating system.

The layout meant much emulation of the Grand Old Duke of York, marching up and down the hill, probably no bad thing given the basically sedentary lifestyle.

Those who had transferred from Bodmin found the weather very much better; though the average temperature was obviously lower than down in the south-west, there was about half the rainfall. Most Crail memories include references to the sunshine, the sparkling waters of the Firth, seals basking on the rock and even glimpses of wheeling larks, gannets and drake eiders as a Wordsworthian distraction from the idiocies of the parade-ground. Some do not. Writing back in 1958 an RTU'd Coder remembered among Crail's drawbacks 'the climate, the inadequate heating, the food was comparatively bad, the working hours long and there was no issue of rum or duty free tobacco'. Debating whether he was better off at Crail or on regular duties, the writer concluded that, 'freedom being the essential ingredient to being well off it matters not a whit whether I am a coder at Crail, an SA [stores assistant] at Chatham or a stoker in Kuala Lumpur. I still have to submit unwillingly for two years to a set of rules under which I lose all my rights as a free citizen and shall not be better off till my release.. . .' And Philip Ivory recalls Crail as having 'a touch of the gulag'.

Maybe so. But as with Bodmin, with which it shared much the same curriculum and staff, Crail's atmosphere worked if the pupils, as they were in most cases, were ready and receptive. 'A kind of frugal university life', remembers one. Myles Burnyeat recollects graduating in the first few weeks from incomprehensible numbers to a point where 'we became accustomed to these foreign sounds. We began to talk. Sentences gradually developed into reasoned arguments. Those of us who had joined straight from school were seventeen or eighteen years old. Others who had been to university were older but still of an age that loves to talk and argue. For obvious reasons our teachers . . . encouraged talk. The more the better so long as it was in Russian. So life became an endlessly argumentative seminar on every subject under the sun. And that went on for eighteen months becoming more sophisticated each week as our Russian grew into ever more subtle thoughts . . .'

Though the schools in Coulsdon, Bodmin and Crail were Service establishments, they were run with a light touch and, to adapt a favourite Army mantra, bullshit was rarely allowed to baffle brainwork, despite the occasional attempt by some Queeg-like officer, usually a newcomer, to 'get a grip'. 'Yew men must get your hice in orda,' yelped a major with the unfamiliar vowel sounds of Belfast. In part that must have been a matter of enlightened policy; the aim was to produce linguists not light infantry.

Perhaps because the military side of life did not predominate, many students have little or no recollection of their higher-level Service superiors, who tended to be figures seen at a distance.

The Russian teachers made lasting impressions, but it is a tribute to, not a criticism of, the character of the individuals who held the positions and the way they did their jobs that few alumni have anecdotes about such figures in the Service hierarchy as Lt Colonels Askwith, Thompson, Rose and Montague, Wing Commander Harrington and Major G. A. Tod, though they are remembered with warmth and respect (though not universally; at least one senior instructor had strong reservations about what he saw as Askwith's excessively narrow military mindset); Lt Colonel

Rose, who moved with JSSL from Bodmin to Crail, earned one student's tribute as having become 'the spirit of the place', even though in schoolboy style his rank was sometimes deliberately mispronounced in conversation to create the nickname of 'Carnal Rose'. Two Brigadiers (E. K. Page DSO MC and J. E. F. Meadmore CBE) were respectively the last Principal of Bodmin and the Principal of Crail from start to finish. Meadmore, born in 1904, had been a very early alumnus of the pre-war SSEES/Paris Russian training programme.

In 1954, continuing a campaign that seems to have started in 1952, four of the foreign instructors – led by a former senator of the Polish parliament – and one British member of staff, backed by their Principal Lieutenant Colonel Montague, wrote to the commandant and the Institute of Civil Servants to complain that 'our salaries were fixed three years ago . . . and are now reduced to £400 p.a. We used to be represented by the National Union of Teachers but when the Burnham Committee gave teachers a big rise we are told we are civil servants and not entitled to it. Our Cambridge colleagues get £600 p.a. and in London 25 shillings per hour [which probably came to the same, assuming ten hours' teaching a week]. Our appointments are technically temporary, so many of us have families elsewhere in the UK, yet we have no travelling concessions. And our posts are not pensionable either.' They requested an increase backdated to 1952. The response is not known but is unlikely to have been favourable.

The schizophrenia of JSSL, the conflict between schoolbook and Sten gun, is neatly brought out in a 1959 report in the *Dundee People's Journal* of an Open Day at Crail. It offered its local visitors 'sideshows and competitions', and students and children joined in 'a concert of Russian singing and dancing'. But also on display were a Centurion tank, driven over from Heaven knows where, Fleet Air Arm equipment, and 'an RAF helicopter gave a rescue demonstration'. It is a pity that Makaroff was not contemplating a production of *Götterdämmerung* at the time, as he might have used some of the equipment to good effect. It is also a blessing that the *Daily Express* was not around to photograph

Patrick Procktor riding into St Andrews on a white horse, a scarf loosely wrapped round his midshipman's uniform, smoking through 'an impossibly long amber cigarette holder'.

But JSSL was geographically and militarily out of the mainstream, to put it mildly, and, especially at the NCO level where most senseless aggravation can arise, its sergeants and warrant officers were themselves by and large not upwardly mobile in their careers. Like the students, they knew a 'cushy billet' when they saw one. Unkind rumour had it that they and many of the officers had actually ended up there as a consequence of some awful mistake they had committed elsewhere. One of the naval officers was alleged to have been exiled to JSSL after running his destroyer head-on and expensively into an unyielding dock wall in the Far East.

The NCOs shouted and chivvied at times, but their hearts were not really in it, as compared to the psychopaths encountered in Basic Training in places like Catterick, even though one senior NCO was said to be convinced that the Nazis he had fought in the Second World War were coming back to get him any day.

For the Army contingent immediate authority was represented mainly by the bulky and benign figure of 'Chunky' Charnley, the Corporal of the Horse – by some military quirk a Household Cavalry rank that in fact was the equivalent of sergeant major in lesser regiments. Addressed in best Western style despite his occasional protests as 'Horse', he supplemented his military duties with the concession to supply the School newspapers and his visits on Sunday mornings, his car laden with quires of the *Observer* and *News of the World*, were eagerly anticipated. 'When are we going to eat, Horse?' was a well-worn joke.

Another well-remembered Crail NCO was an RAF flight sergeant who was utterly convinced, even when shown an atlas, that the shoreline so clearly visible on the other side of the Firth of Forth was not just more of bonny Scotland but in fact the troll-strewn coast of Norway. Another was a quartermaster who, despite the access his job gave him to the best available in everything, had let himself and his uniform go to seed to the point where his tarnished badge and buckles would have served well as the 'before' section of a Brasso advertisement.

One observer has gone so far as to draw parallels between the *kursanty*'s attitude to the military regime and the home-made cultural life that surrounded the school framework, and those 1950s' and 60s' film portraits of life in officer prisoner-of-war camps in Germany in the Second World War, in which amateur theatricals also played an important part.

Although as conscripts the JSSL pupils were there under sufferance, they were hardly prisoners; no one dug tunnels under the Bodmin wire and there wasn't a war on. But their genial contempt for those whom they regarded as in some sense their jailers, and certainly their intellectual inferiors, had many strands in common with the shot of a hutful of polo-necked British actors when a German security Hauptmann comes in to find them playing gramophone records and praises Beethoven as 'a great German'. 'Yes,' one jeers, 'he's dead.'

Men on the Translators' Courses lived in barrack-rooms, were marched about in squads, did military things from time to time, and were called on, admittedly at infrequent intervals, for camp duties such as the overnight Fire Piquet. Tony Blee recalls one of the Piquet commander's duties was to make sure – which, when it was his turn, he failed to do – that the lower camp gates were closed at night, not to keep out the KGB but to keep in the flock of sheep a local farmer was allowed to graze around the runways. (One classically trained student conjectured that the sheep were actually former *kursanty* who had undergone a Circean transformation.) A helpful mimeographed sheet on what to do in case of fire advised the commander that if the alarm was sounded, it would summon the local fire brigade 'and possibly PC Wood, depending on which way the wind is blowing'.

The officer cadets who had finished university and were back at JSSL for a final few months to polish up their Service Russian and prepare for the Civil Service Examination had their own Mess (to which a suspicious hierarchy once refused to supply the *Daily Worker*, one of the few manifestations of 'censorship' we have encountered in JSSL's history), wore white or green flashes on their collars and caps to mark their superior caste, rather like members of Pop at Eton, shared rooms rather than barracks and were almost totally free of military interference. Navy midshipmen switched out of what one later called nostalgically 'those lovely bell bottoms' to 'nasty little navy serge suits with the white caps'.

Outside distractions were few. In Crail itself there was the Music Box Café, with a jukebox to justify its name. Hearing Harry Belafonte's 'Island in the Sun' today still has the power to time-shift Tony Blee back almost fifty years to its steam and Formica ambience; another remembers Elvis Presley's 'Heartbreak Hotel' in the same way, bringing to mind Noël Coward's quip about the potency of cheap music. The Boswell pastiche writer already quoted claimed the local coffee produced 'by boiling goats' flesh in a kettle . . . served the inhabitants for an aphrodisiackal'. Something of the same gamey flavour pervaded the cookhouse, tended by small and not very clean men who, whatever else they were, were not cooks; an outbreak of dysentery around 1958 brought a scrub-down and new equipment but no noticeable improvement in the cuisine, which, as for all non-combatants, was classified, an inquisitive linguist once found out, as 'Army Grade 2'.

For those who preferred their coffee without music, there was The Haven, and for those in need of more potent brews, three hotels, two of which had the coveted seven-day licence allowing them to serve drinks on a Sunday evening to 'bona fide travellers'. They had to sign a special register in the hall to confirm that they had come at least three miles.

Crail did have one of the three oldest golf courses in Scotland at Balcomie Links, described by one aficionado as 'a stunning layout of holes where I did my best to quench my thirst for the game during my service to His and Her Majesties'. Ben Wright was so keen a golfer that he once feigned illness and went AWOL from Crail – a serious offence – not for a romantic tryst in some nearby bothy, or to run home to Mummy, but to drive across the

Tay to Carnoustie to see the great Ben Hogan play. It was a nice coincidence that the links were connected to Balcomie Castle, once the ancestral home of the Learmonth family, of whom, for students of Russian at least, its most famous member was the poet Mikhail Lermontov.

There was also Aird's Cinema, owned by the man who ran the garage, where the front circle seats at 2/3d were at a significant premium over the 1/- rear stalls.

For those in search of brighter lights and willing to take the bus or hitchhike to St Andrews, Airds had competition in the Cinema House, which boasted of its Cinemascope, CineScope and Superscope projection capabilities. One wonders now what the differences were and how the confused projectionist managed to avoid getting the systems muddled. The cinema also offered the chance to reserve its circle seats. St Andrews also had 'The Byre', advertising itself rather disarmingly as 'Scotland's smallest professional repertory theatre' and promising daily performances of the 'leading plays'.

While short on restaurants – even today – St Andrews at least had rather more for the serious drinker especially at 'Kate's Bar', which, unusually for those days and for a country more oriented towards malt-based fluids, offered 100 per cent proof Polish vodka, slivovitz and the lethal Polish honey liqueur krupnik. Bodmin cuisine must by comparison have been dire, since Dmitri Makaroff, recalling the favourable impression St Andrews made on him and his fellow instructors, with its 'ancient university, a spectacular ruined cathedral by the seashore', when they found that 'of course, gastronomically Scotland was far more interesting than England', a memory which the Tourist Board should enshrine for posterity, since most present-day comments tend to be biased in the opposite direction.

In the 1950s, St Andrews' culinary and social highpoint – and to be fair deservedly so – was 'High Tea' in one of the many genteel cafés on the main street, from which for a few shillings one could stagger away stuffed to the gills with ham, eggs, finnan haddie, baps, cake and unlimited pots of very sweet tea. There were also dances, sometimes at the University Students Union, and weekly upstairs in the Town Hall, where the local girls lined up on one side and a pimply mix of hardboiled Scots lads, under-graduates and Crail students shifted nervously from foot to foot on the other. When the music started, each side advanced towards the other, the girls giggling, the boys pretending they were not nervous and sweaty-palmed; when it ended, they separated again like the parting of the Red Sea. Former *kursanty* will kick themselves to learn that, according to one of the St Andrews women students, the JSSL men were thought to be quite a catch.

In July 1956 Crail's 718 student population slightly exceeded the total number of male students at St Andrews, though unlike the lonely linguists the St Andrews undergraduates had 601 women students to bring some sense of proportion to their daily lives!

On a dour and overcast Sunday, it was easy for a JSSL student at a loose end to agree with the nineteenth-century poet who wrote of 'St Andrews by the Northern sea, a haunted town it is to me'. Some did find kindred spirits. Gerry Smith, who at the time was consumed by the ambition to become a jazz musician, hitched rides from Crail whenever he could to play with the university jazz band led by 'Rip' Rippingdale. Another JSSL man, Lance Cavan, played clarinet. Music was an important part of the back-drop to JSSL life, and for many a new voyage, whether concerts in Edinburgh or via long-playing vinyl records, like drip-dry nylon shirts a major social advance of the 1950s; groups of like-minded *kursanty* would contribute to a weekly pool and take it in turns to select a new disc from Brubeck to Beethoven to be played and solemnly discussed.

One translator remembers that the Crail theatre had a Steinway piano – 'How many Service camps could say the same?' – which gave him 'the most powerful musical experience I ever had'. After practising on it for his allotted spell one evening, he was joined by the man who had his name down for the next slot, and they launched spontaneously into six giddy hours of Mozart and Schubert duets for which his fellow linguist happened to be carrying the scores.

As others had before him, Glen Dudbridge played the Harrison and Harrison organ (remembered as a 'splendid' instrument by another of the many JSSL students who were seriously music-minded) in Crail Church, snooker and table tennis in the NAAFI, competed in the JSSL team in the 100 yards race at the Fair in nearby Anstruther, and with a group of friends made it to Edinburgh at Festival time to enjoy the Fringe events and see Yeats's *Purgatory*. Others took piano lessons from the Crail Church organist Mrs Maughn. It is doubtful that any JSSL student knew that in 1739 sleepy old Anstruther had been the birthplace of the 'Beggars Benison Club', modelled on Sir Francis Dashwood's Hellfire Club, 'a society for the collection of good songs, stories, jokes and facetiae of all kinds . . . and an outlet for the most exuberant and outrageous fun and jocularity of the roughest description'. Over 200 years later the fun at JSSL may not have been quite as outrageous as Anstruther, but it was still a key feature of life and a much-cherished memory, whether impromptu cabaret acts, plays, concerts or the school magazine.

A badge, a school tie and a school magazine are prerequisites for any British boys' school with pretensions. JSSL, though unpretentious in the extreme, had all three. (At Cambridge in 1953, at the height of the attempt to replicate university life as much as possible, a scarf was also created, in black, pale blue and red, though it seems not to have lasted long.) An 'Old Boys' association is also desirable and though JSSL does not have one composite alumni group, there are a surprising number of Intake – or Service – specific groups whose members still seem to keep in regular contact – among them The FRINTON SOCIETY, so-called not because its members live in that fossilised seaside village where time stood still around 1935, but as an acronym for 'Former Russian Interpreters of the Navy'.

There was also a *Samovar Song Book* on sale for 6d. First introduced at Coulsdon, and edited by the *kursanty* with staff help, it ran to two editions and included folk melodies, and melancholy and passionate pre-Revolutionary gypsy cabaret songs of the kind that aroused Rasputin to priapic ecstasy. There were Ukrainian nonsense songs, the Russian equivalents of Christmas carols, songs sung by wagon-drivers on the steppes, boot-stamping Cossack choruses and more doleful chants of prisoners and Tsarist Army conscripts, as well as some of the basso-profundo lyrics popularised in the post-war years by the Red Army Choir when they were not busy crushing East European uprisings. It was typical of JSSL's occasional pedantry that its Introduction was a scholarly essay on Russian rhythms, polyphony and harmony.

A vinyl record of Russian songs performed by the JSSL choir under the direction of Mr Skobiej – in an earlier incarnation a seminarist – sold well at four shillings (today's 20p). Later transliterated, perhaps in an unconscious echo of Graham Greene as Mr Scobie, he is remembered by one Crail student as 'a honey-tongued cold-as-ice perfectionist – no sympathy, no encouragement and shockingly high standards'.

For a while there was even an orchestra, known for its spirited renderings of folk songs under the direction of Mr Diakowski.

The JSSL badge was an attempt to combine the emblems of all three Services. It also featured on the tie, advertised by a St Andrews' gentleman's outfitters in 1955 at a price of 11/9d. For those who missed the opportunity to acquire a wearable memento, a specialist store in Darlington still has JSSL gold wire blazer badges on sale for £19. The School even had its own austere Christmas card – no robins or sledges, just the crest and a bow of blue, red and silver ribbon.

The school magazine, *Samovar*, was originally called *Teapot and Samovar* until in his spell as editor Michael Frayn metaphorically dropped the 'Teapot', partly on the pedantic grounds that the two words were not synonymous – a samovar only boiled water, and a teapot was still needed for the final brew. He also felt that *Samovar* 'sounded slightly more obscure and stylish'. The Russian spelling of 'samovar', CAMOBAP, can also conveniently be pecked out on an English keyboard. However, full sets of *Samovar* are hard to find. Until this project stimulated interest,

111

there were no copies in the British Library and there are still none in the Bodleian.

It is even difficult to determine exactly how many issues there actually were; twenty-three seems the best guess; as just one bibliographic loose end, No. 15 never existed since the records and back numbers file were mislaid in the move from Bodmin to Crail and the new editors mistakenly fixed on 16 as the new starting point. To give future researchers one more clue, by courtesy of Terry Wade, the message in the 'small ads' in the Xmas 1954 issue – 'STANTON – all forgiven – FREDA' – is an inside joke using the names of two of the characters in J. B. Priestley's *Dangerous Corner*, which *kursanty* had translated into Russian from cover to cover.

Samovar had its origins in a 'Russian club', an entity whose creation was negotiated with the camp authorities – rather like Koshevnikoff's poetry circle – as a legitimate alternative to the physical exercise otherwise mandated for Wednesday afternoons. The club soon found it actually needed something to do to justify its exempt existence, and thus the magazine was born. Eric Korn, who was another early editor, recalls it as an arena 'for stylistic manoeuvres in which poetic coteries snarled and skirmished – useful preparation for cultural wars to come'. With every intention of keeping up his schoolboy science studies (recently graphically described by his school-friend Oliver Sacks in *Uncle Tungsten*), Korn had acquired access to a tiny laboratory in Plymouth where he and Frayn would retreat at weekends to plan the contents of the next issue.

Though much helped by several of the instructors, notably Mr Oljhovikov, reportedly the son of a Ukrainian Hetman, or chieftain, it was first and foremost a student initiative 'written by the students of JSSL primarily for the students . . . and controlled by the students', a claim borne out by its style and content which contain no hint of any censorship or guidance by the military 'powers that be'.

It had an unusual format in that about half of most issues was in Russian; at least one number even had poems in Czech and Polish. Though the English text could be typeset at a printers, the Russian had to be hammered out on a JSSL typewriter and duplicated, and the whole thing then stapled together, making physical production something of a nightmare. Produced two or three times a year, to judge from the copies we have seen, and priced at 1/6d, *Samovar* varied in external appearance from a rather plain military style reminiscent of a machine-gun manual, to issues such as the big Jubilee number whose covers had vivid woodcut images.

Michael Frayn and Eric Korn apart, the editorial boards and contributors listed in the extant copies do not seem to have included many of the linguists who later made their name as writers. But they did an excellent job, serving up an eclectic bilingual diet of gentle mockery, poetry, short stories, anecdotes, reviews and essays on topics from the learned to the seriously abstruse.

A random walk through a few of the greying pages throws out such topics as 'Glinka's Life and Creativity', 'Worker Priests', the life and works of Fr Rolfe Baron Corvo, and 'Joan of Arc – a Story in Verse' (all of these in Russian). There was a jokey fantasy, also in Russian, about a frustrated instructor who ends up killing off a student for persistent failure to differentiate the pronunciation of the 'soft' and 'hard' versions of the Russian letter L – probably closer to the mark than the writer realised. Another Russian essay asked, 'What's to become of Bodmin?' after its closure, suggesting that it could become a detention centre for Army punishment battalions.

In English there were reviews of 'Rock around the Clock' and *Lucky Jim*, a piece on 'The Psychology of Jung' and an essay on Rimbaud, 'Voyage dans l'Inconscient'. The eye is also caught by a disquisition on 'Christian Influence on East Chinese Art in the 6th and 7th Centuries', which, read and reread by someone who admittedly knows nothing of the subject, has the hallmarks of a delicate practical joke. There was also an essay in a Crail-produced issue by a Norwegian officer on the tourist high-spots of his home country, which suggests the covert training programme for Norway's Sigint effort that had started at Bodmin had continued at Crail.

Despite the 'written by students' principle, *Samovar* did carry one or two pieces by staff. An instructor wrote on his wartime adventures in the Crimea and the brilliant linguist and resonantly named Commander David Maitland Makgill Crichton, who bore a marked resemblance to the late King George VI and who had come to head the RN Section at Crail after a career which had included tough times on a destroyer escorting wartime convoys to Murmansk, provided two accounts of his experience in flawless Russian under the title *One Less U-Boat*. (He sat the Civil Service Interpretership in Russian at Crail in June 1957 and achieved one of the rare Firsts.)

The Commander was a member of a distinguished Scottish Clan, three of whom have served over the more than 130 years of the event's history as Chieftains of The Gathering at the Crieff Highland Games. One of its young men was lost at sea in the Second World War apparently en route to a posting with the Special Operations Executive. David Maitland Makgill Crichton, born in 1881 and described as 'a famous Free Churchman and radical politician', is commemorated with a statue in the town of Cupar, some miles outside St Andrews, marking his victory in what sounds like a tough battle with the penny-pinching Edinburgh and Northern Railway to compel them to provide the townsfolk with a bridge instead of a far less expensive level crossing over its planned new line through the town.

Yet another family member figured in an episode reminiscent of Trollope's *Orley Farm*, when around 1900 a Fife hermit named Johnstone had died apparently intestate, his fortune of some £1 million (a princely sum in those days, let alone by today's values) passed to his nephew, one Lieutenant Maitland McGill [*sic*] Crichton, as his heir-at-law. Ten months later a will dated 1869 and said to be in the hermit's hand, was found, according to the London press 'sewn into the dress of a lady who had died three years ago', and who had herself inherited the dress from an elderly aunt. 'The finding of the will,' the press reported with commendable understatement and a pardonable splitting of the infinitive, 'is likely to very materially affect Lt Crichton's position.'

Various editors had fun with *Samovar*'s format – still used by *Private Eye* – of commenting on JSSL events in the style of an Old Testament text. Since this only works, if it works at all, when the reader has a first-hand knowledge of the events being mocked, it does not merit much reproduction here, though one rather arch set of quasi-biblical verses does turn out to be based on a real event.

'Did we not in times past command that these young men should study greatly upon the tongues of the East? the fictional Prophet records the "House of War" as saying.

'Wherefore then is this great work neglected? . . . Let this place no longer be troubled as is an anthill crushed by the foot of man . . .

'And when this news did come to the knowledge of the young men they did rejoice with an exceeding great joy and the praise of the House of War was loud in the land.'

In fact these celebratory lines record an episode when officer cadets returning to JSSL Bodmin from university for their final few months felt unreasonably pressured by a military regime that seemed to have been deliberately tightened up in one of the periodic attempts by a resentful soldiery to 'teach those poncy linguists a lesson', to borrow a Maresfield taunt. When George Bolsover next paid a routine visit to Bodmin, his London alumni took the opportunity to complain and he in turn successfully lobbied the War Office to relax their grip.

Samovar did take the trouble to thank one retiring commanding officer for 'giving us a lot of rope [but] not an inch further' and to praise another for his kindness. One writer also paid tribute to the instructors at Bodmin for doing a job that was 'difficult . . . boring and very seldom rewarded by good results'.

Obviously the tone of each issue and the advertising content reflect the style of its editor and the energies of its business manager, but the Crail team do seem to have been more successful in persuading the local tradesmen, perhaps already in the habit of supporting the University of St Andrews' publications, to advertise. The Crail issues we have seen have rather more of the 'school magazine' flavour with reports on the doings of the Rugby Club ('at times the hospitality offered to visiting teams was non-existent. On one occasion there was no referee and on several no whistle or ball'), the Hockey, Soccer, Golf and Music Clubs, and the Ski Club, which often found it hard to find skiable slopes within driving distance but whose members perhaps got more out of the dances they held in the Cadets' Mess, with special buses laid on to bring the girls of St Andrews and Anstruther to Crail and take them home again at 1 a.m. The Philosophical Society was also appropriately philosophical about how hard it was to keep itself going.

There was also the theatre, translated from Cornwall to Scotland in what seems, to judge from *Samovar*, an even more adventurous mode. Gogol's *The Inspector General*, with Patrick Procktor as Khlestakov, seems, unusually, to have been relatively straightforward, but the Players soon began to 'ascend the brightest heaven of invention' with Aristophanes' *The Clouds* in English 'with a few snippets of Greek'.

Ionesco's *The Picture*, described by a reviewer as 'incomprehensible but delightful', is reported to have 'rather shocked the good ladies of the Kirk' when put on in Crail, while the audience for Mayakovsky's *Klop* ('The Bedbug') found itself beset by actors dressed up as hawkers selling herrings and fur-lined brassieres. Patrick Procktor and Makaroff later collaborated to repeat the production at the University of London's Students' Union.

As was claimed in the case of one of the Bodmin productions, Kenneth Tynan was said to have come to Crail to review *The Inspector General* but again no record can be found.

We have so far tripped the light fantastic through the mainstream JSSL establishments. For a fortunate few there was a further dimension, that of the University Course at London and Cambridge, whose worlds we shall soon visit. For those who did not pass through the Eye of the Needle and who stayed on at JSSL to complete the Linguists' Course, they might have been briefly disappointed but were happy enough to have got as far as they had from the real Service world and gladly buckled down to six or seven more months of hard work.

They then moved on to Service stations – described later – to hone their technical language skills and acquire a basic grasp of monitoring techniques, after which most were posted to 'user units' – a euphemism for some component of the Sigint system – for the balance of their Service.

The High Road to Scotland

Those who thought they had said goodbye to JSSL for good might find themselves mistaken. One way they might come back was as part of the Reservists programme. National Servicemen were liable to recall in an emergency for several years after demobilisation and in the case of Army linguists also had a three-year obligation to return to one of the Schools for a two- or three-week refresher course; the Navy and RAF reservists went to one of the Sigint establishments. A voluntary correspondence course for former students also operated for a period and at one time had 600 men enrolled, no mean logistical effort on its own. But the reserve obligation – for the administration of which the Services themselves were responsible and not JSSL – seems not to have been invoked uniformly and some men were summoned back for only one refresher course, in one case three years after demobilisation. Others were not called on at all. Nevertheless over its life JSSL funnelled 1,200 reservists through its gates, in addition to the mainstream students, a considerable extra organisational burden for the staff, especially Brian Hawkins. Those who used the correspondence course found it of value in keeping their Russian going, but many fell by the wayside over time and awareness that the scheme existed was not universal.

Those discreetly patting themselves on the back and going off to university would also return, in their case for the final six months of intense preparation for the Civil Service Examination, though this was so far ahead it was best not thought about. *Carpe diem*. Two who thanked their lucky stars rather than congratulated themselves were David Metcalf (who subsequently joined the Atomic Energy Authority) and another RAF colleague who had been told that only six from their Crail intake would be selected for Cambridge, and that they were seventh and eighth. At the last minute they were added to the list, subsequent enquiries suggesting that this was because theirs would be the last Cambridge Course and someone had decided for the six months before Foxton closed that squeezing two extra beds into a back bedroom would not be too difficult to arrange.

8

Ye Fields of Cambridge

Those selected for university after the Second Major Test – the numbers fell over the period of JSSL's life from a Cambridge intake of 100 on Course A, down to twelve on Course M and twenty-four on the final Course T, and tapering down from fifty in London – breathed sighs of relief, tried to suppress any feelings of smugness and vanished, stopping off at Woking in Surrey to collect their allocation of so-called civilian clothes; some claimed the depot there had an arrangement with the nearby Brookwood Necropolis and Crematorium to take suits from its customers who no longer needed them.

A puzzling bureaucratic feature of the arrangements was that at the end of a man's Service he could opt to keep them, usually for some small payment; otherwise they had to be handed back. But what then happened to those 'shoes, brogue, brown', 'hats, trilby, green, officer's', and 'suits, civilian, tweed', and were they recycled for another lucky generation? (The Services' style of putting the noun first when cataloguing supplies was said to have reached its finest hour with the entry many claimed to have seen in a

Quartermaster's List for 'pots, chamber, rubber, lunatic officers for the use of').

In the early planning all three Services had in mind that interpreters needed to be officers, especially if they were to serve as interrogators. The Army and RAF ducked the point by classifying their university candidates as 'officer cadets' and sending them off in the closing weeks of their Service for a run through a Commissioning Board and Officers' Training Course; if they passed, they would then be commissioned into the Reserve. The Navy insisted that all its students who were picked for university should pass a selection board before being given a place. If a man was felt academically qualified but not 'naval officer material', he would sometimes be given the option of mustering out of the Navy forthwith and transferring to the Army or the RAF, if they had unused spaces on the university allotment. Guy Lancaster took that route though he remembers that some loyal Navy men thought going back to service in the ranks as a Coder Special was preferable to life as an Army officer.

Those *kursanty* who made it to Cambridge or London to be trained as interpreters found themselves working even harder. One of them likened JSSL to sixth-form work at school whereas the University Course was very much harder even than his subsequent spell as an undergraduate. Over and above the peer group pressure, and the strong desire to live up to the expectations of charismatic figures like Liza Hill and Ronald Hingley, lay the by now familiar stick of the rejection and dejection that would be the consequences of failure. No one cared to give up the fruits of their virtually civilian life, which was interesting and very comfortable, certainly if compared to the normal expectations of a National Serviceman and by some measures, especially financial, rather better supported than an average undergraduate. Peter Woodthorpe recalls among many happy memories of a midshipman's life the fact that at nineteen or so he was being paid £5 per week to study while back home in Yorkshire his father was bringing up a family on a weekly wage of £8.

There were significant differences between London and

Cambridge in teaching style and atmosphere, in the personalities of the staff and indeed in the accommodation arrangements.

Cambridge was a curious blend of the marginally military, living a quasi-civilian life in one of the various 'Officer Cadets' Messes', and the quirkily academic. A member of Course M captured it in song as '. . . that semi-civvy setup, Where you wear your Woking getup, In that semi-civvy setup faraway'.

Learning advanced Russian under Liza and her team at Salisbury Villas was rather like being at a high-intensity crammer run by a distinctly odd extended Chekhovian family. Though this 'Slavonic heartbeat' was a consistent hallmark of the Cambridge Courses, comparison of memories over the life of the Course there makes it clear that there was a perceptible shift in lifestyle, with the early Courses being encouraged to think of themselves as enjoying many of the academic and social pleasures of university life, and the more segregated and perhaps more disciplined tone of the later and much smaller Courses.

As we have seen, Foxton Hall soon became the sole Mess. Before that and while the Courses were larger, the early accommodation at Newmarket was divided between two large Edwardian country houses in which each spacious room was shared by four *kursanty*, who would rise each morning to the sight of magnificent racehorses being exercised on the neighbouring gallops. Apart from those with an interest in the Turf, the town offered little diversion beyond the usual pubs, a fish and chip shop, and an excellent golf course. Much time – perhaps too much – was consumed by the daily trip, thirteen miles each way, in and out of Cambridge in a 'Progressive' bus, frantically learning word-lists on the outward journey and much given to songs both bawdy and bizarre on the way home. One staple in the repertoire, only to be appreciated by a Russian speaker and a somewhat childish nineteen-year-old Russian speaker to boot, was a song consisting of the word *dostoprimechatel'nost'* ('a sight worth seeing'), repeated over and over in the plural and singular to the tune of '*Deutschland über Alles*'. (For those interested in that sort of thing, the German equivalent, *Sehenswürdigkeit*, works rather less well.)

Lunch was taken at Marshall's Airfield, on the edge of Cambridge, which meant another bus ride, and the rest of the time was given up to learning word-lists and revising the latest set tasks in grammar.

A special feature of The Hermitage into which some *kursanty* on the large early Courses were moved was that meals were served by Danish girls who had come to Cambridge to acquire a 'Certificate of Competent Knowledge in English', a broad-based and pragmatic curriculum. The new residents, for the most part barely adult Englishmen, lavished ill-concealed longing on these (mostly) wasted gifts of the gods.

Living in Cambridge rather than Newmarket changed the character of the Course. Instead of the bus rides, under the sometimes responsible eye of a duty cadet, *kursanty* now enjoyed what Harry Shukman recalls from Course C as a sort of pseudo-student status, a feeling reinforced by regular attendance at university lectures given by members of the Slavonic Faculty.

Like undergraduates, *kursanty* in that early period went everywhere by bike, began using the Slavonic Faculty Library for extra study, patronised restaurants where three shillings would buy steak and chips with onions, or a high-class curry at the Koh-i-Noor in Trinity Street, went to the movies and, in the lazy summer afternoons when they didn't feel like punting yet again, enjoyed the *thé dansant* at the Dorothy Café in Petty Curie, where the adventurous might make the tea and toasted buns more memorable by dancing with a Scandinavian au pair. The Course raised football and cricket teams, and there was plenty of tennis. By contrast Geoffrey Elliott searching his memory for recollections of the closing Course T concluded that men on those early Courses had 'never had it so good'. He would not have known where to find a punt to rent, let alone how to venture out in one. Instead of *thé dansants*, his culinary highpoint was sharing a greasy Chicken Biryani in a café near the station with a future ambassador and a later colleague who made his mark as a translator of French *bandes dessinées* (or comic strips). Any football team raised from Course T would not have lasted more than ten minutes against Foxton Primary School Under-11's Extra B XI.

Douglas House, to which the *kursanty* moved at the end of 1952, had been the Stella Maris maternity home and the neat notices next to the bedside buttons declaring, 'If you need a nurse, press the button,' provoked much mirth; a two-storey cottage at the far end of the large site provided an extra bonus of privacy for the half-dozen or so *kursanty* lucky enough to be billeted there. So easy was life in Cambridge for the early Courses, at least, that it is not surprising that a degree of abuse crept in. Members of C Course were found on more than one occasion wandering around town when they should have been in class. The excuse that they were on their way to the Slavonic Library cut no ice with Liza, who knew a *progul'shchik* ('skiver', the Service argot for a slacker, is a fair translation) when she saw one, and serious warnings were followed by several cases of *kursanty* being RTU'd. As so often in JSSL's history the delicate balance between discipline and learning sometimes tipped the wrong way, and after what they saw as several unfair RTUs and a mounting tide of work for which threats were not a conducive background, Cambridge Course G staged a discreet 'go slow', deliberately failing its tests, until an upset Liza dealt with the problem. (Life on the London Course was far tougher and RTUs were delivered there with no compunction – three late arrivals for class and a *kursant* was unceremoniously handed his return rail warrant. There were no warnings for those detected wandering abroad during school hours – the RTU was instant. No fewer than sixteen were removed from the Course in late 1953.)

This literal and metaphorical overindulgence in strawberries and cream was probably what prompted the authorities in 1955 to replace the languid summer vacation enjoyed by earlier Courses with a brisk spell at the Cambridge University Officer Training Corps, where military discipline was sharpened with drill from a genuine sergeant-major and refresher training on the firing range. 1955 seems also to have been a watershed as the point at which the size of the intakes was scaled back. Though we have seen no record of this in the official files, an article in the university

122

newspaper *Varsity* on 19 July records a ceremony formally marking the 'last of the large Russian Courses'. It was presided over by Lord Carrington, then Under Secretary for Defence, who, in congratulating the four *kursanty* who had taken the top four places in the Cambridge final exam, generously told them they 'could now be considered as bilingual'. The indefatigable Liza also procured a letter from Foreign Secretary Anthony Eden congratulating the *kursanty* engaged on 'these important and difficult studies'.

Having like most sensible young men detested the idea of National Service, Alan Bennett found the Russian Course a 'happy time' and, 'although I did not realise it until later, far more enjoyable than my time at university proper'. Like many but not all, Bennett saw the greatest difference between *kursanty* as one not of class or school but age, the divide between schoolboys and graduates. But his comment in an interview thirty years later that, 'Once we got there, we didn't really have to work very hard. It was just a very, very pleasant life really', is an exception; most *kursanty* found themselves working at a level of intensity they had never experienced before. Michael Frayn reckoned his working day at Cambridge was about fourteen hours.

'We worked very hard. These were very congenial people, they were all good at languages or academics and I have to say I enjoyed it very much. I enjoyed the work and I enjoyed the company . . . Alan Bennett was a great friend and . . . we used to do shows together. That's where he pioneered his sketch of the sanctimonious clergyman.' Frayn, himself a grammar-school boy, conjectured that the JSSL Cambridge experience must have been like being at a public school 'where all one's emotional and educational needs are satisfied within a very small world'.

It was at Cambridge that Frayn and Bennett began to develop not just stand-up routines but a debunking attitude towards perceived pretentiousness, excessive zeal, or 'sound opinions' in their immediate circle; interviewed thirty years later, Frayn said that he was still wary in dealing with his friends from that time in case something he said would inspire their derision. He also remembered as part of the same self-mockery that he and his friends had developed a persona for each other, nominally spoofs but in fact highlighting what were seen as their real characteristics. Frayn was typecast as a man always running late, and unaware – 'Good heavens, why didn't someone tell me' – while Alan Bennett found himself characterised as a retiring literary figure chiefly interested in Virginia Woolf.

Cambridge *kursant* Michael Bourdeaux, who had been the bass soloist in the choir at Bodmin and who, as Canon Bourdeaux, founder of the Centre for the Study of Religion and Communism which later became the Keston Institute in Oxford, fought tenaciously against religious persecution in the Soviet Union, found Russian 'a most beautiful language'. He told an interviewer that the Course had opened the door to Tolstoy, Dostoyevsky, Pushkin – 'the world's greatest poet' – and not least to the extraordinary world of Soviet politics. 'It was the height of the Cold War with the possibility there might be another war. On our second day the instructor came in with a smile and taught us our first compete sentence, "*Umer Stalin* – Stalin has died". It was a time of great uncertainty in international relations and here we were being qualified to do something about it.'

When on the later Courses the accommodation was again shifted out of town to Foxton, the *kursanty* found themselves in living quarters which were a good deal less Spartan than any other Service accommodation they had experienced up till then, in some respects well up to the standard of a middling country-house hotel, with a bar, a library, a dining room, a tennis court, and a distractingly attractive housekeeper; and even though maybe two or three men found themselves sharing a bedroom, it was at least a decent size. But in contrast to any hotel or indeed doss house, the cost of all this to the cadets was a mere 1/6d per day.

Lurking behind brick walls and thick trees, Foxton's clumsy Victorian façade was a natural setting for a Sherlock Holmes short story involving demented doctors and snakes, though Kevin

Ruane recalls 'Daffodil' and 'Tulip' and other plaques on the bedroom doors, the floricultural overtones suggesting it might perhaps have been used earlier as a girls' school.

Again there was a bus from the 'Progressive' Company to run the students to Cambridge and back again in the evening. The students 'paraded each morning with their brief cases' and 'marched' a few yards down the gravel drive to board it. There was also a civilised and comfortable city within relatively easy reach when their workload allowed; in contrast to the experience of the earlier Courses, the Foxton *kursanty*'s 'neither town nor gown' status and freedom from the attentions of the Proctors and their 'bulldogs' was probably a marginal advantage.

Other than a mention in the Domesday Book, Foxton itself seems to have attracted little attention from the world, though in January 1958 the Cambridge University tiddlywinks team ventured out of town down the A10 to Foxton Hall, where a 'record crowd of five' watched them trounce the *kursanty* in a warm-up match for the University's much-publicised tourney against the Goons, their band leader and their scriptwriters a month or so later. Arthur Stockwin remembers earlier lengthy tussles in the Foxton lounge between those who wanted to listen to the Goons and the more cerebral element who favoured Schoenberg. The compromise was Beethoven.

One *kursant* remembers that perhaps the furthest you could travel culturally from the *babushki* and *pirozhki* at Salisbury Villas was a few miles from Foxton to the village of Whittelsford, where its self-styled squire, Kim de la Taste Tickell, a flamboyant bachelor, lorded, or perhaps more accurately queened, it over the Tickell Arms, often decked out in knee breeches and silver buckled shoes.

Neatly drawn by his obituarist as 'the Basil Fawlty of the Fens', Tickell once expelled a hapless *kursant* for daring to poke at the smouldering logs in the fireplace, something for which he claimed *droit de seigneur*. A bemused group of Sunday lunchtime drinkers was once shooed out of the door to screams of, 'I'm not having South London garage proprietors and their tarts in here!'

One of the many no doubt apocryphal tales of the time is that when the teaching staff were invited to a Christmas sherry party in Foxton, one failed to appear. When tackled after the holiday, he ruefully admitted that, having gone to Cambridge station to get the little branch line train that ran to Foxton, his accent had let him down and he had found himself on a mystifying and expensive detour en route to Folkestone, until a kindly ticket inspector sent him home.

The Service side of Cambridge was overseen by Squadron Leader West. A pale man, just short of retirement, and quietly spoken, he had been commanding officer at RAF Waterbeach, one of the first homes for the earliest Cambridge students, and had gained respect by making it clear to students arriving in full military gear that he disliked hobnail boots stamping on his office floor. Like almost every other figure in this story he soon acquired a nickname, in his case two: 'Eliot', after some literary *kursant* claimed to see a resemblance to the poet, and '*Zapad*', as a direct translation of his name into Russian. He usually had the moral upper hand though Geoffrey Elliott recollects West being discomfited when he encountered *kursant* and future historian Nicholas Bethell carrying a battered and curiously curved sporting implement.

'What on earth is that, Bethell?' the Squadron Leader asked in genuine puzzlement.

'That, sir,' drawled Bethell, who even then had a marked *de haut en bas* style, 'is a Real tennis racket.'

Being allowed to wear civilian clothes was a major blessing, though if it was true, as folklore had it, that this was for security reasons, the Services as usual missed the point by insisting – at least for the later Courses – that uniforms had to be donned for the weekly Pay Parade. They were also pulled out of the cupboard for the ceremonial end-of-Course photographs, all carefully preserved in Liza's archives. An alternative legend was that Liza simply refused to teach students in uniform as it created the wrong atmosphere. Even though *kursanty* were free to wear their own clothes, and many did, some were so outraged at what they saw as the theft of two years of their lives by conscription that they refused to compound the crime by wasting their own money, preferring to soldier on in the Woking 'ready to wear'.

Literature loomed large, with *kursanty* reading up in the evenings and expected to talk the next day in class about what they had read – the diet included *The Queen of Spades*, *Family Happiness*, *Crime and Punishment* and Chekhov.

In an early, undated draft of a proposal for the structure of the Interpreters' Course, Liza had declared that, 'It will aim solely at linguistic efficiency. Party politics and political propaganda will be completely excluded.'

Given the background of many of the staff, however, it was impossible to exclude at least some flavour of their views, and early programmes specifically included lectures on 'How the USSR is Ruled', and related topics, such as the collective farm system, on which an objective note would have been hard to strike. Later Courses recall less of this approach.

Looking back on his time at Cambridge, John Field asks himself why the absence of women from *kursanty*'s lives seems not to have presented a problem. For a start, Cambridge in the 1950s 'was a male-oriented town. There were very few women undergraduates – we were in fact not encouraged to mix with any undergraduates at all – and we were also a long way out of the city.' Though some of the older *kursanty* had girlfriends and one or two were married, most of his colleagues were absorbed in music, art and the theatre, and, above all, most of them worked night and day to avoid the RTU.

There might also have been social issues in the Course itself which mixed often temperamental young men from very varied backgrounds in a highly competitive blender, but there were not. In a sense, the great majority of *kursanty*, coming as they had from grammar rather than public schools, embodied the social mobility of the period. This was emphatically not a group that was wedded to its social origins, and whether the students were graduates or graduates-to-be, they looked forward to the future as professionals. One, for example, has recalled that his best friend on the Course had been to a grammar school in Essex and had a place waiting at Cambridge to read Modern Languages, his elder brother had been to Christ's Hospital and was now a senior advertising executive, while their father ran a butcher's stall in an East End market.

Years later a discerning interviewer asked a former *kursant* of working-class background whether he had felt socially at ease in this new world, or whether he had felt a need to adapt. He said that he had felt no such pressure and that is probably true of most of the *kursanty*. The Cambridge Course, as with London and JSSL in its various locations, in effect provided its own environment and shared goals and was throughout its existence a friendly, easy-going, un-class-conscious, barrier-free community. Michael Frayn, who had not been to boarding school, speculated that Foxton might have had some of the same spirit, and remembers that he 'greatly enjoyed the sense of communal life, of being part of a society united in its resistance to authority', though in fairness other than Liza, who could put on an act of great ferocity if needed but who was a benevolent dictator, rather than an authoritarian, or the occasional mild wrath of Squadron Leader West, there was not much authority at Cambridge itself against which to resist.

9

The World's a Stage

If JSSL was a unique and productive school with heady flourishes of theatricality, the Cambridge University Course could be seen as a theatre which served brilliantly as a school. The stage was Salisbury Villas. The producer, director, scriptwriter and leading lady was Liza Hill, the cast her Russian staff and the audience her admiring, hard-working *kursanty*. At moments they could be forgiven for thinking that they actually had walk-on parts themselves in a play within a play on the lines of *Vanya on 42nd Street*.

Eric Korn imagines the scene when Liza got the green light: 'Professor Hill, I like to think, dashed off to Paris with a bagful of contracts to tell her White Russian friends that the good times were back again. No more taxi driving, no more waiting at table. You can wear your straw hat and read them Lermontov, you two can teach them to act Chekhov the way you did at the Moscow Arts and you, madam, you just need to make conversation and teach elocution by example; of course they will call you Princess. But there weren't enough princesses and Petersburg boulevardiers and Moscow Arts juvenile leads to go around. Poles, Ukrainians,

South Russians with throaty genitives like a carthorse coughing, Ossets (one Osset, to be fair) from the Caucasus, Latvians and even, or did I dream it, a Hungarian, took the menial parts, conjugation drills in chilly Bodmin where you could spend most of the morning getting the stoves to light.'

Certainly those on the early Courses must have pinched themselves to make sure that they were not dreaming when they found themselves faced with two Orthodox priests, the saintly-looking Father Vladimir Rodzianko, later to become Orthodox Bishop in Washington DC, and Father Popov, whose ashen face was probably explained by the fact that he had to travel overnight from Manchester to Cambridge for his 10 a.m. oral practice class. Alongside them was the much loved Mrs Hackel, who, Liza claimed, had joined a religious order in London and changed out of her nun's habit into her habitual black suit on the train.

The secular side was represented by Vladimir Pavlovich Saulus, a jovial gentleman with a florid face and bushy white moustache, who had been commandant of the Tsar's personal aircraft and arrived at Salisbury Villas from Bulgaria. A past master of Russian slang and coarse jokes, he caused a prolonged raucous belly-laugh in David Fill's class when explaining the different ways to translate the word 'ball' into Russian: 'In Russia we have three balls . . .' He is still remembered by his colleagues, George Bird and Marina Fennell, for his conversation-stopper in the staff common room: 'Do you know, I met Chekhov.' His father, a doctor whose estate bordered Chekhov's, was attending the famous playwright, and one day asked the young Vladimir to run over with some medicine. 'Anton Pavlovich was reclining on the balcony. He thanked me for bringing the medicine, asked me how I was getting on at school – it was in the school holidays. I told him, and that was all. I never saw him again. But now I think of the many, many things I would have liked to ask him.'

As was the case in the mainstream JSSL, the *kursanty* had little or no appreciation for the difficult, often terrifying paths along which their instructors had scrambled on their way to Cambridge – escapes, prison camps, factory work, families left behind, secrets unspoken – but they did sense the vast cultural and linguistic gulf that separated the émigrés of the Tsarist generation and those who had come out of Soviet Russia. This gulf was much in evidence in Liza's memoirs, but allowance must be made for the fact that these were written when she was in her late eighties and nineties, lonely and beset by all sorts of difficulties.

Liza's insistence that Russian was best taught in Russian had the unusual result that several men and women rejected by the Air Ministry panel for JSSL posts because their English was poor or non-existent were snapped up by her as oral tutors for Cambridge. One, the elegant and sardonic Andrei Romankiewicz, explained to the panel that, as a Polish officer sent to Siberia as a prisoner of war by the Russians, until released as part of some larger political settlement, he had not had much chance to study English. He had nevertheless been rejected and had returned to his night job packing Peek Frean biscuits, but decided to try his luck again, explaining later to Liza that, based on his experiences in the Soviet Union, it was always worth another go, since 'the official you saw first time around would either have been moved on or liquidated'.

One of the better-kept secrets was that the understated and polite George Trapp, born like Liza into an Anglo-Russian family in St Petersburg, and given to beginning anecdotes with the line 'When I was in Helsingfors . . .', was the author of the eclectic and daunting word-lists that were the daily equivalent of learning the Catechism. His work as an engineer and a translator – as well as a brief spell selling shirts at a City outfitters – had given him a peerless Russian and English vocabulary. Liza described him in a slightly uncharacteristic turn of phrase as 'a real white man', meaning that as an instructor he was hard working but above all he could always be trusted.

The cultural tilt at Cambridge was towards the spirit of Russia, its classics and literature which were central not just to Liza's theories of teaching but to the background of so many of her staff from the older generation. John Waine was an A Course entrant who went on the fast track to Cambridge with a Divinity

Degree, not a criterion envisaged by Liza in her original listing of desired academic skills. He was to become Bishop of Chelmsford, so it is not surprising that to judge from a radio interview he gave thirty years later one of the most evocative memories for him was being in a group taken to London by Liza to Easter service at the Russian Orthodox Church, guttering candles, kerchiefed old ladies, the priest's basso-profundo message *'Khristos voskres!'*, and the congregation's reply, *'Voistinu voskres!'* ('Christ is risen', 'Verily, He is risen').

She was inclined to dismiss those brought up in the Soviet era as altogether *'nekul'turny'* ('uncouth' is a close translation), which led to her making quite sharp sheep and goat distinctions, of the depth of which most of the *kursanty* were thankfully unaware.

In the early days the Cambridge staff roster had distinct *Almanach de Gotha* overtones. Many were of a certain age, though Emmy Voznesenskaya – Emmy, Emochka, or Miss Voz to the *kursanty* – was a pretty Leningrad girl in her twenties. Though only about five feet tall, she had a way of looking down her nose that made it plain she regarded *kursanty* as *infra dig*. Probably quite rightly, since she later became a lecturer in Russian Literature at Edinburgh.

Liza also records keeping one lady out of sight for a while as an examination marker in London 'because I did not think her refugee appearance would fit in socially in the Cambridge scene'.

But the roster evolved, and many of the older generation left the scene and were replaced by the mix of first- and second-wave émigrés familiar from JSSL. Even the 'refugee' was allowed to come in from the cold.

While a few cynics dismissed him as a ham, many *kursanty* recall with fondness the elegant, lantern-jawed figure of the former Maly Theatre star Boris Ranevsky, who read stories by Chekhov or Gogol while he sat poised but comfortable in an arm-chair. Poems by Pushkin on the other hand merited an almost Victorian, standing mode, eyes uplifted to some distant horizon, a large well-laundered snow-white handkerchief ready to mop his brow.

The World's a Stage

The splendid Mrs Hackel was a widow whose route to exile had included swimming across a border river into Holland with her late husband. She gave oral classes in groups of six, insisting that her room, where she usually arrived fractionally late and out of breath, must have a large and open window to give her copious drafts of fresh air. A good answer to one of her questions would elicit a beam and a cry of *'Molodyets'* ('Clever boy'). The ultimate condemnation for some howler was a doleful *'takovo slova nyetu'* ('There's no such word'). Even that cool observer Naky Doniach was struck that when he once listened as she read *The Inspector General* aloud to her class for translation, she would still chuckle at some of the jokes even though it might have been the hundredth reading of her career.

As at Bodmin, theatre was an important part of the Cambridge Course. In one sense the whole experience could be said to have been theatrical. The indefatigable Liza had brought over to the UK the happily married Vera Grech and Pavlov – always known by his surname only, like Inspector Morse or the French film star Fernandel. Like Yul Brynner's parents and the Hollywood actor Akim Tamiroff, they had been among members of Stanislavsky's touring company who opted for exile when their 1925 tour reached Paris. There are many memories of Grech reading from *Crime and Punishment*, tears in her eyes as she recounted Sonia's fate. 'Such moments,' D. M. Thomas reflects, 'were very affecting, and made one start to love Russian literature – and the infuriatingly difficult language.' His 'single moment of triumph' came as he recited a Pushkin poem and was later told that, with tears in her eyes, Grech had murmured, 'That young man, he must have Russian parents.'

Like no other instructors, Grech and Pavlov could convey the extremes of Russian histrionics, from melancholy to hysteria, to a wide-eyed and often embarrassed group of *ingénus*.

When they first came to Cambridge in early 1952, Grech and Pavlov directed Russian-language productions featuring only *kursanty*, all of whom look back at the experience as both formative and unforgettable.

In his first term, Harry Shukman appeared in their *Cherry*

Orchard, playing the footman Yasha and declaiming words whose full meaning he had yet to understand. In this first production, all the parts were played by *kursanty*, except for Anya played by 'Miss Voz' and Ranevskaya and the old retainer, Firs, played by Grech and Pavlov themselves. Harry recalls his unease when he had to grab and kiss 'a very pretty, pouting Dunyasha', played by Hugh Johnston in drag. 'I felt much more comfortable in the next production, Chekhov's *Three Sisters*, in which I played the part of Baron Tuzenbakh. All the women's roles were taken by female undergraduates in the Slavonic Faculty, one of whom played the part of the sister-in-law Natasha and was to become my first wife and the mother of my three children.' Alan Fisher scored a cross-dressing 'first' when to achieve verisimilitude in the same role in a different production Lisa lent him one of her bras, which he stuffed with his rugger socks.

Grech and Pavlov – whose theatrical egos often clashed noisily and publicly with Ranyevsky's, compounding the sense of back-stage atmospherics – also produced *The Inspector General* with a cast including Alan Bennett as the heavy-handed policeman, Derzhimorda, Michael Frayn as an inn servant and Eric Korn as Bobchinsky. In an interview many years later Bennett brought it back to mind, 'I really didn't understand half the play, I think I just probably knew my own part without really understanding the plot.'

Frayn remembered that as he made his exit from the stage, he had pushed the door rather than pulled it. It jammed and he was stuck while on the other side of the door the stagehands struggled with crowbars and the audience began a slow handclap. 'My nerve broke and I haven't been back on the stage since.'

Several students kept in touch with Grech and Pavlov after they retired back to their tiny Paris flat in the very Russian 16th arrondissement. Terry Wade was not the only sharp-eyed movie-goer who spotted Pavlov as a Russian waiter taking Alistair Sim to task in the film *Holiday in Paris*.

Liza's relationship with her older staff, and their regard for her, is perhaps best caught in the story of the Plyushkoffs who arrived in Cambridge with two suitcases and an armchair bought from the earnings of their first jobs as émigrés, woolcarding at a Bradford mill. Their dossier, found by Geoffrey Elliott in an archive, is every bit as harrowing in its account of adjustment to life during and after the Revolution, and of terrifying wanderings across Europe, as the life story of Mr Dudariv cited by David Marquand. The tall, sad-eyed Alexei Ivanovich, always impeccably turned out with his trademark bow-tie, was a poet who had never forgotten that when he was a young man the great Alexander Blok had once pronounced some of his early verses to be 'not at all bad' and encouraged him to continue writing. In between his teaching duties on the Cambridge Course, he wrote prodigiously, primarily for the Russian émigré newspaper in Paris under the *nom de plume* of Alexei Ugryumov, or 'Alexei Gloomy', doted on by his wife and admired by his students for whom his lectures on *Crime and Punishment*, combined with the mimeographed *Voprosnik* or Questionnaire on the book that he handed out as a teaching aid, were invaluable building blocks in their studies.

The Plyushkoffs (Madam organised Salisbury Villas singsongs, and ran Snap and Lotto sessions in the coffee breaks, to develop numbers skills) consulted Liza on everything dear to them – including the almost miraculous discovery that the son they had left behind in the Soviet Union was still alive, miraculous since the news came not long after they had offered up prayers for him at the Orthodox Church in Brondesbury. When they died, they left their Cambridge house to its nuns.

Liza was also there at the end. When Alexei Ivanovich died at home after a dignified fight with cancer, Liza and Dmitri Shchipakhin – 'Professor Jimmy' – went over to help lay him out.

The dapper, Shchipakhin was an artist and an *homme polyvalent* who worked as the boilerman, kept an eye on the garden, prepared the staff lunches and supervised the cleaning.

At Madam's insistence, before the undertakers were called, Plyushkoff had to be dressed in death as neatly and respectably as in life, complete with braces and bow-tie. Liza and Dmitri struggled valiantly to get him into his jacket and tidy him up. The only compromise was that, unseen by his widow, his braces were laid flat on his chest under his jacket rather than being slung over his shoulders, on the pragmatic grounds that holding up his trousers was no longer a priority for him.

It was as though here as elsewhere Liza was acting out Lermontov's character in *A Hero of Our Time*: 'fate has somehow led me to the climax of other people's dramas. It was as if no one could die, no one could despair without me. I was the essential character in the fifth act.'

(Confusingly and much to Liza's chagrin, since she preferred to refer to him as 'the Slavonic soul of the house' and 'The Steward', the university records showed the 'boilerman or caretaker' as Colonel Rozdjalowsky, a Serb who had once been an aide-de-camp to King Peter of Yugoslavia. He was always strapped for cash, not least because of a Slav propensity for drink, and he tested Liza's loyalty sorely when she discovered that not all the money he was given to buy groceries for staff lunches was being spent on food. On another occasion she had to get him out of a Cambridge police cell, where he had spent the night rather the worse for wear.)

Less fraught examples of how she fussed for her staff are seen throughout Liza's correspondence, especially with the University. In the summer of 1952 she asked them to instal a bathroom in the basement of Salisbury Villas, 'as our Colonel/Caretaker and the Russian instructors who live in rooms about the town, most of them without bathrooms, would be a much more contented staff if we could provide them with a bathroom and geyser'.

On the other side of the mental green baize door were Liza's staff from the Soviet era, unkindly dismissed in her memoirs towards the end of her life as 'runaways from the Soviet Army, each with his own ideas and supposedly having abandoned Communism'. One suspects the main bone of contention may have been the 'own ideas'. Liza grouched that some of the ex-Soviets were 'majors who would not have been sergeant majors in our army', and who remained slaves to 'pathetic Soviet bureaucracy', though in the final analysis she conceded that they worked hard, were simply trying to make a living and that 'harnessed, they became splendid instructors, dedicated and popular'.

Among the 'Soviet' staff were three ex-Red Army men who liked to stroll to and from work arm-in-arm, a typical Russian habit but one that provoked mirth among their callow students and earned the inevitable nickname, the 'Three Stooges'. The mocking sobriquet seemed rather less appropriate when word spread that the trio were all members of the National Labour Union, an anti-Soviet subversive organisation based in Frankfurt, and two of its members, former Red Army Major Ivanov and former intelligence officer, Major Frolov, both wrote for the strongly anti-Soviet journal *Posev* ('Sowing'). Michael Frayn recalls that Frolov was obsessed by the large amounts of time he had spent in the Army commuting backwards and forwards between Vladivostok and Moscow and liked to remind his pupils lugubriously that 'on the Trans-Siberian railway, people fall in love, people marry and people die'. According to Liza in later private conversation, Frolov, like so many thousands of other Soviet officers in security and intelligence, had been too close to too many executions and had fled to the West after a crisis of conscience.

Another Soviet-era instructor is memorably recollected by a *kursant* as 'a bit forbidding and sinister, the sort of man who, when he caught sight of flowers, looked around for the coffin'.

To judge from her memoirs Liza was less than fond of a woman instructor, Alexandra 'Sasha' Chernysheva, an official with the Soviet Control Commission in Berlin until she defected. Then in her forties and clearly toughened by her early years as a *besprizornaya* – one of the millions of homeless orphans who had wandered wild in Soviet Russia in the early years after the Revolution and were eventually corralled into one of Stalin's early (failed) experiments in social engineering – she is remembered by several *kursanty* as reserved, elegant and a good teacher, who pronounced the Russian word for 'bomber' (*'bombardirovshchik'*) 'as though it were an elegy'. Another expressed a more widely held view than he perhaps realised when he wrote of her wistfully many years later that, 'I had recently seen *Tea and Sympathy* and was rather hoping for something on those lines.'

Alexandra seems to have managed to upset several of her colleagues, one of whom, according to Liza, nicknamed her 'Lordessa' for her supposed aloofness. Later on she also found herself at odds with Liza herself. The proximate cause to judge from the latter's memoirs seems to have been that Alexandra had wandered into the complex electromagnetic field of emotions that made up the relationship between Liza and her 'Sister in Christ', Doris Mudie, whom Liza supported financially and morally with unremitting commitment. She was always at pains to find, and invent, a role for Doris, who fluttered helpfully in the wings of Salisbury Villas, making recordings and copying texts and diffidently giving small group classes in phonetics, even though most suspected she actually spoke little or no Russian.

It is too easy to suggest that Cambridge was 'all a bit of a laugh', or even infirm of purpose. It had its marvellous and irreverent moments, but its students worked very hard. The mixture worked well and in the acid test produced many really excellent linguists. One reason is that while there are fewer anecdotes about the gifted British teaching staff, they too made a critically important and steadying contribution.

Most of the British teachers focused on grammar and thus provided the basic underpinnings without which the rest of the teaching edifice – the vocabulary, the oral work, the literature, and the free-form engagement with the Russian teachers – would not have been possible. In Cambridge these included George Bird, later to move to Crail as Chief Instructor, Higher Grade, whose sound advice to students to learn Chekhov short stories by heart to boost fluency, vocabulary and style was probably heeded more in the breach than the observance; there were also James Larkin, Tony Stokes, David Jones, Jan Horvat (Eric Korn's 'Hungarian'); Alexis Vlasto, who deputised for Liza when she was either away or on sabbatical, and who was the author of *A Linguistic History of Russian* and one of the first pre-war recruits to the GCCS code-breaking efforts. In the early years John Fennell is remembered for the clarity and authority of his teaching and his gift for finding a vivid extempore phrase, such as 'I had just returned from killing my aunt with an axe', to illustrate a point. Fennell, who went on from Cambridge to build up the small Slavonic department at Nottingham, with the support of several *kursanty*, later became Professor of Russian at Oxford.

In the early years Cambridge *kursanty* were also taught by British members of the Slavonic Faculty and attended memorable lectures: Nikolai Andreyev on Russian Thought, Ian Young on Lenin and the Revolution, the bear-like Edward Sands on Pushkin, and Peter Squire (who demonstrated at parties to awestruck students why he had the reputation of being the fastest simultaneous interpreter of Russian in the country) on the Decembrists. The popular Andreyev had spent two and a half years in Soviet camps after being arrested by SMERSH in 1945. This may have accentuated the jovial relish – '*uzhasno bylo, uzhasno*' ('it was terrible, terrible') – with which he recounted some of the bloodier episodes of Russian history. Nicknamed '*Gromkogovoritel*' ('The Loudspeaker'), he was admired by the *kursanty* and adored by the female undergraduates of the Slavonic Faculty whom he called his '*detskii sad*', or kindergarten, one of whom he eventually married. One of their three children is now a tutor in Russian history at Oxford. Another lecturer, Alex Miller, remembered as 'a cross between Gogol and the young lover in Peynet's cartoons, with then unfashionably long hair and a little goatee beard', is said to have moved from Cambridge to The Progress Publishing House in Moscow, a Soviet institution whose product belied its name, and where a number of equally 'progressive' former JSSL *kursanty* also found work for a while.

Liza herself gave occasional lectures on a variety of topics from Russian history to Pushkin's verse, or – one of her hobby-horses – Russian pronunciation. Kevin Ruane remembers a master class on the pronunciation of the letters 'a' and 'o'. 'Unfortunately, the validity of her suggestion that the unstressed "o" in Russian sounds rather like the English pronunciation of the letter "u" in "guns and butter" was undermined somewhat when my friend Willie Ledgard demonstrated the awkward truth that a northern English pronunciation of guns and butter can differ markedly from the southern.' On another occasion she spent a whole morning on how to say '*Da*' or 'Yes'. 'The tongue must kiss the roof of the mouth well behind the teeth and gums just at the ledge of the palate.' Ivor Samuels notes that, 'having demonstrated how she, above all, could pronounce a better "Da" than we, she swep' out'. (Voltaire told James Boswell that a similar dental technique was needed for proper pronunciation of English but that as he had lost all his teeth, he could not master it.)

The effect of Liza on her classes was brilliantly caught by Michael Frayn when he wrote her obituary:

> Suddenly, there she would be, the Professor herself, powerful, unpredictable, her hair swept dramatically back from her broad, always smiling face, with eyes of childlike innocence and inquisitorial penetration, the personification of everything most indomitable and transcendent in the Russian character. Sudden, terrifying questions would be hurled at us. Impossible texts for oral translation would be plucked without warning out of the air, terrible permutations of the different possibilities offered by the Russian verbs of motion, perhaps – going on foot or by some means of transport, perfective/imperfective aspect, determinate, indeterminate or frequentative – in all their various nightmare irregularities. The man who often used to drop in at the house (on foot), she would begin, 'having noticed two geese sliding along the street in a sledge, will tomorrow go several times, either on foot or in an electric tram'. Pause, while she struggled to imagine how to bring this farrago to a full stop, and everyone else in the room waited to see who the finger was going to be pointing at. Then, offhand, thrown away with an impatient wave of the hand, '. . . to see his elderly aunt arrive by balloon from Saratov'. And the finger would be pointing at you, and she would be nodding with eager encouragement, smiling with delight at the effortless correctness with which you were

going to negotiate all those terrible verbs, coaxing the Russian out of you by the sheer brightness of her eyes. As inconspicuously as possible, the first verb would creep out of your mouth, the wrong one, naturally, representing the sort of dropping-in done not by an assiduous pedestrian but by the most infrequent horseman. Instant impatience from Liza. You would be brushed aside, together with all your stupidity, in one characteristically Russian sweep of the hand in front of the face, and the bright, expectant eyes would be shining on someone else. We all imitated her, sometimes to her face, and we all loved her.

But the day-to-day administration of the Course and the dealings with the University and Service authorities took most of Liza's energies, assisted by her secretary Jean Thomas, who, as Jean Stafford-Smith, edited and organised the publication of Liza's memoirs in 1999. Courtenay Lloyd, whom Liza dubbed her 'right-hand man', shared significant parts of the administration. Remembered as having a remarkably clear and simple way of communicating the early problems of conjugation and declension that Russian presents to the beginner, and by Phillip Hanson (later Professor of Economics at Birmingham) for his 'amazing ability to recall from one week to the next who had got exactly which grammatical construction wrong the last time around', Lloyd's Cambridge studies had been interrupted by service in the Navy during the Second World War and a spell as an intelligence officer with the Control Commission in Germany. He graduated in 1950 with a degree in German and Norwegian (part of his war service had involved liaison with the Norwegian Navy). Impressed by a friend's account of the dynamism of the Slavonic Faculty under Liza, he took a one-year course in Russian at her encouragement and joined her team. He taught as well as managed: everything from organising the setting, writing and marking of the weekly test papers, through pacifying Russian instructors with minor problems to being the one who entered a classroom as the lesson ended to make important announcements.

A shy and gentle man prone to blushing, he figures improbably in the archives as the official in charge of discipline and of reprimanding absentees and other miscreants, though doing so must have hurt him more than it hurt them; however, anything as severe as an RTU was handled by Liza herself. Lloyd later married Princess Elena Lieven, who took conversation classes and was also the Russian secretary of the School. She was a tall, good-looking young woman, remembered despite her cosmopolitan background as like the hockey captain at an English girls' school.

But the *kursanty* were by and large far too busy to think much about what went on in the staff room – though the 'Old Adam' was never far away. At one point one of them was said to be 'walking out', in an administrator's prim phrase, with one of the women instructors, while many longed to help the lady who kept the housekeeping ledgers master the intricacies of double-entry book-keeping – alas mostly in vain.

George Trapp's word-lists are a central feature of the collective Cambridge memory. Thirty new words had to be memorised each and every day with a weekly test, a task that looking back fifty years later seems not just impressive but virtually impossible, even for boys fresh out of school or university with high-octane learning skills. Arthur Stockwin kept a complete folder, random selections from which give some flavour of the amazing range: sixty musical instruments from accordion via tambourine to xylophone, insects, sixty birds, all aspects of human behaviour and traits and moods, horticulture, all known metals and elements, legal procedures, education, basic military terminology, fruits, transport, fish and shellfish, bathroom and beauty products. Under 'sounds', *kursanty* were required to learn the Russian for 'din, whisper, snorting, chirruping, clucking and screeching'; and much more. It was as if the editors of *Roget's Thesaurus* and Smirnitsky's Russian Dictionary had combined with the compilers of *The Times* crossword to produce raw material for the ultimate word game. One group felt themselves so pressured by the Lists that they fed them onto a ceremonial end-of-Course bonfire.

Kursanty had the standard JSSL issue Semeonoff Grammar and two dictionaries, English–Russian and Russian–English. The former was bound in blue, the latter, which was somewhat smaller, in red; whether there was anything whimsical in the choice of colours we shall never know. With the advice of Naky Doniach both had been copied – whether by GCHQ or the Air Ministry is not clear – from Soviet originals without acknowledgement, fair game at that time, since the Russians were not party to the Copyright Convention. The Air Ministry also produced *Russian Passages for Translation Practice* with extracts from the Russian classics as well as Soviet writers, such as Sholokhov, Kaverin, Grossman, Fadeyev, Simonov and the satirist team of Il'f and Petrov.

It also included difficult passages by the nineteenth-century historian Klyuchevsky and the Marxist Pokrovsky, and from Russian thinkers such as Berdyaev. There was also a long section of extracts from military histories and war novels, all of a high standard of Russian which would enable even the average *kursant*, admittedly with much hard work, to master Part One of the Cambridge University Tripos and approach the even more demanding Civil Service Examination at the end of the Course with some confidence.

The underlying principle was 'immersion and absorption'. This also meant reading novels and poetry whose relevance to any military intelligence assignment was tangential at best, though the story of battles on the Eastern Front told in *Days and Nights* by the Soviet novelist and war correspondent Konstantin Simonov represented a way of getting across a lot of Service vocabulary in a fictional context. Even though they dated from the early nineteenth century, Pushkin's short novel *The Captain's Daughter* and his *Queen of Spades*, along with Lermontov's *A Hero of Our Time*, provided models of Russian prose at its most elegant and lucid. Kataev's *Lone White Sail* (its title a reference back to a Lermontov poem) offered an early example of Soviet prose at its least propagandistic.

Probably the first book *kursanty* at Cambridge (and at

London) saw when they arrived was an edition of *Crime and Punishment*, showing the stress on each and every word on its 588 pages. Liza had employed a bevy of Russians on this tedious chore, using a Russian text published by the YMCA in Paris, since no Soviet edition was in print, nor would be for several years to come. She never explained her choice. Perhaps she felt it would take its young English readers into the depths of the Russian mind in language that reflected the chaos and hysteria to be found there.

Crime and Punishment was also the source of many themes snatched at the last moment by *kursanty* who were late in preparing for the 'lecturettes' in Russian they had to deliver to their class, in some phases of the Course several times a week. Thumbnail sketches of Shakespeare plays, articles from the *New Scientist* – anything was fair game however complex or infantile. A resourceful *kursant* once used almost half his allotted time putting into Russian the title of a short story by William Saroyan, 'The Man Whose Uncle Had His Head Bitten Off by a Circus Tiger', whose plot was the theme of his lecturette. This technique, intended to exercise the use of vocabulary and increase fluency, was effective and was an idea adapted by the London Course Director, Ronald Hingley.

Another centrepiece was the weekly essay. These were set on the lectures the Course had heard in the week, on a variety of topical themes, on literary figures and, at least once per Course, on the *kursanty*'s own biographies, a subject which looking back with twenty-first-century suspicion might lead one to ask for whom these were actually intended.

The papers of Harvey Pitcher, generous provider of that earliest mention of Service language training in Tsarist Russia, give a good snapshot. He was a member of Course M whose time at Cambridge in 1955–6 coincided with Liza's absence on a sabbatical, and who thus did not experience the full sense of 'electricity in the air'. But her presence still made itself felt, when instructors would say grimly: 'If the Professor were here, she'd never let you get away with such poor work!'

His essay book – stamped on the cover with the EIIR emblem and the note 'Supplied for the Public Service' – includes such themes as 'Teddy Boys', 'Art in the Soviet Union', 'The Race Problem', 'Soviet Propaganda and British Propaganda', and 'What Have Events in Hungary Shown the World?', yet again demonstrating that political themes were not ignored by the staff even as they drove the language home.

The piles of manuscripts, each bearing its author's number rather than name for security reasons, were sent to London to be marked by another JSSL Cambridge legend, (largely but not wholly because almost no one had ever set eyes on him) Count Bobrinskoi. They came back marked out of fifteen – five for grammar, five for content and five for handwriting. Some, like Geoffrey Elliott whose script was illegible in any language, thought this unfair.

The Count's formal marks were augmented by neatly written comments that were sometimes sharp, sometimes funny, and occasionally, if the work took his fancy, illustrated with one of his trademark cartoons. One of Pitcher's essays earned the accolade of a sketch illustrating a nuanced point about various alternative Russian words for 'misfortune': it shows a young man splashing desperately in a vat labelled 'Watney's Beer' and shouting 'Help me out of my trouble'.

To save time the Count also had a selection of rubber stamps made up which he used to highlight the more frequent and egregious grammatical howlers. To draw a line between this exiled nobleman and Kingsley Amis and Philip Larkin at Oxford in 1946 is a stretch, but, as one *kursant* has pointed out, they too felt that stamps with such questions as, 'What does this mean?' and 'What makes you think I care?', were an efficient way to criticise their own and their friends' early poetry.

It is not clear where the Count, descendant of the pre-Revolutionary Bobrinskois who owned the rolling serf-studded Tula Bogoroditsk estates, fitted into Liza's extended family. She records in her memoirs meeting a Countess Bobrinskaya, with her two daughters and her 'seven-year-old son', en route from Russia to England for a holiday in 1912. What is clear is that as the descendant of a noble line whose founder was delicately described in the Tables of Rank as the 'natural son' of Catherine the Great and Prince Orlov, Bobrinskoi fitted in well with Liza's early vision of her teaching staff.

Another technique also followed by the London Course was that of the 'conferences' that figured sporadically in the mid-1950s. John Goodliffe took part in these when he returned to Cambridge as an instructor in September 1953. An English instructor sat at one end of a long table, a native Russian speaker at the other, and four *kursanty* sat along each side. Prepared by Arthur Birse, who had interpreted for Churchill at Yalta and who would leave Cambridge temporarily to interpret at the Petrov spy trial in Australia in 1954, 'scenarios', as the archives show, were vetted by someone in Eaton Square in London signing himself only as 'Charlie'. These scripts might depict the interrogation of a Soviet defector picked up near the Turkish border, or a conversation at a diplomatic reception. The British instructor asked questions in English, the Russian gave his answers, and the students did their best to translate orally both ways. In one conference which stuck in Goodliffe's memory, the Russian, played by George Trapp, came up with, 'I had to climb on to the lavatory seat so as to tie a piece of string to the broken chain.'

The Service side was not ignored; Pitcher's papers also include a translation into English, meticulously corrected by the instructor, of a very technical Russian newspaper article on the principles of liquid fuel rocketry, and a dictated Russian dialogue between two military men.

After the weekly test, failure in which two weeks in a row spelled real trouble, 'the results were posted on the notice-board on Monday before our mid-morning break'. As Harvey Pitcher recalls, 'I can readily picture coming down the stairs at the end of a class; a crowd of *kursanty* affecting cheerful indifference but inwardly anxious is already clustered round the notice-board but by peering over their shoulders it is just possible to make out the one vital fact, whether one's name is above or below the fail line.'

Those on the early Courses who thought their destiny was to interrogate Soviet prisoners of war, sometimes wondered about the relevance of all this literature, all the more since they were supposed to be limited by the Geneva Convention to asking only about name, rank and number. But according to Naky Doniach, the military authorities were persuaded that interrogators needed to emerge from the Course fully equipped to deal with Russians, prisoners of war or not, on an equal cultural and educational footing. Michael Frayn remembered being told that it was a cardinal principle of interrogation for the British questioner to retain the moral advantage by speaking Russian even if his target spoke good English.

In later years when interpreters were more likely to be engaged in higher-level Sigint work, the same principle probably applied in the different context of the conversations they might need to understand. In any case, whatever Whitehall thought, Liza was convinced that mechanical learning was not enough to make an interpreter and that only immersion in the culture would do the job, even if it was limited to the glittering microcosm, that Green Room of the Moscow Arts Theatre-in-exile, that she and her team had created at Salisbury Villas.

The administrative problems of the University Course should have been far less than for the sizeable JSSL itself, as the numbers involved were so much smaller, but Liza's ongoing struggles with the Cambridge University Treasury were far sharper than any arguments she may have had with the Service authorities. Most of her exchanges with the latter were about the academic progress and results of the various Courses and the reason for variances. With the University the issues were usually costs: Why was she spending money on taxis (to ferry teachers and exam papers around Cambridge when they were under pressure to collect and mark them)? Was the newly repaired TV really being used for the Course, she retorted? Who spent what and why at Miller's Wine Parlour? etc.

In the 1954 letter we cited earlier (see page 35), she also put forward to the University a lengthy and plausible case, based on her workload and the results achieved, that her annual salary of £500 should be raised to the £1,000 received by the Director of the London programme – in fact it was £1,150, made up of £650 as a Lecturer plus £500 for running the Course – and which the Services would have been quite prepared to pay her at the outset had the University not stepped in to prevent it on the grounds that she was continuing to receive her professorial salary while all of her energies were in fact being spent on the Service Course.

Her London counterpart, Ronald Hingley, she bridled, was 'a lecturer in the London School of Slavonic Studies; an inexperienced administrator who was sent to Cambridge to learn my intensive methods and after profiting by my experience and material prepared at Cambridge successfully modelled the London Courses on our standards'. In Hingley's view, however, it was Liza who learned from him, and who indeed had begged him tearfully to tell her what to do to improve the standards of her *kursanty*. More will be said below about this fraught relationship.

In support of her pay claim, however, it was indeed Liza who had provided the template. She had also borne a considerable administrative burden. She had had to work out 'a timetable which, when the Courses were running concurrently, involved 440 teaching hours per week for forty-two weeks in the year, which represents more than the number of lectures offered . . . by the entire Modern and Mediaeval Languages Faculty'. She had not just appointed the staff but had to train and supervise them. She had worked hard in 'driving up standards and keeping in contact with the instructors by visiting classes, taking groups for advanced written interpretership, lecturing to each of the Courses in Russian literature and history and maintaining morale by interviews and encouragement'.

Since she was arguing for a pay increase, there may have been an element of special pleading, but Liza's explanation of the workload represented by the system of exams and tests is compelling. A progress test had been held each week with each Course submitting about 250 scripts, meaning that 'an average of about 700 scripts per week for three years have had to be corrected'. In addition there were mid-term and term examinations for each Course with five or six papers each, and an oral examination. On top of all that came the final examination for each Course 'with printed papers and a standard equivalent to that of the Part One Tripos (not only in language but with a knowledge of Russian history and literature being required)'.

She had also had to make time to attend working parties at the Air Ministry in London, visit Coulsdon and Bodmin, and host 'distinguished visitors' from the Service Ministries, the Foreign Office and overseas language-training schools. In short, she felt that she had done her bit to fulfil 'my vocation and my public duty'. She had every right to add, had she wished, that she was also the prime mover of the whole scheme. But the Vice-Chancellor did not agree and his reply was, predictably, negative. Other lecturers were not paid extra for administrative work and anyway the workload was going to go down as the 'large course' came to an end and the numbers reduced.

At the risk of over-working the theatrical theme, we can now shift the spotlight to a scene – the London Course – which had exactly the same mission, to train interpreters to the highest possible standard, but which fulfilled it in a rather different style.

10

London Pride

If Cambridge was Chekhovian, London's tone, set less by the shadowy George Bolsover than by its first director Ronald Hingley, might best be called be 'Stakhanovite', if anyone now remembers that persistently overachieving worker who became a propaganda icon of the Soviet era. But it was far from grim and it achieved results.

The contrast with Cambridge was comprehensive, from the personalities involved, the teaching style, the discipline and the staff down to the students' accommodation. The two institutions, or more precisely their leaders, were fiercely competitive in a way that perhaps only those used to navigating the undercurrents of academic life can appreciate. Hingley, who was highly critical of the Cambridge operation, though he got on well with Liza personally, recalls George Bolsover harrumphing that Liza 'would be better off bringing up a bunch of squalling brats' than pretending to be an academic.

Bolsover's distance from the day-to-day Course meant that Hingley, who directed the Course until 1955, and Brian Toms, his deputy, who took over from him, were the London *kursanty*'s main interface. Both were brilliant Russian scholars, but professional and unemotional; more accurately, with more of the British stiff upper lip than the Slavonic brandishing of the heart on the sleeve, they chose not to let emotion show. Like Bolsover, their backgrounds and personalities were totally different from Liza's, though as we have seen she too was largely self-made and very much self-propelled and had experienced more than her fair share of knocks and setbacks.

Cambridge was Liza's show. However, while Bolsover ran SSEES itself, his day-to-day involvement in the Interpreters' programme was limited, and responsibility for the key early years of the Course – though never the credit if things went well – lay with Hingley. He and his team were acutely conscious of the hovering presence of the man they referred to among themselves as 'The Gaffer' or 'Big Brother'.

Bolsover had excellent Russian but by one account had little time for Russians, whether Soviet or émigré, who, he claimed, were all characters out of Gogol. Another academic who knew him commented, more in grudging approbation of his tough and manipulative personality than in criticism, that, 'He struck me, from the slight contact I had with him, as being "the useful bastard", an asset (and inconvenience) to many an institution as a curb on wayward individualism.'

Born in 1910 and educated at the County Palatine School, he studied Russian at the University of Liverpool, obtained his Doctorate at SSEES, and taught at Birmingham and Manchester Universities. From 1943 to 1947 he served as Attaché and First Secretary at the British embassy in Moscow; one of his main responsibilities was producing *Britanskii Soyuznik* ('British Ally'), a journal with the daunting – some might say impossible – aim of clearing up Soviet 'misconceptions and misinformation' about Britain. It was something of a re-run of a propaganda effort orchestrated in Moscow by the author Hugh Walpole during the First World War to convince the Tsar and his Ministers that Britain was doing all it could to supply and support its gallant partner. As an alumnus of SSEES, Bolsover's appointment must have had the NKVD busily dusting off its old files on London's alleged role in training SIS officers.

He was appointed Director of SSEES in 1947, a major university post which he held for twenty-nine years and to which he must therefore have brought considerable skills, whatever some of his Russian Course staff may have thought of him. When a friend eulogised him for being 'always cautious and prudent in money matters', that may well have been simply a polite way of making Hingley's point that Bolsover had the Northerner's legendary tight-fistedness. Likewise to describe him as man who 'liked to call a spade a spade and could be very blunt on occasion, something that could prove disconcerting for those unprepared for it', may again be a nice way of highlighting what others have called more succinctly his 'legendary rudeness'. But comments from the same friend about Bolsover's 'strong sense of duty and absolute integrity' cannot be left out of the account.

When Bolsover became Director of SSEES, it was regarded by many, in contrast to the view of it held before the war by the NKVD, as what Hingley has caustically characterised as 'a nest of poisonous Kremlin-fanciers' under the influence of the late Andrew Rothstein. Rothstein held a temporary lectureship in Soviet Institutions, a position granted with some reluctance since he had been a leading member of the British Communist Party since its inception. In the 1920s and 1930s, as the Party, like all its siblings worldwide, gnawed at its own entrails and fought to justify itself to its Moscow masters, Rothstein had become increasingly marginalised to the point of being shipped off to Moscow, where he was accused of 'social democratic tendencies'. There, as described by Andrew Thorpe, who has chronicled the history of this troubled period of the Party's often troubled life, Rothstein 'rotted' in a series of menial jobs in the Communist International organisation before returning as a UK citizen to England in 1935, ostensibly to head the NKVD front organisation Friends of the Soviet Union, but in fact as an NKVD officer tasked with agent development. Hingley was shrewd in his assessment of Rothstein's role at this period, since we now know from the researches of David Burke, who is working on a biography of Melita Norwood to be called *The Spy Who Came In From The Co-op*, that it was in fact Rothstein who recruited Norwood as early as 1935 as a Soviet agent in the UK. One day we may even find out whether Rothstein was also the 'mole' known in the NKVD files as 'PROFESSOR' who gave the London *Rezidentura* its early insights into SSEES.

In 1949 Rothstein was told that his contract at SSEES would not be renewed, on the grounds that it was 'unlikely he would be regarded as suitably qualified for promotion to a senior post'. The bland phrasing was vociferously interpreted by some of the staff and students as a cover-up for the authorities' objections to his Party membership, but Bolsover persisted in the decision despite the clamour and appeals to the Convocation – 'and good for him', to quote Hingley again. His father was the remarkable Russian revolutionary, Theodore Rothstein, who had come to Britain as a nineteen-year-old exile from Tsarist Russia in 1871 and spent thirty years as a left-wing activist; for a while, he was a financial 'bagman' between Moscow and London in the heady days when gold and jewels were sometimes smuggled across to the British comrades in tubs of butter. When Theodore returned to the Soviet Union, he served as Soviet Plenipotentiary in Iran before building a career as a senior Comintern official and academic. Even though he had been an old friend of Lenin's, Theodore's survival through the Stalinist era and its anti-Semitic paranoia to a peaceful death in Moscow was an achievement reminiscent of the Abbé Sieyès.

Some in the academic world claimed that Bolsover, 'conservative in taste and politics', had been installed at SSEES to root out these subversive elements and to recruit teachers and students with a safe anti-Soviet outlook. It was part of London Course folklore that if not an officer of MI5, he was one of their trusted emissaries, on the lines of the bluff brigadier who lurked in Broadcasting House in the Cold War years secretly vetting job applicants for the BBC.

Ronald Hingley had joined SSEES in 1947 as an assistant

lecturer after a war which included service with the 21st Army Group, SOE and a brief spell at Bletchley Park, where, he was told, he had been the first to break a Soviet code; he declined an invitation from one of its leading lights, John Tiltman, to work there. He believed that 'maximum intensity' and as much exposure as possible to linguistic material were the key to mastering a foreign language and while still at school had crammed Latin and Greek at a pace which earned him a top scholarship to Corpus Christi at the age of sixteen; he taught himself German by immersing himself in the works of Sigmund Freud and *Mein Kampf*, and went on to tackle Russian in the same way, 'closeting myself with Dostoyevsky and coming out six weeks later blinking but Russophone'. He felt that when he pressed the *kursanty* so hard at their studies, he was not asking them to do more than he and indeed other British members of his staff had done.

Hingley's indignation at Liza's claims to the superiority of Cambridge was trivial compared to the exasperation and frustration he clearly felt he experienced at Bolsover's hands. Like Liza – with whom he had friendly personal relations, as the correspondence between them shows, despite her propensity to one-upmanship – Hingley carried a heavy burden of responsibility covering all aspects of the Course. But she was her own boss, whereas even though Bolsover left it to him to hire and fire and take all the other practical decisions, apart from pay, Hingley always felt exposed to second guessing and had to contend with what he saw as a complete lack of moral or material support. In fact, he often had to bite his tongue to prevent himself from exploding at what he perceived as another of Bolsover's attempts to undermine him, since without a good 'reference' from him, he knew that he would never escape to the freedom of another academic post.

Hingley planned the London Course syllabus, wrote the timetable, hired the best staff he could – and fired those who were not up to scratch – and put into place the 'stringent system' of tests by which the *kursanty* lived and died. London *kursant* Malcolm Brown, who already had a congratulatory First in

English from Oxford, remembers his dismay when his Course was told by Hingley on its first day that they were not 'bloody students' but Servicemen and that every lesson was a parade. 'We were in the University but not of it and the lectures and lessons were not options but as much a part of our National Service as forming fours and rifle drill.' Brown would not have known it but Hingley was equally direct with his Russian staff, telling them that if they did not perform up to scratch, *'ya vam ustroyu skandal'*, a phrase which to nervous émigrés would have had the force of 'You won't know what hit you.'

Hingley's life-long love affair with Russian language and literature, especially his highly acclaimed work as a translator of Chekhov, scotches any suggestion that his focus on the London Course was narrow and pedantic. There may not have been as diverse a group of outside lecturers as Cambridge paraded in its earlier years at least, but *kursanty* were exposed to eminent university historians such as Hugh Seton-Watson. Hingley took the straightforward view that his students were there to learn the language in order to function as interpreters, not as lecturers on Pushkin. What he himself termed his 'habitual severity' was prompted above all by his determination after a visit to Salisbury Villas not to allow the lax standards and discipline he felt prevailed at Cambridge to take root in Russell Square.

It is hard to visualise either Bolsover or Hingley performing the last rites for Plyushkoff; and we can only speculate, though the answer is not hard to guess, what Hingley might have said had he been approached by Michael Bourdeaux, who went to Liza on behalf of Cambridge Course F to ask if they could take the rest of the day off after grammar class to watch the Australians play the University at Fenners. 'Yes, certainly,' she told him, 'and those who don't want to watch cricket can go punting if the weather is nice.'

Hingley looks back on Liza as 'a larger-than-life character who could have doubled as chief instructor on an assertiveness course'. He also felt that she was an early exponent of the art of 'spin', never missing the chance of presenting Cambridge in the most favourable light. Her commiseration with him on his appointment as London's Director, wondering how he could hope to compete with her Cambridge operation, 'which is the crack course and which had . . . all the experience and talent', clearly rankled to the point, as we shall see, where Hingley, apparently not the only party interested in validating the assertions resonating from the rooftops of Salisbury Villas, claims to have brought about what he later called a 'duel' by examination.

Liza had weaknesses – among them bluster and a tendency to over-excitement – and the adulation she inspired among the *kursanty* was not always matched by the view of her held by some of her staff and academic peers. But her weaknesses were more than compensated by the generally high quality of her staff – her droshky-load of eccentrics apart – particularly the university teachers she employed on the Course in the earlier years. Hingley, too, recognises that his choice of British instructors was crucially important in maintaining standards of work and discipline, and in helping him to keep his emotional balance in the face of Bolsover's insensitivity.

The concept of 'management structure' would have been greeted in Cambridge with mild derision and incomprehension. Hingley was more formal, using British 'Heads of Courses', such as Michael Futrell ('a model of competence, efficiency and loyalty'), the trilingual John Nicholson ('the best Russian scholar of all, me included, I wouldn't wonder'), John Warne, Mark Petheram (a tough New Zealander who had trained as a Jesuit), John Richardson, ex-*kursanty* John Roberts and David Rundle (who later made his career at GCHQ), and Peter Norman to take charge of each intake and supervise a group of Russian instructors.

In parallel with the National Service intakes, Norman had been running courses for Regular Officers, also aimed towards the Civil Service Examination. Although future Air Commodore and Defence Attaché in Moscow Ted Williams, who joined Norman's Course in 1951, remembers it as 'intensive. Of leisure, there would be none for the duration', Hingley seems to have thought of

Patrick Prochter

it as operating at a lesser level of intellectual ferocity than he applied to his younger charges, and speaks of a few officers who were capable of being 'promoted' on to the National Service Courses.

Also among this team, which Hingley jokingly called the *nomenklatura*, was Brian Toms, who took over from Hingley when the latter, breathing heavy sighs of relief, took up a Lectureship at Oxford in 1955, spending a few weeks at GCHQ en route trying unsuccessfully to break Soviet Army field codes. Toms is remembered by Hingley as 'a workaholic's workaholic . . . perhaps the most formidable of all', and by Futrell as good-natured and 'a very effective concentrator on essentials, who compiled splendid explanations of Russian grammar with excellent exercises'.

It is the fate of almost all teachers, especially those who push their pupils hard, to be viewed by their sullen charges with a jaundiced eye. This is no less true of Brian Toms, who, while undoubtedly a man of great energy and linguistic skill, tended to be seen from the *kursant* side of the desk as very intense, narrowly focused and even rather humourless, with an 'unfortunate voice and a poorly judged Hitler-like moustache', according to John Drummond's acerbic account. One even unkinder view, drawn in a *kursant*'s contemporary letter home, probably with the bias induced by some bruising classroom encounter, was that Toms was 'totally without imagination . . . his exhortations were never more than low-level threats, his criticisms akin to jeers', though he was known to have come close to a laugh when he fell victim to the kind of joke he probably felt would have been childish even in a class of eleven year olds.

'Please, sir,' one *kursant* piped up, 'what does *tkan*' mean?'

'Tissue,' answered Mr Toms unsuspecting.

'Bless you, sir,' the *kursant* smirked. The pin-drop silence until Toms gave a mirthless cough brought to mind Ken Dodd's quip that no one knew what it meant to fall flat unless they had played the old Glasgow Empire on a Saturday night after Rangers and Celtic had both lost.

The teaser was lucky. If anything, Toms was even tougher than

Hingley. It was, Henry Thompson recalls, a source of much *kursant* joy to discover that his initials were BF. Others nicknamed him 'Brain'.

It probably did not make Toms' task any easier that, as a recent Christ Church graduate, he was not much older than many of those over whom he had authority and that he was arguably as clever as any of them.

Toms was said to have learned the red-backed Russian–English dictionary by heart. Corridor gossip also claimed that he had written a – mercifully unpublished – complete Russian grammar, which devoted no less than 250 pages to numerals alone. He later took an even harder road and qualified as a doctor; he was last spotted by Tony Blee working on the administrative side of the NHS, compared to which drumming Russian imperatives into the heads of flippant *kursanty* must have seemed literally child's play.

The London syllabus, like that in Cambridge, was structured around periodic tests, persistent failure in which led to dismissal far more frequently than at Cambridge. Hingley also claimed that while London's marking was objective – grammar and vocabulary were black or white, right or wrong – Liza's instructors took the intrinsic difficulty of the work into account in deciding what mark to award. However, had this been the case in the earlier years, Geoffrey Elliott, who was at both Universities on the closing Course T, recalls no difference in the way work was assessed.

'Active' work, such as speaking, essays, interpreting and 'lecturettes', was balanced by a heavy reading load, less for its literary content than for its vocabulary, which had to be learned word by word. In written work sloppy writing brought far tougher penalties than an ironic Bobrinskoi cartoon. This was not just to ease the burden on the staff, who marked 100,000 pages of written work a year, but to stop *kursanty* from deliberately blurring the variable Cyrillic word endings when they were unsure of the grammar. *Kursanty* had to mark the stress on every word they wrote, that being an integral part of its meaning.

Numbers too played their part. If putting into grammatically correct Russian 'with 45,983 blind mice' was a challenge, explaining Pythagoras' Theorem in Russian must have been a nightmare, especially if one's grasp of it in English was less than complete. In 1961 Hingley told the Hayter Committee on Oriental, Slavonic and East European Studies that on a three-year degree course the average student of Russian should have received about 270 hours of language tuition; in practice, as classes were not compulsory, the average was lower. In stark contrast, under the 'forced march tactics' of the JSSL system, students had clocked up at least 850 hours in a single year; classes had been compulsory and failure meant removal.

Even the way the *kursanty* lived was different. As we have seen, although in the later Courses the students at Foxton kept themselves rather to themselves, they were within reach of a university town and living in a country house in some style. And as Oscar Wilde once observed, 'Anyone can be good in the country.'

London was London, teeming with temptations. HMS *President*, the quondam hotel in Queensgate Terrace which replaced Sussex Square, was a South Kensington 'ship', and the *kursanty*'s day began by 'going ashore', as the Navy called it with a straight face, on to the pavements of South Kensington through the old mahogany and brass revolving doors left over from its aspidistra days.

In the dusty lobby or on the steps they might encounter some of the occupants of the other half of the building, a prim flotilla of WRNS officers serving in the Admiralty. However, these passing glimpses were about it; the haughty girls wrapped in Kevlar-strength blue serge with 'hush-hush' jobs at the Admiralty were too much like older sisters to be objects of desire, even though Patrick Procktor remembered that on Thursday evenings *kursanty* could go over into the WRNS side of the 'ship', which included the former ballroom of the hotel, for Scottish dancing, permissible perhaps 'because it is something you can do without touching each other too much'.

Geoffrey Elliott was discomfited by a Joyce Grenfell lookalike in the WRNS Mess who offered him a 'Pink Gin' – neat, with a dash of Angostura Bitters, a drink he had not encountered in his adolescent tippling at the 'Jolly Farmers' in Purley; he had to think even more rapidly for an answer when asked, 'Would you like the other half?' Like the drink itself, the Navy's term of art for offering a second round was a puzzling 'first', and for a delirious moment he wondered whether it was some kind of coded invitation.

The mid-section of Gloucester Road has gone through many social transformations. Now gentrified, almost village like, in the mid 1950s it had far more of a Mitteleuropäisch flavour. The long-since demolished mews behind Gloucester Road Underground Station was home to a splendid Polish delicatessen, and in the European coffee house across the street from HMS *President* one *kursant* claims that Maria, the attractive if mature Czech waitress, once pointed out proudly that two serious gentlemen quietly sharing a plate of *strudel* were Rawicz and Landauer of piano duet fame, Viennese music's forever-coupled version of St Cyril and St Methodius.

A few *kursanty* did get to know one or two of their Russian instructors socially, but perhaps because of the more businesslike approach to hiring instructors – no extended family, no priests, no Slav versions of Donald Wolfit or Margaret Rutherford, no one hired because they were 'my brother's first love' – there are far fewer personal reminiscences of the teaching staff. David Metcalf, who like others on Course T had experience of both Universities, found the London staff 'all seemed two dimensional . . . I got the impression they regarded their work as just a job rather than as a mission or a way of life which seemed to be the case in Cambridge.'

However, some instructors did stick in the mind. In the days before the podgy, shoe-pounding Nikita Sergeyevich rose to prominence in Moscow, few *kursanty* saw anything odd in the fact that one of the most quintessentially Tsarist tutors in London was the courtly Mr Khrushchev. Or that another tutor, an irascible émigré of Soviet times, bore the same surname as the Soviet Politburo heavyweight Lazar Kaganovich.

It is a comforting confirmation of the eternal verities that, work or no work, testosterone was still surging so that after nearly half a century many London *kursanty*, when asked to name an instructor they remember, bring instantly to mind Kiev-born Lyuba Volosevich, nicknamed 'Flossie' (as always with nicknames, not to her face), whom they describe as a 'bright young blonde', 'small, blonde, lively, approachable and easily embarrassed' and 'beautiful in that rather harsh Russian way'.

Many of the same hot eyes noticed an 'agreeably vivacious thirtyish Serbian divorcée' named Kosara Gavrilovic, remembered by Hingley too as 'a notable life-enhancer'. While not inducing the same reactions, the cheerful Wagnerian-built Madame Alkhazova could swiftly reduce *kursanty* to stuttering incoherence with her well-timed morning question, 'Well, gentlemen, what did you read in the newspaper today?' Mrs Cholerton, along with a somewhat younger Mrs Knupfer whose husband was deeply embroiled in émigré politics, are remembered for being pleasant, competent and, within the limits of the discipline imposed, easy-going.

A Polish grammar instructor, Mitek Gigiel-Melechowicz, had lost both hands and an eye in a grenade accident in the war and had 'something like blunt scissors' in their place. *Kursanty* watched in awe as he used one set of hooks to insert the blackboard chalk deftly into the other. Off duty his dexterity in balancing and downing glass after glass brimming with vodka, without spilling a drop, was also a minor legend. Even the lower rungs of the staff ladder epitomised the difference. Below stairs, Cambridge had its Slavs from Central Casting, 'Professor Jimmy' and the bibulous Colonel Rozdjalkowsky, to stoke its boilers and supervise the cleaners. London's janitor, 'Old Ivory', was an ex-Serviceman straight from a Pinter play, who kept a mynah bird in his basement. He once asked Ronald Hingley, 'Ever 'ear of that Colonel Lawrence, sir? 'im what was in Arabia? Well, I was 'is 'angman.' He also claimed to have doubled as the chief flogger of recalcitrant Arabs. 'Cor, you should've seen the claret flow.'

Though no reading lists have come to hand, and their content may well have varied over time, there is anecdotal evidence that *kursanty* found the diet rather heavily skewed against the classics (one student commented sardonically that his Course must have been issued with Turgenev's *Fathers and Sons* by 'administrative oversight') and towards Soviet-era novels about the war and science fiction, all designed to build contemporary vocabulary. 'More utilitarian' than Cambridge, another remarked. Given the aims of the Course, this is quite understandable even if it made the going tough. The students on one Course at least, and perhaps others, solved the problem of having to learn the words while doing their best not to read the turgid texts by forming syndicates, whose members would take turns to gut the allotted pages and produce an ad hoc vocabulary list, which the whole syndicate would then learn.

Though writing at any length about an individual student is a departure from our general approach, a history of the Russian Course in London inevitably brings up the name of Jeremy Wolfenden, the brilliant, overtly homosexual son of a distinguished British public servant. The portrait of him by Sebastian Faulks in *Three Fatal Englishmen* is of a rare but complex talent. He was admired and loved by many, though John Drummond, who was with him in London, wrote in his autobiography that Wolfenden had 'something strongly unlikeable about him', a view reinforced by his hiding behind dark glasses even in winter and deliberately wearing unmatched socks 'to irritate people on the Tube'.

Wolfenden actually wore the glasses because he was sensitive to light, a problem which affected his JSSL studies. This may have been the reason that when Malcolm Brown and others on the following London Course went on to Bodmin for their final 'orientation' and preparation for the Civil Service Examination, they encountered Wolfenden, who had been 'backcoursed' to catch up.

Remarks attributed by Faulks to Wolfenden such as 'We can't all be brilliant but I find it helps' and, when someone challenged his accent, 'I don't speak pure Russian – I speak the language of the Moscow racetrack' are precocious, though very much in his

style. (To those who might find the idea of such a capitalist
attraction alien to the dour years of Communism, it may come as
a surprise that there has been a racetrack in Moscow almost con-
tinuously since 1834, with only a brief closure after the
Revolution in 1917. It served the regime by encouraging the
breeding of high quality military horses, and gratified the needs
of a betting public with a Tote gambling.) Wolfenden's claims,
however, do not square with contemporary memories of a *kursant*, that at Bodmin at least he was 'certainly no star; on the
contrary he was quiet in class, one of the crowd and yet according to Faulks he had studied Russian at Eton before being called
up and so should have been better than most of us'. (Faulks
records that at Eton Wolfenden had won a Newcastle Prize in
Russian.)

Malcolm Brown's memory of the Bodmin Wolfenden as 'a man
who did not contribute greatly, who seemed in fact to be always
hurrying away, withdrawing, avoiding involvement, heading elsewhere', contrasts sharply with his image of Wolfenden's
school-friend and fellow *kursant* Robin Hope, 'a major contribu-
tor to our small society, with a permanent air of good humour and
relaxed elegance'. Brown felt that Hope, who had played Olivia in
the Bodmin production of *Twelfth Night*, in which Brown himself
played Viola, 'combined an almost Wildean wit with an outstand-
ing linguistic flair'.

Ill health prevented Wolfenden from taking the Civil Service
Examination, and he left Bodmin to spend the last phase of his
Service helping Hingley, who remembers him as 'good company',
on the administrative side of SSEES. Mark Frankland, who had
been in the same group as Wolfenden and who recounted with
great sensitivity in his own memoirs a relationship he had with
another Bodmin student, remembers gossip that Wolfenden and
another Old Etonian went to homosexual clubs. 'Neither made a
secret of what they were and I cannot remember anyone express-
ing outrage. Among young people like us it scarcely mattered that
homosexual acts were still a crime.'

The simplest guess nearly half a century later is that at Bodmin

Wolfenden was not well, bitterly bored – an *ennui* characteristic of his schooldays – and simply marking time before effortlessly scaling some of his generation's heights, a First at Oxford, a Fellowship at All Souls, a job on *The Times* and then the *Daily Telegraph*. When, sadly, he seems to have found himself caught between the upper and nether millstones of SIS and the KGB, stress drove him to step up his already excessive drinking; he died far too young, much missed.

Though compared to Cambridge London might have been expected to offer far more in the way of distractions, diversions – and even dangers of the kind courted by Wolfenden – the reality was that work took over. Some like Peter Woodthorpe, who found that he could cope with the workload relatively well, look back with great pleasure: 'And there I was in London in civvies, learning a language, travelling on the Tube, £5 [a week] in my pocket, with intelligent, funny people. Playing bridge, going out [to the theatre], falling in love – everything . . .' While still in awe of the workload, Tony Cross, now Professor of Russian at Cambridge, found his year in London 'wonderful. Civvies, weekend passes to go home to play cricket in the summer, with my fiancée at a London college and many remarkable people, exceptional linguists, great characters . . .' Others also found time to make occasional sorties to concerts, ballet and the theatre, but by and large the pressure of work, the fear of being RTU'd and the shortage of money kept noses to the grindstone in a way that demonstrates either the keenness, or more likely the fearfulness and herd mentality, of that generation.

Ted Braun, Professor Emeritus of Drama at Bristol University, recalls that, for a twenty-three year old with money enough London itself was a powerful incentive to remain on the Course. '1956–7 was an extraordinary time to be there. I remember *Look Back In Anger* and *The Entertainer* with Olivier as Archie Rice at the Royal Court, Paul Scofield in the première of Eliot's *The Family Reunion*; there was the revelatory first visit of the Berliner Ensemble, the London première of *West Side Story*, the first performance of a Tippet Symphony at the Royal Festival Hall, Lisa

della Casa singing Strauss's 'Four Last Songs', Ken Collier playing New Orleans jazz in a basement off Charing Cross Road,
Chris Barber in Soho, the best of world cinema at the Academy,
the Curzon and the Paris Pullman in Drayton Gardens. And of
course just across Russell Square there were the riches of the
Courtauld Collection, my first direct experience of great painting.' And Brian Verity recalls a Donald Wolfit production of
Macbeth at the King's Theatre, Hammersmith, with a young
Harold Pinter as the second murderer.

The final Interpreters' Course, T, spent half its time in
Cambridge and was then transferred to London, giving its *kursanty* a unique opportunity to compare and contrast the two.
David Paisey's summing up probably reflects the consensus that,
'Cambridge was beautiful – comfortable, cultured and relaxed.
London was harder-going academically maybe because the staff,
not having had Liza's constant benevolent presence, seemed less
friendly and more demanding.' Glen Dudbridge saw it even more
starkly at the time as a regime of 'hysterical pressure', though he
did manage to see the Moscow Arts Theatre's short Chekhov
season and films by Cocteau and Andrzej Wajda. John
Drummond, whose Course arrived when a new system was being
tried out for grammar teaching, had 'never worked so hard in my
life', echoing David Marquand to the letter. Patrick Procktor saw
a Diaghilev exhibition, paintings by Francis Bacon and even did
some 'rather botched experiments' painting with a palette knife
the view from what even thirty years later he still called his 'cabin'
in HMS *President*.

One *kursant* on a later London Course found time to indulge an
appetite and a skill for professional bridge, encouraged by the
willingness of the rather grand establishment he patronised to
grant him credit when the cards turned against him. In the end,
heavy-set men called round for a discreet chat with the bemused
officer in charge of HMS *President* and somehow or other the
matter was sorted out.

The Alice in Wonderland protocol of the Services revealed
itself in strange ways. For the Army *kursanty* a bowler-hatted

major would appear from the War Office, a placid Scottie dog at his heels, to hand out the money at the formal pay parades, for which uniform had to be worn. The RAF decreed that while the rest of the *kursanty* queued up with trays each evening to collect their dinner at a serving hatch and eat at group tables, Ted Braun, as the only Regular Officer on his Course, was given his own table and was served by a waiter.

Alumni of both Courses and detached observers can speculate which University produced better linguists, which imparted more 'feel' for Russia, which Course was better run, and which had the better teachers. Neither Liza nor Hingley had any doubt that theirs was the better approach.

Both of them held Naky Doniach in high regard, and both felt, with equal justification, that he was an ally. In his role as the Air Ministry's Inspector, Doniach soon saw that the differences between the methods and the approaches at the two University Courses could become a problem. But as it was in his nature always to foster the creative rather than the destructive urge in people, he encouraged both Liza and Hingley, gave them each the support they needed, and was a paragon of even-handed friendship in his dealings with them.

As Hingley recollects, it was he who brought the problem out in the open by a direct challenge, persuading the Air Ministry that a straight competition should be staged between London and Cambridge A Courses to 'settle the matter'. C. P. Snow might have amused his readers by fictionalising such an academic skirmish. But though there may well have been an element of London saying 'Now we'll see who's best' as a reaction to Liza's unremitting application of the one-upmanship ploys of Stephen Potter, in the end the explanation may be less adversarial.

As we have seen, the pressure to produce interpreters had been such that the London and Cambridge men on those first Courses had gone direct to their Universities, and were thus starting Russian from scratch without the filtering and testing process subsequently applied by JSSL. The Air Ministry may well have thought it fair to orchestrate an even-handed test less as a matter of competition than as a practical check to see how the first Courses were meeting their objectives and whether any teaching weakness could be identified and corrected, or whether the methods of one institution seemed to be more effective than the other. Courtenay Lloyd, as well as some of the *kursanty* involved, recollects the event as being simply a trial for the real thing.

In any event, in September 1952, A Course – ninety-one from Cambridge and forty-three from London – sat a mock Civil Service Interpretership Exam. To ensure a level playing-field, the examiners who read out Russian material for précis work started at the beginning of the morning in London and then drove to Cambridge so that they could do the same there; equity would therefore not be upset by having unequally clear or timed diction.

The results show that while only two *kursanty*, one each from London and Cambridge, and both from the RAF, attained First Class Standard, fifty-two Cambridge candidates failed, as against only fifteen from London. It was no doubt this figure that caused Liza's discomfort at an outcome that Hingley felt 'destroyed the pretensions of the Cambridge Course to superhuman status'. It may not have been quite the 'Game, set, match' he claimed, but it was still a comparatively poor showing.

It prompted Liza to write to the RAF that comparisons were not always meaningful; Cambridge took a rather longer view of its students' potential so did not RTU them as readily as London, experience having shown that given enough help and attention they could improve. She also allowed second chances, so that a man relegated to Bodmin or Crail might be allowed to return if his work got better. As a result, she argued, the number of passes expressed as a percentage of students was bound to be lower at Cambridge since they culled fewer men. Neither protagonist seems to have taken into account that in the early years the London Course was half the size of Cambridge. Experience of the later, smaller Courses and of the post-JSSL schemes suggests, hardly surprisingly, that better results were obtained with smaller groups.

Liza was so put out and so determined to fathom the causes that, very much out of character, she solicited the opinions of B Course as to what they thought might be wrong with her methods. A dozen or so lucid, mature letters are to be found in her archive. There were suggestions that lectures on the Soviet armed services were of no value, and the same was felt about the university lectures; there was not enough oral practice; the point of watching Soviet films on Saturday mornings was defeated by the English subtitles (Liza took this one to heart and thereafter no subtitles were to be seen); there was too much idle time, and zealous students were not rewarded with more free time to study on their own.

The conclusion was that the London *kursanty* were doing better because they were given more homework, and because there were fewer distractions and tougher conditions. They worked harder and the chief focus of their efforts was simply to master the language and avoid the cultural 'frills' so dear to Liza's heart. When the still, albeit temporarily, discomfited Liza asked Hingley what she should do, he suggested that she get rid of most of her Russian staff; this may have occasioned the departure from Salisbury Villas of some of the ladies in the early nest of gentle-folk.

However, the competition was not over. 'A' Course, Cambridge and London all together, sat the final – real – Civil Service Examination in Bodmin in February 1953. One candidate got a First, and he had been at London. Of the Cambridge cohort of seventy-four candidates, twenty-five failed (i.e. 33 per cent), while eleven of London's forty-one candidates, or 26 per cent, failed. The rest, as before, were scattered fairly evenly throughout the Second Class, with one 'Londoner' leading the field, followed by three 'Cantabrians'. On balance, it can be said that while the trial run vindicated Hingley's claim that London was doing a better job, the real exam, six months later, might indicate no more than that those who failed a second time were students who, if they had done a preliminary stint at JSSL, would never have made it on to the University Course in the first place.

While the head-to-head rivalry may not have continued in such an intense form, Liza may have gone on learning or been encouraged to learn from experience, since the folk memories of later Cambridge Courses suggest a pattern of increasingly more work and less play, whether in punts or on the stage. Whether the proverb is right and the boys emerged duller as a result is unknowable.

But at the end of the day the best we can do by way of a final judgement is to listen to Naky Doniach, who, while always kind and tactful, was certainly objective. He concluded in an interview thirty years later that academically both Universities had been 'neck and neck'. The 'strong emotional appeal' of Cambridge created more enthusiasm, but the London *kursanty*, 'many of whom were so good', achieved a high standard 'in spite of everything', working 'until they did not know where they were. It was a very, very hard life.'

When Geoffrey Elliott managed to everyone's stupefaction, not least his own, to scramble breathless into the First Class foothills, Liza somehow tracked him down to his grandparents' house where he was on leave and sent him a congratulatory telegram in transliterated Russian, which must have caused much head-scratching in the Post Office. Since the final and critical phase of his training had been at London, a phase of solid hard work which he feels probably tipped the balance in his favour, she was also exhibiting her usual gift for claiming 100 per cent of any available credit.

11

Hearing Secret Harmonies

The combination of JSSL and the University Course took up so much time that for many of the interpreters the examination marked the end, or close to the end, of their National Service. But for the linguists coming out of the Translators' Course at JSSL it was a different matter; they had a job to do. As we have seen, from the start of its initial and Most Secret deliberations Whitehall itself was clear that the main beneficiary of all the hard work, all the teaching, all the administrative effort and all that very considerable investment over the Cold War period, was to be the Sigint organisation.

However, even relatively recent references to JSSL have gone no further than to refer coyly to its students going on to unspecified 'user units', or performing 'basic translating duties relevant to British intelligence'. Until they went from JSSL to whichever Service station was to train them in intercept techniques and beef up their Service-specific vocabulary, most linguists had little idea about the work they were to do.

The JSSL system maintained a bland vagueness about the end use of all the study and effort. Michael Frayn, for instance, does not recall hearing a single mention of 'GCHQ' during his entire time at JSSL, Cambridge and a brief first spell at the Intelligence Corps Depot at Maresfield. Even when the linguists were actually engaged on intercept duties, the stress on compartmentalisation and the 'need to know', rigorously perpetuated from the Sigint world in the Second World War, meant that very few of the linguists understood where what they produced fitted into the larger Sigint framework. One who probably did was Michael Alexander, later knighted as a senior Ambassador; his father was the chess champion C.H. O'Donnell Alexander, one of the driving forces behind Bletchley Park's and later GCHQ's codebreaking victories.

These chapters are emphatically not an exposé of signals intelligence in the Cold War, let alone an attempt to explain its contribution to policy-making. Skilled and highly readable researchers, notably Richard J. Aldrich in the UK, the US author James Bamford and Olav Riste in Norway, whose country had close ties with the US and the UK in Sigint operations, have shed much new light on the subject generally. Michael Smith's own contribution to the book entitled *Action This Day*, edited by himself and Ralph Erskine, gives a fascinating insight into the early years of Sigint, especially against the Russian target.

Nor do we seek to cover or readdress the Sigint operations aimed at diplomatic or commercial targets, or those at the sharper end of the spectrum for which National Servicemen were highly unlikely to have been used. The taps on the Soviet cable lines in Vienna and Berlin are the most notable examples of the latter. There are other tantalising glimpses; for instance, Richard Aldrich's reference to a British team posing as archaeologists in Northern Iran and monitoring Soviet radar and missile tests, is a nice echo of the First World War Palestine Exploration Fund, which provided cover for non-archaeological investigations by Leonard Woolley and T. E. Lawrence. Olav Riste cites 'Operation Log Cabin' in August 1954, when a 'British national called Philip' and a Norwegian crossed into the Soviet Union from Norway to tap a strategic cable line. Presumably Philip was a Russian speaker and it would be nice to think that he was a JSSL product. If so he may have worked for SIS, though the fact that when they got back three days later tests showed that they had tapped the wrong cable suggests he may have been better suited for British Telecom.

Our aim is simply to try to explain the operational jobs most of the linguists did and give a general idea of how this large effort was organised.

The starting point for young men leaving JSSL for this new world was one of the technical training stations. In the early 1950s, Wythall, outside Birmingham, seems to have had a central role mainly for the RAF but to some extent also for the other two Services. It is remembered by an RN Coder as 'unpleasant . . . patrolled by guards with Alsatians'. It ran a ten-week course 'on the inner workings of radio, how to tune a B40 to various frequencies and how to listen to Russian military traffic through the static. We practised endlessly to hear fuzzy Russian conversations between ships, planes and tanks . . .' They also learned to distinguish between Russian military signals and Polish air traffic, to follow the Russian at ever lower signal levels and write down streams of Russian numbers dictated at a pace which accelerated at each session.

The RAF element of Wythall was later taken over by a camp at Pucklechurch, about seven miles from Bristol, on the site of the murder 1,000 years or so earlier of King Arthur's grandson, King Edmund, by a banished robber named Leoff, an early echo of a *Blackadder* script. History then leaves it largely unremarked until the Second World War, when it operated as the Bristol area's focal point for the storage, repair and deployment of 'barrage balloons', the hydrogen-filled anti-aircraft deterrents which so many *kur-santy* remember hovering in Dumbo-like serenity in the permanently unclouded skies of their childhood. Pucklechurch was not exclusively RAF, however, since one RN Midshipman recalls a spell there teaching basic Russian to Coders and working on an elementary grammar textbook.

Pucklechurch is remembered by former Coder Special Alan Smith as a rural village where the local bobby was so startled to hear four other Coders – in civvies – conversing in Russian that he took them for spies up to no good near a hush-hush defence establishment and – briefly – arrested them.

Royal Navy linguists also passed through HMS *Mercury*, another 'stone frigate', or shore-based establishment masquerading as a ship, high and dry on a hill twenty miles north of Portsmouth. Once Lady Peel's Leydene Park estate (when the RN officers sent to commandeer it during the Second World War arrived at the *Brideshead*-scale mansion, the butler announced, 'The men are here, your Ladyship'), its baronial hall rapidly grew into an agglomeration of Nissen huts, prefabricated buildings and, reportedly, underground bunkers in 160 acres of land. *Mercury* also trained newly joined telegraphists and signalmen – and women, there was a large WRNS contingent – in the basic communications arts. One faded 1944 photograph shows a group of young ratings engaged in 'a standard flashing exercise'.

The linguists were designated as 'Coders Special', no doubt, as Jim Reed suggests, 'to fox the Russians, and our fore-and-aft rigs [i.e. jackets and ordinary trousers not tunics and bell bottoms] had a special white band around the peaked cap, perhaps to suggest we would surrender without an irregular verb being fired'. They were treated with a mixture of derision and wary respect. One recalls the Tannoy blaring, or technically 'piping', the noontime call 'Hands to Dinner'. After a brief pause the same voice, but now affecting a Kenneth Williams 'high camp' style, trilled, 'Coders to Lunch'. Whether dinner or lunch, one odd memory is the cooks' fondness for serving 'huge boiled onions'.

Gerald Seaman remembers other 'pipes', ambiguous to the untutored ear. 'Liberty Men, Fall In' meant that those off duty could leave the camp rather than being an exhortation to leap over the side, while 'Up Spirits' was not the title of a new light-hearted musical review, but the welcome announcement that it was time for the daily tot of rum. Coders not old enough to qualify were given lime juice from the Rose's Estate, which was still operating in Dominica; the diluted retail variety was but a pale green imitation. The evening drink, which, in the dressing-

gowned world they had left behind was 'cocoa', was here mysteriously known as 'kai'.

The Intelligence Corps Depot at Maresfield figures so large in
the afterlife of many *kursanty* that it merits review on its own
later, but the pattern in the later 1950s seems to have been to give
the Army linguists their 'tradecraft' training at what the files identify as the 'Ministry of Defence Voice Intercept School' housed
within GCHQ itself; one interpreter recalls filling in time by
spending several weeks at Benhall, one of GCHQ's two sprawling
sites in Cheltenham, taking civilian-clad JSSL linguists through
endless, and by that stage in their training very tedious, numbers
drills and dictation exercises.

The Intercept School was later transferred to The Royal
Signals centre in Loughborough. In 1963, long after JSSL had
closed and as GCHQ continued to expand inexorably, its admin-
istrators decided that they needed to take back a hut that had
been used for many years as a store where the arriving linguists
would leave their military gear and scramble gratefully into their
so-called 'civilian clothing'. When a party led by Roy Giles, for-
merly Cody Fellow at St Antony's, Oxford, swung open the doors
to start clearing the hut, the musty reek, the scurry of mice and
the piles of gnawed and nibbled khaki uniforms serving as nests,
revealed that many of the arrivals had been in such a hurry to shed
the visible symbols of their servitude that some haversacks had
been slung on the shelves still containing the uneaten residue of
the packs of rations issued for the train journey. All that was now
left were a few shreds of the contemporary newspapers in which
the packs had been wrapped. There were even a few rounds of
rifle ammunition. Relatively unscathed at the back, perhaps
because even the mice had some dress sense, were stacks of unis-
sued civilian clothing.

Once trained in the black arts, the linguists found themselves
part of by far the largest UK intelligence body. While data for the
period of the Courses is not available, we know that by the mid-
1960s Sigint employed more people than the entire Foreign Office
at home and overseas.

At the start of our story we saw the planners wrestling with how to get information and early warning from a Russia that was a world to all intents and purposes closed for the more conventional intelligence hunters sniffing for secret truffles under the forest roots. So Sigint was the key. Leaving aside the critical issue of finding Russian speakers, which we have addressed, the task was actually not that difficult, a matter simply of refocusing the interception, code-breaking and analytic efforts so recently directed against Germany against a new target in a different language; same melody, different lyrics, more or less. The song had been played before, and was neither an exclusively British preserve nor a Second World War phenomenon. As far back as the outbreak of the First World War, as Hew Strachan has noted, the Germans, the British, the Russians and the French were all reading and, at times, jamming each others' high-level diplomatic communications. And in September 1914 Joffre's 'Order of the Day for the Battle of the Marne' was intercepted and read by the German High Command well before it reached the French front line.

As the First World War waxed and waned, the Germans deployed a powerful wireless network based in Nauen, just west of Berlin, whose range enabled it to reach China, southern Africa, the northern part of South America and well into the US and Canada. Relay stations in China, the Pacific and Africa meant that the High Command's signals could span much of the world. The other side of the coin was that, rather like the Enigma in the war that followed, the very sophistication and power of the system encouraged its use, and multiplied the opportunities, quickly seized, for its traffic to be intercepted by Britain and its Allies.

German intercept operations were also successful. Nor were radio games and deception a Second World War invention. In 1915 a British station in Sudan found the wavelength of a Zeppelin that had left Bulgaria carrying a cargo of arms for the German Army in East Africa, and successfully transmitted a phoney message ordering it to turn back.

After the Armistice and the Russian Revolution, the British

interventionist 'Dunsterforce' set up a Sigint network in South Russia and Persia which supplied the British Cabinet into the 1920s with 'an impressive volume of Soviet decrypts', bearing mainly on Moscow's efforts to create problems for the empire in India, an operation much helped by Admiral 'Blinker' Hall's recruitment of ace Tsarist code-breakers into the Admiralty's interception service. It was to prove a small world, since one of them, a one-time astronomer turned naval officer and then cryptologist, Pyotr Pashchenny, later 'turned up mysteriously' in Germany, according to a German semi-official history. Nicknamed 'the old man of the mountains', he provided much valuable support for the Abwehr and Wehrmacht in their own efforts against Soviet signals. As late as 1940, an Army wireless unit in Sarafand was still quietly taking, i.e. monitoring, Russian diplomatic traffic.

However, the Cold War Soviet intercept effort had been given its head start not from Russian traffic taken directly but, in a neat twist, from German intercepts. The Wehrmacht had put considerable resources into monitoring Red Army and Luftwaffe traffic on the Eastern Front and when their intercepts were passed back to Berlin on the Enigma channels, they were duly vacuumed up and read by the powerful machinery and equally powerful intellects at Bletchley Park. These operational and cryptological insights into the Soviet machine were given a great boost as the war ended by the Allied TICOM ('Target Intelligence Committee') missions, which rushed into Germany and seized among other treasures of the German intercept efforts against Russia 4,000 documents, manuals and other material and equipment; it took three freight cars to haul them back to the West. All of this must have been an invaluable foundation when the British and US effort was ramped up in the 1950s.

The Sigint world into which JSSL passed so many of its students was a far cry from today's super-sophisticated, space-based, worldwide network in which increasingly virtually no word or e-mail message can go unheard or unread, no website unchecked, and no chat-room exchange unremarked.

Hearing Secret Harmonies

At its hub, as it is today, was Government Communications Headquarters, GCHQ, the 'Queen Bee' to whose Cheltenham hive the workers sent their daily packets of food from the outstations in the form of intercepted messages. Though it sat at the centre of things, Cheltenham preferred to hide its light under a stack of bushels. A rare glimpse of how it saw its role in life, written in heavy and carefully drafted bureaucratese, is in a 1960 memorandum, cited by Richard J. Aldrich. Seeking to justify a request for a bigger budget for scientific and engineering resources, Cheltenham described what it called

> the main permanent activities of the organisation. Signals have to be heard, intercepted and recorded. There is a large and complex problem of data processing before the recorded data can be analysed. Analysis is of several sorts – of the wave-form, of the information coding, the circumstances and message content of the signals. It has to be seen whether Communications networks can be reconstructed by fitting together many scraps of information; whether Signals plans can be deduced, whether ciphers can be recognised, isolated and broken. Non-communications signals – radars, navigational aids, data transmissions and so on – present a range of problems very different from traditional communications. From all of these processes directly and indirectly arises a mass of information that has to be synthesised together with 'collateral' information in order to produce semi-finished intelligence. At all stages of this process there has to be a positive print taken from the negative and use made of the experience critically and constructively in order to enhance the security of British communications.

A snapshot of the scale of the intercept effort in Germany comes from a recently published history of one of the main RAF Sigint bases at Hambuhren, which in 1954 ran no less than eighteen monitoring outstations, though many were probably small mobile units or direction-finding installations. They included

Fort Spijkeboor, which sounds almost as though it had been left over from another war altogether.

Hambuhren's own staff of some 220 included fifty-three monitors, thirty-six of them coded A, denoting Russian-language qualifications, five D for German, two E and ten F, for Czech and Polish. There was also a 'permanent civilian representative from GCHQ'. As an indication that Cheltenham's role was rather more 'hands on' than the bland mission statement quoted above might imply, when Hambuhren was closed in 1957 and its operations divided between Berlin and Scharfoldendorf, the first reference cited as the basis for the RAF's Operational Order for the move is 'Government Communications Headquarters S/0527/100/3'.

Where did the worker bees toil and spin and what was it they actually produced? As to where, the First and Second World War had battlegrounds whose names are etched in folk memory. The National Service linguists' Sigint roll of honour in Europe is rather more mundane but for those who passed that way, equally evocative. RAF Wythall, Gatow, HMS *Royal Charlotte* (known to its habitués as *The Royal Harlot*), HMS *Royal Albert*, RAF Cheadle, Loughborough (where among other specialisations Morse intercept training was undertaken), RAF Digby, Birgelen, Langeleben, Scharfoldendorf, Uetersen, Butzweilerhof, Hambuhren, Cyprus and others. There were wet tents on German hilltops with the intercept sets housed in smoke-filled and sweaty permanently parked trucks nicknamed 'Gin Palaces'. Plain vans with whip antennae that roamed border roads, seemingly innocent trawlers that pitched and tossed around the Baltic and the Black Sea, Lancasters, Lincolns and later modified Comets lumbering alongside and sometimes deliberately into East Bloc airspace, or naval vessels with seasick Coders Special perched uneasily below decks. There was even an ammoniacal converted toilet in the British Military Train than ran nightly from the West German border to Berlin, its carriage blinds drawn tight by Russian edict, in which an operator crouched over his set, the door always 'Engaged', seeking to pick up military traffic as the train clattered across the Soviet

Zone. Heath Robinson arrays looking like large clothes-drying racks on Berlin airport rooftops concealed from prying by corrugated plastic sheets designed to look like water tanks. Wire riggings and coils strung out among pine trees.

Martin Coombs, who spent five months in Uetersen outside Hamburg monitoring Russian aircraft for the RAF, remembers an episode when the nastier side of Service life obtruded and one of his colleagues, David Salmond, wrote in exasperation on his monitoring pad, 'I AM NOW CLOSING THIS RECORD DOWN AS I HAVE BEEN ORDERED TO CLEAN THE BOGS.' Whether this *cri de coeur* reached the analysts at GCHQ is unknown though the earnest sergeant in charge of them had assured them, 'The messages you record from Russian aircraft are taken by security staff acting with great speed to Whitehall where they are interpreted by experts.' Coombs, Salmond and their colleagues wondered just what the experts made of their work since 'most of what . . . we heard over our radios was either incomprehensible to us or was a record of long chats between pilots about their wives and families back home. This at least gave us another view of the evil Communist empire!'

The same unit also went on passive strike against irksome restrictions on wearing civilian clothes. The flow of monitored messages suddenly dried up. Nothing was actually said, though hints that this impasse might vanish if the clothing rule were changed soon produced the desired result without the need for confrontation.

From 1948 to 1950 Uetersen had also been home to an RAF German-language school. Some of its Russian Sigint alumni have formed a group styled 'The Old Uetonians'.

The hub of the British Army Sigint operations in West Germany in this period was No. 1 Special Wireless Regiment, originally formed in Aldershot in 1934 as 'a small independent War Office controlled unit' called No. 2 Wireless Company, and by May 1945 settled in the garrison town of Minden.

By 1953 No. 1 Special Wireless Regiment had grown to a scale calling for a new permanent home, and one as far as possible from any attack from the East. Birgelen, fifty kilometres north of Aachen close to the Dutch border at Roermond, was selected and the Regiment moved into the new 'Mercury' barracks, proud that in the transfer process it had lost not one day of 'operational cover', i.e. intercept work.

As the official history of the Intelligence Corps shows, whatever name changes it went through the Group or Regiment always had a Siamese-twin Intelligence Corps unit, in the wartime years designated a Wireless Intelligence Section but sometimes also carrying the telltale adjective 'Special'. The Signals personnel provided the technical support, the Intelligence Corps the linguists and the analysts. A website set up by former members of No. 1 Special Wireless Regiment actually has on the left of its Home Page the Royal Signals crest and to the right that of the Intelligence Corps. Corps linguists sent to Germany on Sigint duties had to replace their green Corps shoulder flashes and floral cap badge, the much derided 'Pansy resting on its Laurels', with the more prosaic blue flashes of the Royal Signals and its badge of Mercury, winged messenger of the Gods. In fact the alleged pansy is a rose, incorporated for its symbolic significance – *sub rosa* – as a mark of the ability to keep a secret.

Later in 1953 the Regiment set up 'The Royal Signals Detachment, RAF Gatow' in Berlin, an anonymous building on the road that ran through the pine trees along the northern perimeter of the airfield, well-remembered by many JSSL linguists. They recall that the airfield buildings had survived the flattening of Berlin surprisingly well, the only signs of damage being the heads and swastikas ruthlessly hammered off the eagles which still remained, set in stone on the Kaserne walls.

Some like Gerry Smith recall being struck by the quality of the high-ceilinged living accommodation used not all that many years back by Goering's Luftwaffe aces and their crews. With central heating, double-glazed windows with broad sills, top-class bathroom fittings and even parquet flooring, it was a stark contrast not only to any British military installation of the time but also to many contemporary British homes. Indeed, compared to much of the rest of Berlin, still shell-scarred and damaged twelve years or more after the end of the war, it seemed almost as though Gatow had been providentially spared for the benefit of its new occupants.

The world changes so fast that it is hard to recall how Berlin was in the 1950s. Today there is no Wall. Nor was there back then until the 'concrete diplomacy' of 1961. The Soviet Union recognised West Germany in 1955 but Berlin remained a disputed, contentious, tense island at the eastern edge of what had been the Soviet Zone of Occupation and which in fact still was, though *de jure* it had become the 'anti-Fascist' German Democratic Republic. Access to Berlin in those years was by one rail line from Helmstedt and a parallel autobahn, and three air corridors from Hanover, Hamburg and Frankfurt, all tightly dogged by Soviet patrols. Berlin itself was divided into US, British, Soviet and French Sectors, their boundaries clearly delineated but not controlled.

By many accounts espionage and subversion were the city's main 'growth industry' with its main centres the KGB base in the former St Antonius Hospital in Karlshorst, the US Berlin Operations Base on the Clay Allee, a British military base a few miles away and the French secret service centre in the Quartier Napoleon. Their officers, agents and sources, often working for more than one master, were everywhere, from red-light bars to the glossy restaurants on the Kurfürstendamm and even the Soviet War Memorial on the British side of the Brandenburg Gate, used by the KGB for early recruiting contacts with potential assets since it was under the protection of the Soviet honour guard who patrolled the Memorial with metronomic precision.

Though it must have been hard for its often bored operators to appreciate, the Sigint effort mounted from Berlin and across Germany was an important though unglamorous part of this whole effort to warn, to build a picture and to watch.

RAF Gatow adjoined the East German border and was thus literally on the front line, though it had a measure of protection in also being the base for a Scots infantry regiment, the unparalleled ferocity of whose squat, kilted soldiery on and off duty had earned them the wary respect of Berliners, one of whose tabloid newspapers had nicknamed them the '*Giftzwerge*', or 'Poison Dwarfs'.

However, even though as we shall see operational security in Gatow was clearly tight, security in a wider sense was rather relaxed. New arrivals were given a lecture about the risks of catching some anti-social infection from the ladies of the night who gathered like sad, chirping sparrows outside the NAAFI Club on the Reichskanzlerplatz. Many but not all were also read a warning about the risks of wandering around alone in East Berlin and banned completely from the city's overhead railway, the S-Bahn, since it ran into and out of East Germany itself so that failure to understand the map, or a hastily snatched snooze, could mean a very *mauvais quart d'heure* for the unwitting passenger.

Most of the men of Gatow stayed within a fairly humdrum circuit bounded by the NAAFI, the Sergeants' or Officers' Mess, the bars and cafés around the Wannsee lake, the Berlin cinemas, the bratwurst stall by the Spandau bus-stop and for special occasions the alluring and inexpensive – since it was subsidised by the French taxpayer – cuisine of the flagship Maison de France on the Kurfürstendamm, whose bookshop offered all the classics of French literature alongside the equally classical green-jacketed works of the Olympia Press. Others found comfort in the centres run by various churches for British Servicemen; Wesley House in Spandau and its Padre Len Stafford are fondly remembered. Many also drew heavily on the cultural life of the city. Ted Braun remembers the Ring Cycle, *Der Rosenkavalier*, *Mathis der Mahler* and the world première of Schoenberg's *Moses und Aaron*. But as with many others on the Gatow teams, he felt as free to visit the Komische Oper in the East as the Stadtische in the West. A Gatow contemporary of his remembers being part of a group of linguists that slipped across to the East to hear a stellar performance of *Evgeny Onegin*, wearing civilian clothes that with hindsight must have announced their Britishness as much as if they had been clad in khaki, and mingling with an audience dotted with uniformed Soviet officers, probably some of those whose conversations were being taped day by day.

Others crossed over to buy records and even Russian books (with one Western Mark worth four Eastern, the attractions were considerable). Jazz fanatic Gerry Smith played alto-sax in the quartet led by pianist and camp barber Peter Grohman, without anyone apparently querying the fact that the drummer and bass player were East Berliners and that in a busy schedule of concerts and broadcasts the quartet performed several times in East Berlin. One of Grohman's predecessors is remembered by an RAF monitor as asking disingenuously why so many of his Service colleagues inadvertently used the Russian '*da*' for 'yes', instead of '*ja*', when trying to speak German. The RAF men had been told that they were not to admit to anyone in Berlin that they spoke Russian, though it is claimed by one that the passenger manifest of the daily British Military Train to Berlin, a copy of which was punctiliously given to the Russians at the Zone Border, listed the trade of RAF linguists as 'Russian translator'.

Another site of which we have a good record is one of the Army's forward intercept outstations at Langeleben, 900 feet up in the hills between Braunschweig and Helmstedt, where the task of its team of signals operators and Intelligence Corps linguists was 'to keep an electronic watch on the group of Soviet Occupation Forces in Germany . . . Opposing the British Army of the Rhine on the North German Plain was the crack 3rd Shock Army with its HQ in Magdeburg [to the north of which] was the Litzlinger Heide, one of the largest (Soviet) training areas in East Germany . . . as its nearest point lay within fifteen miles of the border the fear was of a surprise attack . . . launched against the West following on from large-scale Soviet manoeuvres in the Heide . . .'

The main destination for RN linguists in the mid-1950s was the monitoring station first at Cuxhaven (remembered by Oliver Thomson as 'a former German Navy barracks with bombed submarine pens nearby and the odoriferous Onassis whaling fleet to windward'); it was moved in July 1955 to a purpose-built facility constructed on a former seaplane ramp, across the water from the

U-Boat Memorial at the Baltic end of the Kiel Canal. Alan Smith recalls the 'perverse *frisson* we used to get on the way to our watch station, crunching through the snow of a Schleswig winter and singing Russian marching songs as we passed the small German Navy Mess quarters'.

Gerald Seaman, who had a place waiting for him at Oxford to read Music, gravitated rather naturally towards his chosen field accompanying a fellow Coder Special in German *Lieder* on the chapel piano and joining two choirs. 'The Male Voice Choir had an elaborate initiation ceremony complete with many songs of Freundschaft and Brüderschaft, all accompanied by generous drafts of lager.'

Some thirty years later Cuxhaven – HMS *Royal Albert* – and its monitoring operations were the setting for the TV play *'Bye, 'Bye Baby* by JSSL alumnus, RN Coder Special and screenwriter Jack Rosenthal. Another Coder Special, Sydney Bernard Smith, later poet, playwright and actor, wrote in a lightly fictionalised account of his work there:

> . . . you got to know the voices . . . Every six weeks or so they would change frequency and would disappear off the air. Then a great stir spread though the room. Every available set was directed to the task of relocating them. When they were found again with a new set of call signs you would gradually identify the same old voices. They became your friends by proxy. You pictured them sitting in their huts in sub-Arctic conditions swathed in furs and mittens cutting their fags in two, lodging them fatly in cigarette holders and smoking them to the last millimetre using that upside down forefinger and thumb grip favoured by the instructors in Bodmin . . .

There was some mixing of services and several Coders Special found themselves working alongside linguists from the Army and the RAF (as well as civilians) at an important signals hub in Cyprus, which also had a sizeable Army contingent and was directly linked to GCHQ. In 1959 an official memorandum described Cyprus as an 'indispensable and irreplaceable centre for providing Y service intelligence' and was home to some 1,000 Sigint personnel. One of its advantages was the combination of geographic and ionospheric co-ordinates that made it a natural collection point for long-wave traffic from Soviet missile test grounds in the southern USSR.

One linguist recalls his time in Cyprus as 'tiring and monotonous – incessant [intercept] watchkeeping and nights guarding the camp against EOKA terrorists', even though he did get a spell on board the frigate HMS *Torquay* which was patrolling the Mediterranean around Cyprus to intercept arms shipments intended for EOKA, presumably because its area of operation was also a fertile one for the collection of Russian traffic. One RN group was posted to a US monitoring station on the Black Sea coast of Turkey under conditions so secret they were not allowed to tell their families where they were; the consolation was that they were paid at US service rates.

We now have a snapshot of where the monitors operated. What do we know about what they actually did? And what did the material they gathered contribute? The first is far easier to answer than the second.

The physical experience of most will have been broadly the same wherever they were and to whichever Service they belonged: the disorientation of shift work, the windowless, smoke-filled room, the neon lights, the slowly turning spools of recording tape, the endless cups of tea, and snatches of Russian scribbled on to ruled pads. Senior linguists, designated as 'scanners', and quite often interpreters with the rump of their service commitment to complete, listened in to make sure that the operators were tuned into the Soviets rather than Sibelius, checked the message logs for anything significant, replayed some of the key parts of the recordings at more leisure to see what else could be distilled, and wove the product into the daily 'take'.

Considerable amounts of material were produced; by one informed account as much as 80 per cent of it from Soviet Air Force intercepts, with military and naval traffic 10 per cent each.

This is not surprising given the initial strategic focus on the risk of air attack and also the number of brief reports a pilot and his controller exchanged prior to and during each flight compared to the more laconic style of the Soviet Army and Navy. It is difficult to get a measure of physical volume since the fragmentary records diligently unearthed by Andy Thomas refer simply to 'groups' of five letters each, or 'messages' with no indication of length or content. He notes that in 1951 the Navy Direction Finding Monitors were sending GCHQ 184,000 groups of Sigint material a month, while a 1954–5 record from an RAF intercept station in Hong Kong, presumably targeting mainly Chinese traffic, notes that forty to sixty intercept positions were in operation and that between 20,000 and 45,000 messages were intercepted monthly. However, there is no way to know how many of these were voice messages and how many Morse or teletype intercepts, which in all likelihood formed the bulk of the material.

Reminiscences of Gatow, which housed both RAF and Army units, are probably as representative as any. At one level, remembered by Gerry Smith, the work was 'monotonous and could be mind-numbingly boring. We operated a shift system of eight hours on, eight hours off for two (or was it three?) days, followed by two rest days.' The basic task, the end product of all the JSSL cramming, was to write down messages from Russian aircraft that were 'almost always very brief and formulaic: the callsign of the station being addressed, the callsign of the aircraft and then usually a numbered code message terminating with the word "*Priyom*" ("Over")'.

Smith recalls a typical message as '*Yachmen! Ya Nivyanik. 24 vypolnil. Priyom*' ('Barley! This is Marguerite. 24 complete. Over.') Ted Braun, who supervised the RAF team at the time, reflected that the main excitement came when the Russians periodically changed callsigns, 'to throw us into confusion. In fact, human carelessness soon gave the game away: "*Govorit zemlyanika 557 – yob tvoyu mat' – kryzhovnik 207!*" ("This is Wild Strawberry 557, no, fuck it, Gooseberry 207!") . . . I was often in awe at our young operators' skill in picking up the most scrambled messages . . .'

Hearing Secret Harmonies

As we shall see, the monitors were never given any real insights into the significance of what they recorded, and it is unlikely that they would have realised the possible value of a simple mistake with a callsign, such as that just quoted, since it enabled the analysts to track Russian units and their movements with great accuracy. A post-Second World War study of the German success against Russian traffic suggests that even back then brilliance in the science of code-breaking was less of a factor than the windows inadvertently opened by carelessness in using and reusing codes and callsigns, repeating garbled messages *en clair* and even simple late-night chit-chat between bored operators about their girlfriends. Indeed the study pointed out that the Germans had made almost no headway against NKVD traffic, since the secret police operators were far more disciplined than their Service counterparts and never broke the rules. Even in the heat of battle and retreat they were scrupulous about destroying any compromising documents that might give clues to their code systems.

There were moments of drama. Gerald Seaman remembers, 'A young Russian pilot took off as usual but after some time he appeared to lose contact with the control tower. His voice became quite frantic crying "*Ya vas ne slyshu, vas ne slyshu!*" ["I can't hear you, I can't hear you!"], and eventually there was a muffled explosion followed by silence.' But these moments apart, other than giving the intercept operators an even better grounding in Russian numbers and the Russian terms for often obscure flora and fauna, it is easy to see that on its own, and all the more after weeks of the same sort of thing, much of the traffic had no real meaning or interest to its interceptors. One exception was the Army side of Gatow, where, at the same time as Smith and his RAF colleagues were trying to stave off boredom by clandestinely tuning in to Voice of America, a team of Army linguists on the other side of the building were targeting a more interesting stream of traffic which anecdotal evidence suggests was a high frequency multiplex teleprinter and voice channel used by senior Russian officers. One operator remembers that signals were unscrambled with the aid of a homely DIY table-top device of the kind that enabled the British to comfort themselves, as the US drew inexorably ahead in Sigint investment and new technology, with the thought, quoted by Riste, that 'we use our heads, they use the instruments'.

Even though it was intended as a 'line-of-sight' transmission via a system of relays, the ionosphere and cloud conditions could play strange tricks, and one of the Gatow operators recalls that while most of the traffic was local and military, he once monitored a long and very domestic conversation between a Red Army general in Vladivostok and his wife in Moscow.

Another instance of the strange effects of the ionosphere is that news of the death of Stalin, remembered by Michael Bourdeaux and others from the excited reports of their JSSL instructors, first broke in the West via Reuters' monitoring station in Hertfordshire, which regularly picked up the midnight long-wave broadcast beamed from Moscow to the Soviet Far East in which the next day's *Pravda* and *Izvestiya* front pages and editorials were read out at dictation speed and carefully transcribed for publication at the other end of the Trans-Siberian Railway.

Though procedures varied over time and by Service, as a general rule the intercept outstations communicated their 'take' back to their co-ordinating units and to GCHQ – and also to their US counterparts via the US Sigint relay hub at Chicksands – over teleprinter links using the punched-tape equivalent of the one-time pad. There were three levels of report. The 'spot' summary, which in the news agency and wire service world would have been a 'flash' message, was banged out immediately when an intercept seemed to record or suggest some significant new development. The technical summary, sent out daily, gave the skeleton outline of what traffic had been logged on which frequencies and at what times, and what callsigns had been used. This was followed up with the intelligence summary, based in large part on the reviews by the scanners, trying to put some flesh on the bare bones and report in simple terms the apparent significance of the intercepted traffic. Back in the UK Ministry officials with appropriate indoctrination and clearance saw key Sigint intelligence distributed from Cheltenham in BJ's (so-called from the blue-jacketed folders in which they circulated under strict security), while the ultimate distillation of the whole process – military, diplomatic and commercial – was the periodic Comintsum circulated by GCHQ to its partners around the world; twenty copies went to Washington.

To back up the teleprinted reports, a full set of carbons of the Army 'logs' from the Gatow Station plus the underlying tapes were delivered daily under armed guard to the SIS and another set to the US Army Security Agency Unit, the latter hidden up several flights of rubble-strewn stairs behind a steel door and a Coca-Cola machine in a seemingly disused building at the side of Tempelhof Airport. This Aladdin's cave of technology was manned by tanned and amiable operators who had learned their rudimentary Russian light years away in climate and geography from Crail or Bodmin at the US Defense Language School overlooking the Pacific in Monterey, California.

Amid a fanfare of form-filling, the Gatow courier was issued with a Webley pistol in a webbing holster. There were also six rounds of ammunition. But these came inside a roll of thick brown paper tightly sealed with red wax; it was no doubt assumed that had the car been ambushed by the Soviets, they would have been content to wait while the courier ripped open the package and loaded up. If the seal were found to have been broken when the courier returned, a formal Court of Enquiry would follow.

If the records of Hambuhren are representative, these tapes and hard copy went back to London via the British diplomatic bag. The Closing Order already quoted noted among many other administrative details that the last 'routine delivery of diplomatic mail' from the Unit via British European Airways in Hanover was to be made on the 25th of October.

The accounts of which the above are a representative sample risk making monitoring work seem boring and far less significant than it was in real terms. Answering the guilt-inducing First

World War recruiting poster question, 'What did you do in the Great War, Daddy?', by saying 'Actually, sweetie, I listened to the wireless all day', risked falling a bit flat.

To an extent these accounts simply reflect the understandable frustration of young men who, having had an enjoyable and challenging time at JSSL, were now cooped up working unsociable hours at something whose value they did not understand, that they knew would only last for a few months, and that had little or nothing to do with any future career. They also reflect management's failure – whoever management was – to understand how best to motivate them and make them feel included, understandable perhaps in a world now half a century away where the Service part of the structure expected men to do what they were told and not ask questions. This was hardly new; one of Wellington's officers in the Peninsula War, when letters and dispatches were the target of energetic interception and decoding efforts, wrote that 'a Staff man is not with secret till he gets pretty high in the Department'. This was compounded by the fact that, no doubt quite rightly, Cheltenham valued secrecy and the 'need to know' principle above all else.

But perhaps the overriding reason that the work lacked 'edge' was that it was not part of a life-or-death world war. It was defensive, the Cold War equivalent of *die Wacht am Rhein*, an electronic Maginot Line or, to borrow an analogy from Richard J. Aldrich, the ether-borne version of the 'trainspotting' surveillance mounted by the Resistance against German military rail traffic in Occupied Europe. The fact is that their efforts were a key part of the reason that nothing happened. There were few if any strategic surprises, and the Soviet order of battle was known down to the colour of the shoulder flashes on a tank gunner from Omsk rattling around in the muddy fields of Saxony. It could be argued that the very fact the Soviets knew that most of what they said and did, most of the verbal and electronic signals they sent out, were being 'taken down and might be used in evidence against them', was a major element in the West's deterrent structure. The voice, Morse, radio-telephone and telex exchanges between Russian signals operators and their submarine and tank commanders, pilots and air-traffic controllers, and between staff units and officers at various levels in the chain of command, that the monitors painstakingly plucked from the air day by day, were fragments, the little stones that made up a tessellated pavement: a pavement the monitors themselves would never get the chance to view as a whole. However, as they were recorded, replayed, analysed, decrypted and collated with information from other sources both overt or covert, over the years they grew into an immense database of knowledge.

Thanks to Sigint, the West knew a great deal about the organisational structure, strengths, equipment, defences, callsigns, codes, signals networks and order of battle of all three of the Soviet armed forces and their missile testing and launch systems and had a keen understanding of how the Soviet command and control system worked, especially when it felt under threat. Another value of this enormous database and familiarity was that any change in behaviour or procedures that might have significance could be readily picked up by comparative analysis.

But all of that was difficult to appreciate when drowsiness and boredom set in at 3 a.m. in a smoke-filled room.

Listening was one thing. Active steps to stir up the other side's radar and radio networks were another. Understanding how the Russian radar and control systems would respond under perceived threat of intrusion or attack was an essential piece of the intelligence jigsaw.

We know that in the early years of the Cold War both the US and British sent aircraft crammed with electronic gear and operators on 'ferret' missions to probe, tease and often cross Soviet borders and airspace listening for radar and direction-finding reaction, for the callsigns and procedures of ground stations and intercept aircraft. James Bamford records that over the years these missions cost the US forty aircraft and 200 men. President Yeltsin set up a special commission in the early 1990s to find out what had happened to these airmen, but it came up with nothing.

Nothing official is known of any similar British losses incurred as part of their contribution, which included RAF Lancaster and later Comet flights in co-operation with GCHQ in West Germany, around the Baltic and in the area of Lübeck; the British even participated in the early U2 overflights of the Soviet Union. It has been claimed for instance that an RAF Lincoln, which crashed over East Germany in 1953 killing six of the seven men on board, was on a probe mission. The Navy also used similar techniques involving submarines around Murmansk and high-speed torpedo-boats in the Baltic and the Black Sea. JSSL alumni, all volunteers on double pay, were aboard a torpedo-boat which 'drifted' into Leningrad harbour, apparently with positive results from an intercept standpoint.

Sensitivity to public reaction to what might be regarded as deliberate 'provocations' may explain the sharp reaction of the authorities in 1958, when two left-wing undergraduates, former Royal Naval linguists, found themselves in front of the Bow Street magistrates. In an issue of the Oxford magazine *ISIS*, given over entirely to the emotive issue of the day, nuclear disarmament, they attempted to lift the lid on these activities.

ISIS, which always relished any chance to *épater le bourgeois*, published an article by two former Naval linguists protesting what they saw as dangerous provocations:

All along the frontier between east and west from Iraq to the Baltic and perhaps further are monitoring stations manned largely by National Servicemen trained in Morse and Russian avidly recording the last squeak from Russian transmitters. In order to get information the West has been willing to go to extraordinary lengths of deception. British embassies usually contain monitoring spies. When the Fleet paid a 'goodwill' visit to Danzig in 1954 they were on board. And since the Russians do not always provide the required messages they are sometimes 'provoked'. A plane 'loses its way'. There is no controlling the appetite of the statistical analysers at Cheltenham . . .

The next issue – this being a small world – was edited by the recently demobilised National Serviceman, fresh from JSSL Bodmin and the Intelligence Corps, the future playwright and screenwriter Dennis Potter, who was already establishing his reputation for being 'brilliantly intelligent, spiky and ambitious'. His first initiative as editor was to leap to his fellow linguists' defence. As a result of the article, he wrote, 'People who were on the Russian Course were questioned and apparently one of the questions was "And what did you do to stop the article being published?" I was on the Russian Course. Let's all spy on each other.'

Perhaps not surprisingly letters of support from Kenneth Tynan, Christopher Logue, J. B. Priestley, John Berger, Doris Lessing, Enid Starkie and other CND stalwarts failed to sway the authorities and the authors found themselves facing three months in jail. Quite rightly this exercise in bureaucratic hypocrisy did not prevent one going on to become a senior academic and the other a leading publisher.

While we have not found, or indeed looked for, any evidence one way or another on this point, to the extent that there were British operations of this kind it would as with other 'sharp end' Sigint manoeuvres seem logical that National Service linguists would not have been the first choice to man them given the political sensitivities; Regulars or demobbed linguists, now civilian language officers, might have been thought preferable.

12

Dump in the Downs

Most of the JSSL students who served in the Army spent some time at the Intelligence Corps Depot. Most of them loathed it and would agree with Alan Bennett that 'Maresfield was a horrible camp . . . it was worse than Basic Training.'

'The trouble with Maresfield in the 1950s,' a Regular Officer sniffed years later, 'was that there was no regimental pride.' How could there be, when the Corps had only been reconstituted in a hurry during the Second World War in the implausible setting of a commandeered Oxford College with early leading lights who brought to mind Churchill's comment to the commandant of Bletchley Park, when he first set eyes on his motley crew of code-breakers: 'I told you to leave no stone unturned but I did not expect you to take me literally.'

Then in 1948 an Army directive cast the Intelligence Corps back into a professional limbo that lasted, in the words of its historian, for 'ten lean years'. In a repeat of their reactions after the First World War, many War Office brass-hats thought of the Corps as an unmilitary organisation that could be tolerated in time of war but had no real role in peacetime, and in this Blimpish spirit the Corps was officially restricted to a small nucleus of specialists in air-photo interpretation and counter-intelligence, as well as what its History calls 'a few linguists' for document study and refugee questioning, a decision that sits oddly with what we know of Whitehall's contemporaneous concerns about the risk of war and the need for translators and interpreters.

Intelligence officers in the Army's operational formations were no longer to be drawn from the Corps and it was not allowed to recruit permanent Regular Officers directly from Sandhurst. Officers who transferred into the Corps were not eligible for Staff College and thus unlikely to advance beyond the rank of major. It was not until late 1957 – too late to make any positive impact on the collective JSSL memory – that it began to be adequately recognised in the Army structure, and to become what its History calls 'The Corps Renewed'.

Geoffrey Elliott recalls an almost surreal experience when he was first posted to Maresfield in the late 1950s:

> When I got to Victoria Station, I eventually found this remote
> platform over at the back near the Classic cinema. A steam
> engine was hissing quietly, attached to three or four carriages that
> were painted brown rather than the usual Southern Railway
> green. I climbed into the middle one and found it was a genuine
> Victorian or Edwardian parlour-car, with armchairs, a centre
> table, antimacassars, sepia photos of Eastbourne . . . I had it to
> myself and the whole thing was like a Hitchcock movie. I half
> expected Basil Rathbone and Dame May Whitty to follow me in
> and that the train would puff off into a time warp and end up in
> Ruritania . . .

Most of the recollections of 1950s' Maresfield come from those who were there as conscripts, on sufferance, and in the case of the linguists with an attitude that was resentful and generally well north of supercilious. They thus tend to accentuate the negative while ignoring the positive – the high degree of professionalism the Corps brought at all levels to British security, counter-intelligence and in later years risky counter-terrorism work in the field; understandably, since they neither had any idea of nor interest in that side of things. So since it is the linguists' story we are telling, the picture is inevitably out of balance as well as outdated by half a century.

Archaeologists, even those concerned with the nearby Roman iron-works sites, are unlikely ever to excavate the Depot remains. If they did, and if they could understand what went on, they would find an odd mix of the military and the mysterious. Militarily, where the road now curves elegantly into a housing estate there was a guardroom, three cells for malcontents and a dormitory for the guard. It was not clear quite who offered the threat against which the guard was mounted so solemnly every evening – the odds of Russia invading East Sussex were slim, but the Depot went through the motions nonetheless.

Outside the Maresfield guardroom was a full-length mirror in which those on duty could check that they were in the best possible shape – blancoed belt taut around the waist, twinkling brass buckles with no function in life except to be Brassoed daily, and trousers folded down about two inches over the tops of those magnificently redundant pieces of British kit, the stiff webbing gaiters. The super-keen dropped a loop of bicycle chain down each trouser-leg to hold the folds in place.

Down the slope past the guardroom and the barber's shop, where a visually challenged psychopath shaved heads for a shilling, loomed the Orderly Room, the Depot's centre of gravity, lair of the virtually invisible commanding officer, and the all-too-visible Regimental Sergeant-Major Balfe, remembered by a late 1950s' visitor as an impressively upright figure who resembled one of those wooden statues of Ludendorff onto which patriotic Germans nailed their Loan Subscriptions in the First World War. Conveniently opposite it was the parade-ground, and up the slope the NAAFI, the gymnasium, the Sergeants' Mess and, at a comfortable distance from the *hoi polloi*, the Officers' Mess.

Opposite the gym was the sports field, on the edge of which four sackcloth dummies oozing straw, intermittently used for bayonet practice, hung forlornly from a wooden gibbet like some latter-day Tyburn Tree. When less than strapping young linguists rushed forward bayonets outthrust, fluting the 'bloodcurdling yells' called for in the Training Manual, the effect was rather less Rorke's Drift than that of an amateur cast in its first rehearsal for *Oh, What A Lovely War!* at Bridlington Repertory. It would have gratified them and horrified the instructors to know that 130 or so years before, the Duke of Wellington had also shown himself up as less than crisp at the basic martial arts, when the same fields were part of the Maresfield estate of his ardent admirer Lady Frances Shelley. On a weekend shooting party he performed, one might almost say, more like a linguist than Britain's greatest warrior, when with three successive shots he peppered a dog, hit a keeper's ankles and lodged a few pellets in the arm of a startled cottager as she hung her washing out to dry. She was given a guinea for her pains.

These standard building blocks of any encampment were surrounded by some specifically Intelligence Corps features, all of them grouped under the vague heading of 'The School of Military Intelligence'. A cluster of Chinese artillery captured in Korea was stashed away in the woods behind 'Ling Wing'. There was the Field Security Training Wing, with its eclectic display of steel fences and varieties of barbed wire, and its sample prisoner-of-war cell with microphones hidden in unlikely spots – one was the door handle. Another distant set of huts was where more robust interrogation techniques were said to be tried out under the direction of a fat major with high blood pressure behind a sign that blandly announced 'The Joint Services School of Psychological Warfare'.

There was also 'Ling Wing' itself, which, in addition to the cluster of accommodation huts and 'ablutions', contained 'The Study Centre', where the linguists filled their time with intelligence tasks said to be 'Top Secret'. Like Dennis Potter's hero in *Lipstick on Your Collar*, whose job in the War Office was translating the football pages of the Soviet Army newspaper *Red Star* because they might contain intelligence snippets, Guy Lancaster was set to work at Maresfield translating the *Great Soviet Encyclopedia* as a 'task of national importance'. (When sometime in the 1970s Robert Maxwell published his own English edition of this classic example of Soviet mendacity, Leonard Schapiro's one-word review of it in *The Spectator* was, 'Why?') Future Churchill biographer and historian Martin Gilbert pored over maps and newspapers from the Caspian, the Caucasus and Soviet Central Asia. (How these newspapers reached Sussex from the depths of a closed society is a matter of conjecture.)

Tony Blee remembers being handed a map of Germany and a table of ranges of various Soviet artillery pieces and told to model them all on the map, using copper wire for the shell trajectory and cotton wool for the impact points. Some confusion between metres and yards – they were after all linguists not physicists – left many strands of wire dangling in midair. Harvey Pitcher applied his skills to translating Russian Service manuals, including how to set up a field latrine, 'knowing full well that waves of previous *kursanty* had translated the same manuals before us'.

In between peeling potatoes and black-leading ovens in the cookhouse, Private John Goodliffe, recently qualified as an interpreter and already armed with an Honours Degree in French, would also read the Soviet papers, in his case ignoring the headlines but making a careful note of the names and any minor details that were given about personalities such as tractor drivers in Omsk who had overfulfilled their norms.

This make-work effort echoes the more serious British 'Press Reading Rooms' which operated in the Second World War in neutral capitals such as Lisbon, Stockholm and Istanbul, and which did actually produce useful background intelligence from a careful study of newspapers from the countries around them. Another, rather more shadowy manifestation of this type of work was the so-called Central Asian Research Centre, improbably but discreetly located over the Kardomah Café in King's Road, Chelsea, where beginning in the mid-1950s a small number of former JSSL students were employed or picked up the occasional freelance translation assignment.

Some of the same sort of work was done elsewhere in London. After a 'very boring' spell at Maresfield translating Russian pam-

Mrs Chernysheva.

Liza Hill, George Trapp, Mrs Hackel and Mr Plyushkoff.

Outdoor lesson with Marina Fennell, Cambridge 1952.

Weekly test at Cambridge, 1954.

'Morning parade' – waiting for the bus at Newmarket, 1954.

A cartoon of
Dmitri Makaroff
which appeared in
Samovar.

Alan Bennett and
Michael Frayn,
summer 1953.

Finale of
The Tenebrae
of St Petroc,
Bodmin 1955.

Curtain call for *The Cherry Orchard*, Cambridge 1952. Second from left Harry Shukman, fifth and sixth from left Pavlov and Grech, ninth from left Emmy Voznesenska, tenth from left John Waine, extreme right John Goodliffe.

Dennis Potter at Bodmin, 1953.

D. M. Thomas.

Peter Woodthorpe as Boris Godunov, Bodmin 1953.

A working day in
Russell Square, 1951.

Queensgate Terrace, in its earlier days as the South Kensington Hotel. In JSSL's time WRNS lived to the right, *kursanty* to the left; the ballroom was first floor right.

'Bye 'Bye Baby: Ben Chaplin and other monitors in Jack Rosenthal's TV film.

phlets, Dennis Potter found himself in the War Office, working as an analyst in MI3(D). He later described his work both factually and fictionally. As a matter of fact he remembered that his section 'dealt with the Soviet Army, where it was, where it had been, where it was going. The information came in partly in code [probably a reference to Sigint] and partly overt. There was an incredible amount of crap. We had to read documents, soldiers' letters and all the Soviet military newspapers, because as with all newspapers someone would make a mistake and reveal the name of a place or person.'

Geoffrey Madell found himself in MI10 sifting through piles of Russian newspapers and magazines looking for items of technical or scientific interest, which since he had no scientific background must have been a rather hit-or-miss exercise.

Even allowing for that, the feeling seems to have been that the linguists needed to be brought down to earth with a sharp reminder that they were now back in the Army after a 'cushy' time at JSSL, or, worse still in the eyes of the regular NCOs, university. Though the ringing condemnation dates from Bodmin, Drill Sergeant Dear surely reflected the feeling of all regular NCOs dealing with linguists when he barked despairingly about, 'All those fucking officer cadets wot all comes back from Cambridge all fuckin' 'omos.' ('Chunky' Charnley clearly had something of the same less than liberal view when one Saturday morning at Crail those involved in one of the theatrical productions were released from parade instead of having to set about the menial housekeeping chores known as 'fatigues'. In what Peter Roland is surely right to describe as 'the most bizarre command ever issued on a British parade ground', he released the aspiring thespians with a bellow of 'Makaroff's queers, fall out!')

This division was accentuated from time to time when some particularly keen Maresfield officer would decide, in Terry Thomas's trademark line, that the linguists were 'an absolute shower' and had to be taken in hand. A Major Klinghardt, surely out of the pages of *Catch 22*, is remembered as having brisk notions about what was needed.

Cleaning latrines as a way of making the point comes up too

often in memories for the technique to have been coincidental. Indeed, it was in a way the genesis of this book when, in a biographical sketch in *The London Review of Books*, Alan Bennett mentioned in passing that he had cleaned a Maresfield Sergeants' Mess urinal 'with his bare hands' after he returned from Cambridge, reminding Geoffrey Elliott that he too had been given the same task several years later; and although he had at least been provided with a razor blade to ease the task, his handiwork had been marred by an officer insouciantly splashing alongside as he worked. This memory after so many years more surreal than distasteful in turn led, with no apparent logic, to the thought that the whole JSSL saga deserved a record, then to a broader solicitation of reminiscences and finally to this history.

Among those with the same memories of military micturition were Geoffrey Madell, who performed wonders with a washcloth and Vim, and Michael Miller, who had the luxury of a knife. Miller also recalls the 'bathhouse roulette routine' in which a luckless linguist would be given an hour before the commanding officer's inspection to swab down the bathhouse and clean sixteen or eighteen baths which were 'normally so encrusted with grime . . . that they resembled lava rock pools'. As there was never enough time to clean them all, the gamble came in guessing which bath stalls the CO was likely to inspect, clean those and get out of the way. The right guess brought the gambler's thrill of backing winners; getting it wrong meant being marched before the CO the next morning and being awarded yet more cleaning duties, known in Army argot as 'jankers', a word probably imported from the days of the Raj.

The record is unclear but in the earlier years of the system Army officer cadets who had completed their Interpreters' Examination and had only a short time left before they returned to civilian life, too short to be posted anywhere, seem to have been sent to a War Office Selection Board and, if they passed, had a brief spell at a training unit and were commissioned as second lieutenants. This is perhaps the only point in the JSSL system where camaraderie occasionally broke down since inevitably some of those commissioned took their new rank and its demarcation lines rather too seriously, like newly appointed school prefects, and tended to shun their erstwhile companions other than to return their mocking salutes in a way that was invariably regarded as pompous and self-important. All the more since in the early days those who failed the Board or the Unit were demoralisingly demoted right back down to the lowest form of Army life, a humble private soldier, and in retaliation exacerbated the gulf by adopting the demeanour of an extremely Bohemian detachment of the Artists' Rifles, in a display of what the Army's official list of military offences termed 'dumb insolence'.

That any linguists could ever have the potential to become officers might have come as a surprise to those who drafted the early selection guidelines stipulating that men with 'officer potential' should not be put forward to JSSL.

The officer selection process, which was in the arthritic hands of the Regular Army, meant exposure to the worse sort of alluvial British prejudices from which most *kursanty* had been sheltered in their time at JSSL. Ivor Samuels, who went through it when the Suez Canal was nationalised, was asked by a Neanderthal interviewer how he as a Jew could 'swear an oath of allegiance to Her Majesty when in your heart you owe allegiance to another state'. 'But Britain and Israel are fighting on the same side, sir.' 'That's got nothing to do with it. You can't have dual allegiance. Who knows what will happen when the Middle East blows up again? What side will you be on then?' Samuels knew perfectly well which side he was on, but the doubt had been voiced and the result was a foregone conclusion.

As National Service wound down, the commissioning option seems not to have been offered and returning cadets were re-classified as sergeants. This made for other tensions and the Sergeants' Mess became an uneasy place. Regular Corps NCOs who had earned their three stripes the hard way resented the 'poncy linguists'. Those who were fond of hurling the charge must have felt it even more justified when, as recollected by Eric Matthews (Professor of Philosophy at Aberdeen), hut inspections revealed a predilection on the part of JSSL alumni to decorate their bedside lockers with vases of wildflowers picked from the surrounding woods.

Likewise, the nouveau-striped felt equally resentful at the loss of their quasi-officer status and their white flashes, and the two elements kept a wary distance – a gulf made deeper by the linguists' noticeable absence from the Mess's more liquid Saturday night bacchanalia, though this was probably due less to snobbery than a realisation that as drinkers they were rank amateurs and no match for the veteran Field Security topers reliving tough times in Malaya, Cyprus and Suez.

Back in Maresfield from Cambridge to finish off his Service, Guy Lancaster recalls being given a 'very hard time'. One officer suggested that they had only volunteered for the Russian Course to avoid going to Korea. His version of 'the treatment' was cleaning the Sergeants' Mess after a Saturday night party, with the overpowering stench of stale beer and vomit.

But there were also better moments and good people. The writer and actor Ian Flintoff, a Bodmin product, remembers acting in *The Duke in Darkness* in a production directed by a Regular Sergeant who had been in the theatre in civilian life. Maresfield also saw the first performance of Flintoff's play *Staking for Red*, which he directed himself and which he recalls getting 'rave reviews' in the local papers.

Dennis Potter's fictional reworking of his Whitehall spell in *Lipstick on Your Collar* struck a chord with another *kursant*, who recalls that in the final stages of the London Course the Army members of his intake were summoned to appear in the upper reaches of the Old Admiralty building in Whitehall looking out over Horse Guards. A bantam-cock NCO in a blazer and flannels lined them up along a draughty anonymous corridor and told them, '"This place is so secret even me Mum doesn't know I work 'ere."

'No one said what we were being interviewed for and at the end no one said you had passed or failed. It was only when we compared notes over lunch that it dawned on us what it might have been about.'

As the end of his two years in the Army approached, D. M.

Thomas was sent to West Germany for a few weeks to monitor Soviet tank manoeuvres and to practise interrogation: 'name, rank and number'. He was graded 'suitable for low-level interrogation after further training', having asked 'a mean-looking émigré, *Kakoi vash chlen?*" ("How is your member?"), rather than "*Kakoi vash cheen?*" ("What is your rank?")'

The Navy was, as so often, ahead of its sister Services and before the end of conscription had already cut down its intake to the point where JSSL members were the only National Servicemen left in its ranks.

After his naval service and university, Mark Frankland was recruited rather more formally by the Secret Intelligence Service – a relationship that he soon outgrew for reasons which he describes very straightforwardly in his autobiography *Child of My Time*. At his final interview, 'in a house near Hyde Park' after a session of predictable questions and equally predictable answers, the telephone tinkled on the desk in front of him. He picked it up. The voice at the other end greeted him in Russian and launched into a dialogue about the weather, the London theatre and foreign travel, a sneaky test both of his Russian and his reaction to surprise.

Though outside the scope of Maresfield, it has to be said that the Navy was just as good or bad as the Army in finding odd jobs for its newly qualified linguists with time to kill before leaving the Service. A posting as a general duty officer on a destroyer or minesweeper required no Russian, and knowing the whole of *Boris Godunov* was no help to Peter Woodthorpe, who, to his shocked disbelief, found himself appointed Divisional Officer at Portsmouth, 'in charge of a company of seamen never having been on a ship in my life'. Leading the annual Nelson's Parade out of the barracks, he swung his sword so far out that bystanders were forced to duck, while he got the giggles.

Myles Burnyeat's post-Course experience was no less surreal. Posted to a Fisheries Protection vessel and clearly having nothing to contribute in the way of seamanship, his captain set him to work updating the ship's Manual of Regulations governing disciplinary offences, by making insertions and changes sent out from the Admiralty. He discovered that 'buggery was the offence undergoing revision. I was a very innocent twenty years of age. Law depends on exact definition. The Navy's previous definition of buggery had evidently proved inadequate. The revisions to be glued into place in the ship's copy of the Naval Regulations were detailed and systematic. Days of concentrated effort, and as many years, before I learned that the results might have been of interest to Proust,' whose works he had recently begun to read. 'Back in my bunk, Albertine was still female.'

But as far as can be known, which is not very far, not that many JSSL men went into SIS. Most, as we saw, found themselves armed not with Walther PPKs but more mundanely with earphones and government-issue HB pencils.

13

The End of the Affair

In 1959 two factors converged to bring the Russian Courses in the form most had known them to a close, though a smaller scale effort continued. The first was the imminent end of National Service, which had been anticipated since 1956 and which dried up the reservoir of potential talent. The second was the realisation that even if it came to war, still a risk but on the scale of things perhaps less likely than it seemed in 1947, the Armed Forces had built up a large enough reserve of Russian linguists to cope with most foreseeable needs.

The Ministry of Defence had begun to reassess its needs as early as August 1956. Its Service Language Training Committee agreed that JSSL's alumni would be a valuable asset if it came to mobilisation, but could not contribute very much to the peacetime needs; by the time they had completed their training, little of their full service would be left. In the world that had evolved since those early, anxious days in the late 1940s, the JSSL scheme had become a less attractive investment in terms of the peacetime return on money spent.

The Committee left out of its reckoning, perhaps because it was projecting forward, the contribution made by National Servicemen who had been trained at JSSL as monitors and who were performing that task at the time.

As the Services shrank, and along with them their interception role, the government's agencies increasingly employed civilian language staff, not just in Russian. These, it should be pointed out, were civilians engaged in many cases as short-term contract officers rather than Servicemen in civilian clothes. A few years previously, as Richard J. Aldrich has noted, there had been concern in some quarters about the influence of the trades unions among GCHQ civilian staff, notably the Electrical Trades Union which had been involved in an 'embarrassing domestic security case' at Cheltenham in 1954. However, these concerns were in all likelihood related less to linguists than to the large numbers of technical staff within GCHQ – its signals technicians, operators, engineers and so on – and already in 1956, when the Committee discussed the peacetime need for linguists, it had noted that GCHQ would be completely civilianised in this respect in the near future. The Admiralty had already 'civilianised' its UK-based intercept stations and the other two Services were doing so where possible; and by 1960 the civilian elements in all three Services were merged at GCHQ as The Composite Signals Organisation. Yet again we come across instances of the blurring of demarcation lines; one Cambridge alumnus re-engaged as a civilian junior linguist officer in the late 1950s found himself on an RAF station in East Anglia attempting to tackle Soviet air-force codes rather than applying his language skills as such.

In developing their plans the Admiralty and Air Ministry recognised that in many jobs a pure language specialist was no use, and that what was required was a man with a Service background who could also speak a language. One way was to offer financial and other inducements to Regular Officers to learn a language.

In December 1957 the Committee Chairman confirmed that discussions were continuing with the Directors of the Courses at

Cambridge and London and that arrangements for running down the Courses were being made. This was to prove a slow process; though the JSSL entry in November 1957 was not offered the university option, the last Interpreters' Course T did not sit the Civil Service Examination until February 1959. We do not know Bolsover's reaction in London, but the archives show that Liza put up the most vigorous opposition to closure, in vain. Whether there was a touch of disingenuousness to her fight is hard to tell; even in the earlier years of the Course she had conceded privately that 'our plans after we have trained our 900 [interpreters] are still vague' and that Cambridge could only offer staff 'a temporary commitment'.

In 1959 a Ministry of Defence working party discussed the future of Crail. The view was expressed that there were definite advantages to be considered in keeping some kind of military language-training centre after the end of National Service, not least because the military would exercise complete control and 'we should be able to train exactly according to our own requirements'. In what would have been felt as a blow to the *amour propre* of both University Directors, one member of the working party voiced the quite reasonable view that, 'The snag at universities was that the training there was too academic and did not cater for the essential military aspect of a language . . .' At the same time, the Committee saw the advantage of using the existing instructors at Crail, many of whom could teach more than one East European language.

The cost of language training in 1959/1960 was £250,000 (or a quarter of what the costs had been at the scheme's inception) and by 1960/61 the cost of running Crail was further reduced to £150,000, of which academic staff salaries accounted for £43,000 and administration and maintenance the balance. The working accommodation was seen as unsuited for academic purposes, and with the student population down to seventy-three, and the staff 160, far too big. On the basis of the numbers under training, the cost per place worked out at about £2,150 compared to £540 per place at residential teacher training colleges.

The Committee then faced a choice: either to keep JSSL but transfer it from Crail to somewhere like RAF Leighton Buzzard with a saving of about £40,000; or to dissolve JSSL and let each Service run its own language training. In the end they decided on the latter course.

The Regular Army element of Russian training transferred to the Education Corps Depot at Beaconsfield, the RAF and Navy moving first to Tangmere and later to North Luffenham; one third of the JSSL teaching staff found themselves out of work. The new arrangements were expected to save £60,000 a year, meaning that language training as a whole would cost £265,000.

There is a record of what seems to have been a separate Intelligence Corps initiative to teach Russian to its Territorial Army unit, 22 Intelligence Company, originally formed from a mix of JSSL graduates and NCOs trained in operational intelligence. With the ending of National Service – which suggests that the project was launched in the late 1950s – the Company, its History records, 'had to turn its attention to the teaching of Russian, often from the beginning . . . remarkable success was achieved thanks particularly to the work of a team of teachers headed by Major B. S. Fitzjohn'. This may well be synonymous with the would-be hush-hush, polyglot 'Joint Services Interrogation Unit', also a Territorial Army section with which several former *kursanty* – journalists, stockbrokers and novelists among them – became involved as reservists, and which did much of its weekend training at Maresfield. One of its alumni recalls that they would be collected at the local railway station in vehicles emblazoned 'M19 INTERROGATION UNIT'!

There is another more dramatic version as to why the Courses ended, namely that they had been penetrated by the Russians.

It is not clear whether the story relates to the entire JSSL initiative or just the Cambridge element, but in any event its dates do not mesh with the known facts. It is the version peddled by the disgruntled ex-MI5 officer Peter Wright (described in her memoirs by Dame Stella Rimington, former Director of the Security Service, as 'that strange and untrustworthy character'), who claimed in *Spycatcher* that though there was no hard evidence of such penetration, the allegations that had been made were compelling and that the Security Service 'decided . . . the safest thing was to close the School down'.

However, the source of the allegations was the controversial Soviet defector Anatoly Golitsyn, whose assertions about moles in the CIA succeeded only in turning its counter-intelligence efforts inside-out for many years. Golitsyn spent four well-paid months in London, claiming in the course of his debriefings that the KGB had successfully infiltrated the Russian Course. Wright claims that Golitsyn spent days poring over the personal files of people who had gone through the Cambridge Course, and that 'we even conducted language tests on some of those he felt of particular interest to see if we could detect from their idioms whether they were picking up Russian words from their KGB controllers. It never paid off,' Wright admits.

Rather more to the point, however, is that Golitsyn came to London only in 1968, by which time Cambridge in the form we have reviewed it here was history, as were Crail and Bodmin, and there can have been no students to subject to tests with Golitsyn behind the arras listening for Soviet vulgarisms. Also, by then the scaled-down post-National Service versions of the Course were sailing, and continue today to sail, successfully on.

Even though Wright's version does not make sense, it is not to say the effort overall was not targeted by Soviet intelligence. Indeed as we saw, they were already sniffing around in London in the 1930s. It would be surprising if they had not continued, and equally surprising if the Security Service had not kept a watchful eye on things.

One Crail alumnus recalls that the class-lists, which identified every student, were posted right by the unguarded gate of the teaching section of the camp, readily accessible to any passer-by. But in the 1950s any Russian hood nervously holding down his kilt in the breeze would have stuck out a mile in the East Neuk or Bodmin Moor. Likewise, even though the opportunities for Soviet emissaries to get alongside the Course were arguably better in the academic and cultural melting pot of Cambridge, Eastern Bloc diplomats needed Foreign Office permission to travel even that far out of London, and their presence, or that of any of the large team of KGB and GRU officers masquerading as TASS or *Pravda* correspondents or cultural attachés in London, would have come to notice very fast. *Pravda* in fact knew very well where JSSL was and what it was about. One of the most unusual souvenirs of Bodmin, treasured for years by Alan Fisher, is a 1955 air-mail wrapper in which the School's subscription copy of the Communist Party newspaper was sent from Moscow addressed to 'The Principal, Joint Services School for Linguists, Walker Lines, Bodmin, Cornwall, UK'!

We are therefore left with the thought that any KGB overtures were most likely made first in London, all the more if over the year *kursanty* fell prey to sexual or other pressures.

Several London alumni recall heavy warnings that put 'Red' centres, such as Collett's Russian and Chinese bookshops, out of bounds. In fact, the manager of the Russian shop from the late 1950s well into the 1960s was himself a former *kursant* at Cambridge, and many other former *kursanty* who went on into academic Russian studies could barely function without maintaining an account and making regular visits to the shop.

At one point the HMS *President* authorities made the bland statement that *kursanty* should not worry if they noticed that they were being followed – they were, but it was simply as part of a training programme for plain-clothes officers of the Military Police.

It is unlikely that Russia will ever open its archives to reveal its own awareness of what the West was up to. Even without the Berlin Tunnel operation, which was unearthed in 1956, and whatever else George Blake, who arrived in Berlin in 1955, told his handlers about Sigint along the way, there were enough cases of penetration or straight defection after an initial major breach of US security in 1948 to have given them a good idea of how intensely they were targeted. In 1952 a British civil servant with knowledge of the intercept system as well as of the Foreign

Office's own communications set-up had been caught passing secrets to the Russians. In the early 1960s the defection of an Intelligence Corps signals NCO must have provided valuable insights. All the more in later years was the case of Geoffrey Prime, who had offered himself to the Russians while serving at Gatow and then gone on to work as their 'mole' at GCHQ. Prime's character – he was actually unmasked as the result of serious sexual offences – was repellent, but we do not know what the motives were for his betrayal. That these cases – thankfully few and far between though damaging – came after the JSSL era suggests that the bright young intellectuals on the National Service Courses were not heavily targeted by Russian intelligence. Robert Evans, later Reuters correspondent in Moscow, thought that at least by the 1960s the 'Sovs were pretty laid back' about JSSL. He recalls that he used to take tea from time to time with Donald Maclean, whose name, like those two Slav saints of old, is forever twinned with Liza's early and unsaintly student Guy Burgess. The defector 'seemed to think [JSSL] served the cause rather than the reverse by introducing so many impressionable young men to the wonders of Russian culture'.

One reason JSSL students were less vulnerable may be that, unlike Maclean's time as an undergraduate in the 1930s, there were fewer great causes: no Spanish Civil War, less numbing unemployment and poverty, and no appeasement of Fascist dictators, to which clandestine help for the Communist cause offered a secret and therefore thrilling panacea for middle-class guilt. And, above all, as the 1950s passed, Communism was being ever more clearly exposed in all its cruelty and falsehoods. That left only money and blackmail as tools for KGB recruitment and, as all agent runners know, they are not the most reliable levers.

The Russians had no illusions about what was going on. A recurring theme in the memories of JSSL alumni on Sigint service is that of Russians transmitting messages of the 'Happy Christmas to all our listeners' variety, or in one instance reading out map references during a tank-training exercise which, when plotted by a bored British analyst, turned out to be those of Gatow. The early history of the RAF Signals unit at Hambuhren records more than one instance of Soviet military mission cars, which were allowed to drive around the British Zone as their UK counterparts were in the East, taking a keen interest in the station as they cruised slowly past.

Several claim as true the story of the record said to have been requested on BBC Radio's 'Two-Way Family Favourites' programme, beamed from London to the British Army of the Rhine, by a linguist from Gatow, back in the UK for demobilisation. His request for 'The Inkspots' version of "Whispering Grass" for all the boys in Gatow', while a nice inward joke, gave away half a codeword that most regarded as somewhere north of Top Secret, a security breach big enough to have him garrotted at dawn behind the NAAFI with his own earphone leads.

Eastern Bloc curiosity did not stop with the Course. Over the years that followed several *kursanty* reported to the London authorities instances of what seemed overly keen interest in their Russian training by Soviet and other diplomats. Martin Gilbert reported back that, while on a lecture visit to Budapest, he had been asked about Maresfield, its layout and what went on. His interlocutor had suggested meeting in Paris to discuss it further. Gilbert made his report in London, did not go to Paris and heard nothing more.

John Riddy, using his JSSL training to teach Russian in Bombay, was invited to give private English lessons to a group of Russian 'heavies', a relationship that came to an abrupt end when one pulled from the raincoat he insisted on wearing even at the beach in tropical heat what he claimed were photostats of all Riddy's Cambridge test results. He suggested that if Riddy were to go back to the UK and join the Civil Service, his upward mobility would be sponsored by unseen hands in return for co-operation. Riddy reported the 'dangle' to the High Commission and, like Gilbert, heard no more.

Shortly after Patrick Procktor finished National Service in 1956, he went to Moscow as an interpreter with a British Council-sponsored mission by the Amalgamated Society of Weavers. When he got home, he received 'a weird little note' inviting him to an address in Queen Anne's Mansions. Ostensibly it was to discuss his application to join the Naval Reserve but his interviewers were much more interested in his trip, declaring that under the terms of the Official Secrets Act he should have asked permission first. His application for the Reserve was 'passed over'.

We have little knowledge of what the Russians might have been up to in intercept work, but some slight indication that things were just as active on the other side of the Curtain can be seen from the KGB's 1961 report to Khrushchev that in the previous year it had decrypted 209,000 diplomatic cables sent by representatives of fifty-one states. This was the successor to the pre-war operations run by Gleb Boky, a serial womaniser but brilliant organiser (not that the latter skill did him much good; like thousands of others, he was shot out of hand in the Purges), whose intercept group is said to have collected prodigious quantities of political and diplomatic intelligence.

However, since the KGB focused only on operations against diplomatic intelligence, commercial and of course domestic targets (much of its work being undertaken via bugs and taps rather than radio intercepts), while its even more secretive 'neighbours' in the military intelligence service, the GRU, ran the Soviet equivalent of the Y Service, this must be only the tip of the iceberg.

Many years after his time in Germany, one RAF linguist had a convivial evening with a Russian academic who asked where he had learned the language. When he replied that he had been a translator during National Service, the academic laughed: 'In that case I know what you were translating – *radioperekhvatki* [wireless intercepts] – we were on the other side of that operation. My father was Soviet Naval Attaché in London in the early 1960s. The attic of our flat in Kensington Palace Gardens was stuffed with radio equipment!'

The question arises whether there was any matching Cold War effort by either Soviet Service to train English speakers for Sigint or code-breaking purposes. It is a nice conceit to think that Bodmin or Crail might have been replicated in a windswept cluster of huts somewhere out on the steppes, where deserters from the Catering Corps taught estuary vowel sounds, or that Salisbury Villas and Russell Square might have their mirror images in the suburbs of St Petersburg, where starched old Scottish nannies left high and dry on the banks of the Neva after the Revolution, or wet-eyed dewlapped defectors, took serious, bespectacled young Soviets through Enid Blyton and the finer points of cricket's 'Leg Before Wicket' rule, or squeezed them into crinolines and bustles to perform *The Importance of Being Earnest*.

The reality is far less dramatic. In contrast to Britain's situation vis-à-vis Russian, according to a former senior KGB officer, English was even then part of the school programme for senior pupils throughout the USSR, and most institutes and universities offered higher level English courses which it would have been relatively easy to augment with more intense specialised technical training; though when Liza encountered a team of Soviet interpreters soon after the war who claimed to have spent four years studying English in Moscow, she was typically dismissive of their 'slipshod' abilities. In the early JSSL planning days Liza had perceptively pointed out that the Russians regarded their complex language as part of their 'defence' against outsiders and were always keen to play down any thought that it could be mastered by foreigners. Hence their generous offers even in Tsarist times to supply foreign visitors and diplomats with interpreters of their own, who could conveniently play a dual role as 'minders' and who probably had a far better grasp of English than their halting efforts sometimes suggested.

JSSL, as 5,000 men knew it, closed. 'Not a drum was heard, not a funeral note.' Russian training, however, went on. As the programme evolved through the 1960s, 70s and 80s to meet changing 'customer' needs, and the designation 'translator' was replaced by 'linguist', Beaconsfield-trained Regular Officers and NCOs – the former reverting for some years to the pre-war pattern of rounding off their studies with four months with émigré families in Paris, of whom there must by then have been a shrinking supply. It also drew pupils from the Foreign Office and notably the Japanese diplomatic service. In 1968 the School ran a six-week Interrogators' Course, but whether this became a regular element of the curriculum is not known.

If any of the KGB old guard, with their keen suspicions of what the Russian Course was really all about, had seen it, they might have felt vindicated by a 1976 photo of a Beaconsfield classroom. On the blackboard in the background are chalked neatly in Russian the separate phrases, 'amphibious tanks', 'Out of danger' and 'Inside the Kremlin'. The explanation that they were written up to reinforce a grammatical point about the use of the genitive case would have cut no ice with the analysts at the KGB's Yasenevo Centre.

In 1982 the Foreign Office set up its own language-teaching arrangements. The School must have missed its leavening of their talented and amiable representatives, but it would not and could not ever be the same.

14

Remains of the Day

The spirit of that brilliant and under-appreciated effort, started so many years ago in such a different world when there was a known enemy to face, lives on in the memories of its now far-flung, multi-talented student body. Many of the main characters, and almost all the physical assets, are gone.

Liza died in 1997, a Dame of the British Empire. At the time of the award a Yugoslav colleague remarked that the recognition was simply the Queen returning to Liza the noble title of her Russian mother which Liza had lost by having a British father.

A year earlier she had brought to an end twelve stormy years of a late life marriage to a Serb aristocrat, an event that had astonished her friends and by her account – she referred to it as 'wickedly destructive enslavement' – brought her much sorrow. She had struggled financially and physically to nurse Doris Mudie until the latter's death in 1970. They are buried side by side at Grantchester.

The core of Liza and her passions is neatly caught by the terms of reference of the Dame Elizabeth Hill Memorial Fund established in her honour, which gives preference to applicants who want to work in 'paleography; mediaeval literature or art; the monastic tradition of the Orthodox Church; or the study of the Slavonic contribution to geography, historiography or the history of science'. And she would have been delighted that by the year 2000 Cambridge had a small but flourishing Orthodox Church of its own, albeit not with Russian priests, under the benign patronage of 'St Ephraim the Syrian'.

George Bolsover, appointed CBE in 1970, retired from SSEES in 1976 and died on Easter Day 1990 while at worship in his Parish Church. It has been said that Bolsover's legendary thrift had profound theological foundations: like the prophet Job, he took a poor view of the frivolities of the modern world (as exemplified *inter alia* by the staff of SSEES over whom he presided). When once it was put to him that there were after all certain basic human rights, such as security on the streets, he replied, 'You have only one right: to die.' But when he invited people, including staff members, to his home, he was the perfect genial and hospitable host, for as he also said, 'You might as well enjoy yourself, for you never know where your next meal is coming from.' He was devoted to his family – and his pets too, a dog and a tortoise – and made a point of maintaining a cordial relationship with those at the bottom of the university hierarchy such as doormen or porters, whom other academics might treat with disdain or negligence. Ironically for a man branded by his Party comrades as 'ultra right', Bolsover's SSEES target, Andrew Rothstein, became a founder member of the 'new' hard-line Communist Party of Great Britain, which arose like a foot-and-mouth diseased Phoenix from the ashes of the discredited old organisation in 1991. He died in 1994 comforted, one hopes, by the award of the Order of the October Revolution in 1983.

After being used for various University functions, including the Department of Experimental Psychology, Salisbury Villas in Cambridge, where foreigners once taught Russian to Englishmen, now houses a school that teaches English to foreigners.

The Hermitage in Silver Street, after a spell as a graduate college called New Hall which later moved elsewhere, is now part of

Darwin College. The Grove at Newmarket was for many years a residential nursing home and is now awaiting demolition and rebirth as luxury flats, while its companion, Cecil Lodge, has been refurbished as offices, and a number of up-market homes occupy the space in between.

Walker Lines, Bodmin, became an industrial estate. Though the Course lives on in Cornwall in a few local memories and in the form of an icon – 'a richly coloured representation of Christ with a large silver halo shown blessing the world' – presented by the departing JSSL to the local church, the School's departure was another in a string of losses suffered by the oldest town in Cornwall.

In the late nineteenth century it had seen Truro designated as the cathedral city. The Duke of Cornwall's Light Infantry head-quarters in The Keep was closed when the regiment was disbanded. The jail, the law courts and the police headquarters all went, too, contributing to the sense captured by a current guide-book to Cornwall that 'an air of regret for what might have been still seems to linger in the town'. Even the asylum closed; local hopes that it might become the cornerstone of a new University of Cornwall remain just that.

When JSSL Crail shut down in 1960, the village went into eco-nomic hibernation until it became apparent that it could profitably reinvent itself as a tourist destination – a role which it seems to be playing with energy and success. *Tempora mutan-tur* . . . it was a happy coincidence to see recently that one of the teams slated to test themselves on Balcomie Links was the 'Russian Ladies' Amateur Golf Society', all the way from Moscow.

But though the village flourishes, what was once HMS *Jackdaw* and then the bustling JSSL is not easy to visualise as the place so many *kursanty* remember. 'Wreck of forgotten wars, to winds abandoned and the prying stars', its fences are now sagging, its roads are overgrown and empty, and many of the buildings are boarded up and falling apart. Others are used as a pig farm, from which echoes a sinister bubbling and squealing chorus, while chest-constricting odours roll down the hill.

Surprisingly, since they were laid in the Second World War, the runways are still in remarkable shape and are used for motor and motorcycle trials, while weekend car-boot sales flourish among the hangars. Local gossip about the site's development as a housing estate and shopping centre has remained just that, due in part to stout resistance from Heritage Scotland. JSSL gave Bodmin an icon as a memento. Other than the buildings, the only memorial at Crail is an inscription in the cemetery recording the passing of Mr Politkowski, one of the Polish-born instructors. A long way from home.

After a spell, according to rumour, as a mental home, the Officer Cadets' Mess at Foxton Hall was bought for redevelopment as an out-of-town office, but burned down, much to its insurer's chagrin, before completion, and the site is now a cluster of executive homes. Coulsdon Camp is almost invisible having been replaced in the 1960s by four large blocks of flats; the Guards Depot next door has also 'gone residential'.

After decamping from Maresfield to Ashford in Kent, the Intelligence Corps is headquartered in the Defence Intelligence and Security Centre at Chicksands in Bedfordshire, a location that had earlier played a pivotal role in Sigint as the main collection station for the ULTRA traffic which was then sent on to Bletchley Park. Its officers, bolstered nowadays by an *esprit de corps* and a professionalism forged in support of many complex and dangerous episodes in the post-war world, now look out on the world from a Mess in the expensively converted twelfth-century Gilbertine Priory at the hub of the Centre. There can be few if any left who remember, let alone pine for, those distant days of The Chequers, now marketing itself as a historic coaching inn with a good dining room and interior-decorated bedrooms. Maresfield Depot's last official residents were arguably even more disorientated than the Linguists – several hundred Ugandan Asians who spent six months there after being expelled by Idi Amin in 1972. Its site is now split by a bypass; part is a fire brigade training school, part a leisure centre, and part housing, some of it expensively executive.

RAF Oakington became an Army barracks for many years and is presently 'under offer' by the MOD's estate agents. Until a development plan for 5,000 houses is approved, it is being let to the Home Office as an Immigration Reception/Detention Centre, and in September 2001 was the focus of a High Court case in which four Iraqi Kurds claimed that the Government had abused their human rights by keeping them in detention there. None of the 'asylum-seekers' in 1951 would have had such complaints.

Queensgate Terrace has been transformed into an elegant block of flats. The local planners insisted that the revolving doors through which so many *kursanty* shambled had to remain in place as of architectural interest. More understandably they imposed some restriction on the de Morgan tiled fireplace in the lobby. The ghosts of *kursanty* mouthing word-lists, and the elegant spirits of all those remote black-stockinged WRNS, are now left to drift ectoplasmically along the close-carpeted corridors.

Pucklechurch was declared 'inactive' in 1959, when the RAF Language School moved to Tangmere. In 1962 part of the site became a Remand Centre and more recently £35 million was committed to building a new prison there.

Moves to develop HMS *Mercury* in ways that match its commanding position seem from press reports to have been mired in continuing difficulty. Part is now yet another cluster of executive homes, but as recently as 2001 the site was slated by a countryside lover as 'an architectural eyesore unique throughout the length of the South Downs Way'.

In 1959 No. 1 Wireless Regiment underwent yet another metamorphosis – it is impossible to know if these changes over the years were designed to keep first the Abwehr and then the GRU off the scent, or simply the result of bureaucratic whim – emerging this time as 13th Signal Regiment (Radio). In 1967 the Army Signals detachment in Berlin moved from Gatow to the towering new intercept headquarters under joint US Army and Air Force direction at Teufelsberg, the artificial hill created out of Berlin wartime rubble on the site of a fortunately uncompleted Nazi weapons research institute designed by Albert Speer, where, under the colours of 3 Squadron, it worked alongside the RAF's 26 Signals Unit.

The Regiment closed Mercury Barracks in Birgelen in late 1994, sixty years after its predecessor was formed in Aldershot. By that point it had grown to be a multi-acre site, and had a resident US liaison officer, with a UK counterpart at the US intercept HQ in Augsburg. Birgelen is now a golf club and its 'Ops Building', where over the years so many British linguists trained to hear the so often inconsequential, but in its totality essential, chit-chat of so many other men of their own age but a different nationality across the Iron Curtain, is now the Clubhouse, where German businessmen now chit-chat about nothing more meaningful than their handicaps and the Euro exchange rate.

When the RAF moved out of Hambuhren in 1957, the site was taken over by a West German Army 'communications' regiment, perhaps continuing the same sort of work. The site is now a housing development. In an echo of those beheaded Luftwaffe eagles which linguists remember still adorning the walls of Gatow in the 1950s, a West German NCO who sent a 1990s' photograph of an Army ceremony to the site's meticulous historian, Peter Jackson, claims (as no one else seems to have spotted in so many years when British Servicemen stamped up and down the cobbled yard) that the light-coloured bricks set in patterns within the darker cobbles were still arranged in the shape of swastikas.

After JSSL Dmitri Makaroff worked until into the 1980s as Russian coach at the Royal Opera House; in 1986 he was ordained as a Russian Orthodox priest, later moving to the Greek Orthodox Church of which he is now an Archimandrite. As a quasi-*sanctus* if not *deus*, *ex machina* he travelled from Rome to London to join a recent gathering of JSSL veterans, his beard doctrinally long, his hair in a knot, but with his black robes of office discarded for the icy evening in favour of a warm cardigan. His partner in drama, Vladimir Koshevnikoff, died in Beaconsfield in September 1978.

The world turns and what was once a base for Goering's

Luftwaffe and then RAF Gatow is now home to a Museum of the 'new' Luftwaffe, one of the highpoints of which is an ME 109 fighter.

GCHQ continues to go from strength to strength. JSSL alumni played key roles in its operations and senior leadership. When Liza celebrated her eightieth birthday party, 'a coach-load' of former Cambridge *kursanty* went up from Cheltenham.

What remains of those hard-won language skills? For those who went on to work with the language, the skills and vocabulary are obviously still there. But even for those who did not, it is remarkable how much has stuck after so many years. Peter Woodthorpe's fluent recall after thirty years of the Tsar's first big speech in *Boris Godunov* may reflect an actor's skill but as heard in a BBC interview the accent is impeccable. This is not surprising for a man whose early professional commissions included the central role in forty episodes of the BBC Third Programme series 'Russian for Beginners'.

Though his life went in a different direction, even Alan Bennett claimed to remember the Russian for 'rolling barrage'; and, tackled nearly fifty years on, Cambridge *kursant* (Sir) Peter Hall took a pad and scribbled down from memory Lermontov's poem 'The Officer Cadet's Prayer'. Others, like Keith Bilton (who went on to a career in social work), have esoteric and fragmentary recollections; in his case his (rather attractive) instructor Miss Ivanova conceding during an extempore English to Russian translation class at Cambridge, based on an extract from *Silas Marner*, that 'it was impossible we should know the Russian for "the glowing embers of the weaving loom". She translated it for us, and *"obuglivshiyesya goloveshki tkatskogo stanka"* is forever engraved on my memory . . .'

Henry Thompson, who read Russian at Oxford and went on to teach it alongside his responsibilities as a housemaster at Winchester for thirty-six years, remembers Course T's 'daily words' dug from Heaven knows where by two of its more scholarly members and including such conversation-stopping gems as '*enot*' ('racoon'), '*ketmen*' ('a Caucasian navvy's spade') and '*duvalo*' ('a wall in Tashkent').

Anthony Hippisley, Head of Russian at St Andrews University, was hastily recruited in 2001 to interpret for the salvage crews working on the sunken Russian submarine, the *Kursk*. So hastily, in fact, that he had no time to equip himself with an up-to-date Russian naval dictionary and instead took along his old JSSL Crail notebooks of 1958. He reported to the FRINTON Newsletter that, 'Altogether this was a welcome refresher course, and an opportunity at last to use training acquired over forty years ago.'

Sir Edward George, now Governor of the Bank of England, can still find the right words from his Crail and London memory banks to greet counterparts from the Russian financial world, though he has not had occasion to use it much more professionally since the Bank of England sent him to Moscow State University in 1964. The aim was to allow him not just to brush up his Russian but also to get to know Central Bank and other officials. That his stay happened to coincide with the ousting of Khrushchev suggested in later years to an imaginative journalist eager for copy that the Governor might have had intelligence connections; a comment to which the best response from a man with forty-two years of unbroken service to Threadneedle Street might well be the Russian vulgarity once ungrammatically blazoned in whitewash on the roof of Walker Lines.

Though he had picked up Russian again on retirement and translated a couple of books, Geoffrey Elliott had not spoken a word for forty years, and was frankly terrified when called on to interpret for three stoutly monoglot Russian detectives visiting Bermuda on the trail of a Yeltsin-era financial scam. 'The first half hour was all stuttering and stammering, then it just seemed to come back. My proudest moment was putting into words that seemed perfectly comprehensible to the Russians the statement from the owner of the cliff-top villa where the fraudsters and their *koll-gerly* had set up shop, "They had the OK to set up the company to polish the diamonds, but were having trouble getting residence permits here, so I gave them a six months' lease with an option to purchase." Even George Trapp could not have thought that one up. From what murky brain recess words like "residence permit" emerged, I just can't imagine.'

And when Ivor Samuels introduced himself in a London gallery as a JSSL alumnus, Patrick Procktor 'gazed at me balefully and said, *"Konstantin Gavrilovich zastrelilsya. Zanaves"* ("Konstantin Gavrilovich has shot himself. The Curtain falls")' – the closing words of *The Seagull*.

15

Weighed in the Balance

Even though it was by a long chalk the lesser of very many possible National Service evils, and a large number of young men had the time of their lives in the process, and were reshaped by it, the Russian Courses had a serious purpose, to meet what was seen as an urgent defence need at a time of crisis. How does the balance-sheet look?

It was an administrative success, carefully thought out and structured at all levels, a tribute to all those sung and unsung in these pages who were involved in the planning and administration and so committed to its success. Its staff were well chosen, its syllabus carefully devised to achieve the best possible results for its stated aims and though, as we have seen, there were inevitably a few haphazard elements in so extensive a selection process, over a nine-year period its talent-spotters did a fine job of identifying those students who would benefit from the training first as linguists and then as interpreters, as evidenced both by the results and by the successful careers of so many of its students in later life.

Also, despite the occasional snapback by military men driven to professional despair by seeing their values so comprehensively mocked by cocky young men who seemed predestined for a better future than they might hope for, it was thoughtfully run by its Service overlords.

Training men to fight unthinkingly as a unit in the heat of war demands rigorous discipline and harsh conditions. Imparting and nurturing language skills need a different environment. The multi-faceted JSSL system and those who ran it saw the force of this and on the whole got the balance right, in the face of the Armed Services' reputation for muddle-headed bureaucracy and the unfair mantra that 'Military Intelligence is a Contradiction in Terms'. JSSL was after all a military establishment and required some measure of discipline. The authorities were adroit in holding over their students the 'iron hand' of the RTU threat inside the 'velvet glove' of life at JSSL, or even more so university, though we are inclined to think that this was on balance less of a factor in making the students work hard than the natural competitive pressures of a peer group.

It was an educational success on three levels. First, its methods worked very well in their fast-track development of language proficiency. As the BBC's Kevin Ruane has noted, 'Having witnessed the difficulties experienced by others in later decades as they tried to learn the language in supposedly ideal conditions, i.e. in Moscow itself, I have to say that the Joint Services Russian Course must have been among the best courses ever devised anywhere. It was direct and it was kept clear and simple.' There were other views too. Looking back at Cambridge Harvey Pitcher concedes its 'remarkable success' but attributes this more to the unique set of circumstances and the atmosphere in which the Course operated 'rather than the quality of the instruction which in some ways now seems amateurish and old-fashioned'. On the other hand, though he got good marks in the Civil Service Examination, Glen Dudbridge found the 'regime of total saturation' counter-productive and, based on his later success in the even more daunting task of mastering Chinese and then teaching it, feels that to achieve their best results students need to be self-motivated.

Second, despite the necessary focus on Service terminology and, for interpreters, oral fluency, the Schools also awoke their students' minds to a new world and a rich new culture, history and literature. The theme that has come through strongly, indeed overtaken only by the constant recollection of how cold it was, in so many of the memories *kursanty* have been kind enough to share with us is what we might summarise as the long-lasting, indeed still strong, 'mind-opening effect' of this exposure. Moreover JSSL's success gave the lie to the notion that the English were not good at languages. In fact, they were renowned in the seventeenth century for their mastery of European tongues, but these skills were arguably lost with the growth of Empire; its rulers could impose English wherever they went and the ruled were keen to master the language of power, so that English began to predominate in much of the world

Third, Liza's promise that JSSL would create a generation of students going on into higher Russian studies was soon vindicated: in 1954 the number of undergraduates in the Slavonic Faculty at Cambridge went up from around twenty to one hundred, the large majority of them former *kursanty*. Comparable figures were to be found at Oxford and other centres of Slavonic learning.

True, the high-point of teaching Russian in schools and universities in the 1960s, for which Liza had made such a compelling case back in the late 1940s, has long passed, as successive government cuts have both reflected and accentuated the decline in interest among Britain's youth, though the decline was briefly halted in the late 1980s when the Soviet Union under Gorbachev became once again a centre of intellectual interest.

Despite this, it is nevertheless also true that the solid foundations of Russian studies on which present-day university departments were built, and the excellent Russian teaching offered in (lamentably few) schools, owe much to the many *kursanty* who went on to academic careers in the 1960s and beyond.

Another by-product was the establishment of academic contacts in the Soviet Union, where JSSL men and their later students established close friendships, as well as valuable quasi-diplomatic contacts, with Russians on various levels.

The Courses were a defence policy success in that they kept the Sigint battlements manned for many key years, built a cadre of Russian interpreters to be deployed if an emergency arose, and created a resource pool for the Foreign Office and its less visible affiliated services including GCHQ. Long-delayed recognition of JSSL's role came in the form of an invitation prompted by personal contact to join the ranks of Ex-Service Associations at the Remembrance Day ceremonies at The Cenotaph and the Royal Albert Hall in November 2001; recognition, but tinged for some by the chastening thought of how long ago all this was and that all those bright *kursanty* are now close to being ranked alongside the veterans of Ypres or el-Alamein.

The JSSL scheme was also, and in some ways most importantly, a social success. It was extremely enjoyable, rewarding and challenging for most of those who took part. Its students, as we have seen, were diverse with hugely varied interests but they had no problems finding like-minded souls, and in the overwhelming majority of cases, cemented by a common purpose, got along very well. Virtually none of the memories we have been privileged to share make much, if anything, of any social gulf, or 'us and them' divisiveness. It was also a social success in that it demonstrated to young men who may have lacked self-confidence or sense of purpose, or felt their career horizons preordained, that they had the talent to succeed. For those who had been to university it offered a new learning challenge. For those with places waiting it rounded out their minds in ways rather different from conventional sixth-form studies; in the case of the Interpreters' Courses, it provided valuable 'orientation' for the conventional university life that was to follow, and for all involved put them to productive use in ways light years removed from the harsh realities and unrealities of National Service life.

Did it change people's lives? This is a dramatic question, which was certainly not part of the planners' original thinking or the instructors' mandate. It is one to which a composite response is impossible but we believe that in many cases it did, and in most it had a lasting and almost invariably positive influence.

First and foremost there was the boost to self-confidence we have just mentioned. Second, had they not been through JSSL, those young men who went into the academic world to study and then teach Russian might otherwise have followed completely different career paths or taken up another subject. Young men who sought a career in the diplomatic world, in journalism, broadcasting or international business, found that they were launched on the job market equipped with a highly marketable skill. Others, whose talents were already growing, such as Michael Frayn or D. M. Thomas, were able to add to their creative output the ability to make thoughtful and enduring translations of Russian literature. Alan Bennett ventured on to the stage. Yet others like Dennis Potter and Jack Rosenthal took the JSSL part of their lives as rich raw material. David Lloyd-Jones, who arranged the music and directed the choir for the *Tenebrae of Petroc* in that freezing church in Bodmin, was clearly set on the path that would lead to his distinguished career as a conductor and musicologist, but would he have further continued his interest in Russian music that produced a scholarly edition of *Boris Godunov* and would he have conducted a wide range of Russian operas – in many countries, including Russia itself – without that initial stimulus from JSSL? He says, 'No, I could not possibly have given the commitment that I have to Russian music and culture in general if I'd not made a determined effort to get myself on to the course in the first place and to hang on by the skin of my teeth for eighteen tortured but wonderful months among a great bunch of fellow students.'

Whether or not Malcolm Brown would have got one of the early general traineeships at the BBC without the Russian Course, it is highly unlikely that had he not had that background, he would have been involved in major programmes about the Soviet Union, including a memorable film of a tour around Russia and Central Asia by that veteran of the Great Game – and bearer of the bad tidings about Bodmin's closure – Sir Fitzroy Maclean.

Martin Gilbert would certainly have achieved great things as an historian in any event but might not perhaps have produced, as one of the first academic fruits of his JSSL experience and his spell at Maresfield specialising in maps of the Soviet Union, his 1971 *A Russian History Atlas*; several of his later books have had a considerable Soviet/Russian content, especially his histories of the First and Second World Wars and the Second World War sections of his Churchill biographical work.

The same is true of Patrick Procktor RA. It was talent, not the Russian Course, that gave him a glittering career as an artist. Would it have been any different if the call-up had not pulled him out of a Holloway builders' merchants and had someone not spotted the talent that qualified him for the Course and introduced him to a new world? Maybe; maybe not. Certainly the £5 a day he earned from several interpreting assignments with the British Council in post-Course years gave him the leeway to paint and create at a critical juncture.

Harry Shukman could not have imagined in 1951 that in two short years he would be qualified as a Civil Service interpreter, or that in 1954 he would be selected to go to the USSR for three weeks as the interpreter from Nottingham University on the first student visit since the war. Or that in 1956 he would be asked to interpret for the Chairman of the South of Scotland Electricity Board for the Scottish part of the visit of Georgy Malenkov and his delegation of Soviet power engineers. 'Perhaps some background in electrical engineering came in useful for the technical stuff,' he reflects, 'but when it came to translating our zombie-like visitor's speeches, every one of which included the same line from Robbie Burns – "A man's a man, etc. etc." – I was thankful for all those Wednesday afternoons with Koshevnikoff in Bodmin!'

Finally was it value for money, a notoriously difficult test to apply to any public sector initiative? JSSL as a whole would qualify as a success by that measure too. Unlike more visible parts of the public sector, it did exactly what was asked of it, to time and, judging by the absence of Treasury complaints, within budget, turning out the Russian linguists whom the planners knew – even if the young men involved did not – were vital to the country's intelligence preparedness. It also spotted and trained the interpreters.

The value for money analysis is more difficult to apply to the interpreters' component of the programme on its own simply because the full span of the Interpreters' Course took up almost the entire span of National Service. As a result in most cases the Armed Forces could not deploy the university-trained *kursanty* on active duties and thus saw no direct return on their investment, even though they had them in reserve had the Cold War become hot. In a way that is a quibble since, for the country, it was in the shorter term a prudential insurance against a day which thankfully never came. At a mere £839 a head, the cost was a premium well spent, as indeed was the investment of time, money and energy in all those painstaking hours, days and years put in by so many young linguists recording Sigint traffic.

In the longer term, as we have seen, educationally, culturally and even socially it must have paid for itself many times over. That in the process JSSL and especially its University Courses gave many young men a unique experience and a wonderful time is a bonus for which all – the co-authors foremost among them – give heartfelt thanks.

In the words of Naky Doniach, who saw the programme through from start to finish, 'It was a great *tour de force*.'

Acknowledgements

Special thanks to all those *kursanty* and staff members who wrote letters or in many cases longer notes, some of them comments in response to the book's first edition, from which we were inevitably only able to quote selectively; we hope all will feel adequately represented. We feel privileged to have been allowed to share so many personal memories. At the same time it is obvious that these are only a small sample of JSSL experiences and that there are many more anecdotes untold, teachers and pupils unmentioned, later careers unremarked. Also fifty years on, memory refracts and plays tricks.

We hope, though, that we have captured the essence of what it was all about.

So that the memories unrecorded here should not be lost, the authors will deposit all their working papers with the Special Collections Department of the Brotherton Library at the University of Leeds, together with a contribution towards cataloguing costs, so that other *kursanty*, families and future generations will have access to the fullest possible picture.

It is always invidious to differentiate between levels of

gratitude, since even a small nugget of information can be of great value, but this book could not have been started without Brian Hawkins and Michael Lee, who broke the ground for this study. Our thanks must also go to Vincent Dowd, transcripts of whose 1986 interviews with the Rt Rev. Sir John Waine KCVO, the late Naky Doniach OBE, Sir John Drummond CBE, Alan Bennett, Mark Frankland, Michael Frayn, Peter Woodthorpe, Patrick Procktor and Harry Shukman himself he generously made available to us and which have been of great value; and to Ronald Hingley for giving us the London perspective with refreshing candour (he retains the copyright in his comments). Sir John Drummond, Alan Bennett, Patrick Procktor, Michael Frayn, Peter Woodthorpe and Bishop Waine were also helpful and patient in tracking back over many of the interview points. As readers will not have failed to notice, Procktor also captured his own colourful memories of colourful times in his illustrations.

Equal thanks go to Kathleen Cann of the Cambridge University Library and Elizabeth Hill Archive; Mark Gamsa of Queen's College, a most diligent research assistant; Michael Sterenberg and Christine Thomas of the British Library; Reg Sheppard (himself a graduate of JSSL) and the staff of the Bodmin Museum, whose memory and researches provided much of value; Kim Cooper of the Cornish Studies Library, Redruth, for her help in finding photographs of JSSL Bodmin; Jonathan Armitage and the staff of the Crail Museum and Heritage Centre who helped with background information and went to much trouble over *Samovar* copies; *Bomb* Magazine; Maureen Reed, Local Studies Librarian, Dundee Central (Wellgate) Library; Emma Camplejohn, General Assistant, School of Slavonic and East European Studies, University of London; Margaret Mumfield, Local Studies and Archives, Croydon Central Library; Roger Packham, Chairman, The Bourne Society; as well as Anthony C. Hall, antiquarian bookseller and Bodmin linguist, with special thanks for the loan of his copies of *Samovar*; Richard Davies of the Special Collections Department, Brotherton Library,

Acknowledgements

University of Leeds, who also helped with *Samovar*, the Harvey Pitcher Course papers, the Vladimir Koshevnikoff archive, and much else besides; Keith Argent and John Goodliffe for the A Course 50th Anniversary newsletter and their recollections; and Navy archives researcher J. H. M. Gulley.

And to our fellow *kursanty*, members of pre-JSSL courses, instructors, specialists in various areas, and friends – Richard J. Aldrich, Julian Andrews, Patrick Andrews, Catherine Andreyev, Vin Arthey, Paul Barker, Arnold Bell, Robert Louis Benson, Keith Bilton, George Bird, David Birt, Tony Blee, Don Bower, Edward Braun, David Brighty CVO CMG, Malcolm Brown, David Burke, Myles Burnyeat, Canon Martin Coombs, John Creasey, Tony Cross, Glen Dudbridge, John Eidinow, Robert J. Evans, Marina Fennell, John Field CMG, David Fill, Alan Fisher, James Fisher, Ian Flintoff, Paul Foote, Michael Futrell, David Garood, Sir Edward George GBE, Sir Martin Gilbert CBE, Col. Roy Giles CBE, Jeffrey Gray, Stuart Griffiths, Sir Peter Hall KBE, CMG, Phillip Hanson, Michael Herman, Derek Hopwood, Philip Ivory, Harry Jack, David G. Jones, Gordon Jones, John Keep, Adam Kellett-Long, Eric Korn, Courtenay Lloyd, David Lloyd-Jones, David Lyall, Geoffrey Madell, Dmitri Makaroff, David Marquand, Eric Matthews, Tom Mayer, Jack Meadows, David Metcalf, Don Mickley, Eric Miller, Michael P. Miller, Robin Milner-Gulland, Edward Morgan, James Muckle, Martin Nicholson, David O'Connor, Edward Orchard, David Paisey, Stewart Platts, Harvey Pitcher, Patrick Renshaw, Jim Reed, John Riddy, Peter Robbins, John Roberts, Peter Roland, Jack Rosenthal, especially for making available the script and a video of *'Bye 'Bye Baby*, Kevin Ruane, David Rundle, William Russell, Peter Scott, Gerald Seaman, Peter Selby, Peter Slot, Alan Smith, Gerry Smith, Sydney Bernard Smith, Harry Spence, Arthur Stockwin, Geoffrey Sudbury, Peter Taylor, Peter Tegel, D. M. Thomas, Henry Thompson, Oliver Thomson, Andrew Thorpe, John Tofts, Ron Truman, Oleg Tsaryev, John Upson, Brian Verity, Terry Wade, C. T. Walker, Michael Webb, Marcus Wheeler, David Wilby, Ronald Wilks and Peter Wilmshurst.

Collective and warm thanks to all the various *Samovar* editors, contributors and Business Committee members whose unsung and in the main anonymous work all those years ago help preserve the flavour. The authors especially wish to thank Linda Osband, who edited the manuscript with scrupulous care.

Websites: RAF Museum Tangmere; Fishponds Historical Society; Royal British Legion Garats Hay; No. 1 Wireless Regiment, Royal Signals; Royal Signals Detachment Langeleben; booksforgolf; the Town of Crail; Cambridge Footlights; RAF Gatow Signals Unit Research; RAF Uetersen; RAFLING; Royal Naval Communications Association; The Intelligence Corps; town of Bodmin; Royal Burgh of St Andrews.

Fay Elliott and Barbara Shukman have both contributed much to this project, despite having had to live with it for far too long, and they deserve our special gratitude.

And, on the basis that the last shall be first, our thanks to the memory of Liza Hill for her energy and inspiration, for her teaching, for her memoirs, edited with affection and skill by Jean Stafford-Smith, and for carefully building for posterity a personal archive of the Russian teaching programmes which has been the cornerstone of this work.

The authors accept full responsibility for the use they have made of all these valuable resources.

Select Bibliography

The following books and papers have been of much value in preparing this study:

Aldrich, Richard J., *The Hidden Hand*, John Murray, London, 2001.
— (ed.), *Espionage Security and Intelligence in Great Britain 1945–1970*, Manchester University Press, Manchester, 1998.
also 'GCHQ and Sigint in the early Cold War', in *Intelligence and National Security*, vol. 16, No. 1, Frank Cass, 2001; with Michael Coleman, 'The Cold War, the JIC and British Signals Intelligence', in *Intelligence and National Security*, vol. 4, No. 3, Frank Cass, London, 1988.
Andrew, C., and Mitrokhin, V., *The Mitrokhin Archive*, Allen Lane, London, 1999.
Bamford, J., *Body of Secrets*, Doubleday, NY, 2001.
Bennett, Alan, *Writing Home*, Faber & Faber, London, 1995.
Blake, George, *No Other Choice*, Jonathan Cape, London, 1990.

Bradford Westerfield, H. (ed.), *Inside CIA's Private World*, Yale University Press, London and New Haven, 1995.

Carpenter, Humphrey, *That Was Satire That Was*, Gollancz, London, 2000.

—, *Dennis Potter*, Faber and Faber, London, 1999.

Clayton, Anthony, *Forearmed: A History of The Intelligence Corps*, Brassey's, London, 1993.

Costello, John, and Tsaryev, Oleg, *Deadly Illusions*, Century, London, 1993.

Craig, Sir James, *Shemlan, A History of the Middle East Centre for Arabic Studies*, Macmillan, London, in association with St Antony's College, Oxford, 1998.

Cullingham, J. D. H., 'Memories of Couldson Common Camp', in *The Bourne Society Bulletin*, no. 187, Caterham, February 2002.

Davies, Hunter, *Born in 1900*, Little, Brown, London, 1998.

Drummond, John, *Tainted By Experience*, Faber & Faber, London, 2000.

Faulks, Sebastian, *The Fatal Englishman*, Hutchinson, London, 1996.

Flicke, Wilhelm, *War Secrets in the Ether: German Code Breaking Success and Radio Espionage during and between the World Wars*, Aegean Park Press, Laguna Beach, USA, 1994.

Forsyth, Frederick, *The Devil's Alternative*, Hutchinson, London 1979.

Frankland, Mark, *Child of My Time*, Chatto & Windus, London, 1999.

Gaddis, John Lewis, 'Intelligence, Espionage and Cold War Origins', in *Diplomatic History*, vol. 13, No. 2, Blackwell, Oxford, Spring 1989.

Hawkins, Brian, *Russian Language Training in the Services: A Personal Memoir*, n.p., n.d.

Holloway, David (ed.), *The Fifties*, Simon and Schuster, London, 1991.

Hudd, Roy, with Hindin, Philip, *Roy Hudd's Cavalcade of Variety Acts*, Robson Books, London, 1997.

Select Bibliography

Hughes, Michael, *Inside the Enigma, British Officials in Russia, 1900–1939*, Hambeldon Press, London and Rio Grande, 1997.

Jackson, Peter, *Hambuhren–Lower Saxony, A Military History, 1939–1999*, p.p Wheatley, Oxford, 2001.

Lahr, John (ed.), *The Diaries of Kenneth Tynan*, Bloomsbury, London, 2001.

Lee, Michael, 'The Joint Services School of Linguists', in *The Linguist*, vol. 38, No. 4, London, 1999.

—, 'A Special Generation of British Speakers of Russian', in *Vestnik Evropy*, vol. III, Moscow, December 2001.

McEwen, John, *Patrick Procktor*, Scholar Press, Aldershot, 1997.

Melinsky, Hugh, *A Codebreaker's Tale*, The Larks Press, Dereham, 1998.

Melvin, Ronald (ed.), *The Guards at Caterham*, Guardroom Publications, Old Coulsdon, n.d.

Murphy, D. E., Kondrashev S.A., and Bailey, G., *Battleground Berlin, CIA versus KGB in the Cold War*, Yale University Press, London and New Haven, 1997.

Plotke, A. J., *Imperial Spies Invade Russia: The British Intelligence Interventions, 1918*, Greenwood Press, Westport, Conn., 1993.

Potter, Dennis, *Lipstick on Your Collar*, Channel 4 Books/Faber and Faber, London, 1993.

Procktor, P., *Self Portrait*, Weidenfeld & Nicolson, London, 1991.

Rimington, Stella, *Open Secrets*, Hutchinson, London, 2001.

Riste, Olav, *The Norwegian Intelligence Service 1945–1970*, Frank Cass, London, 1999.

Roberts, John C.Q., *Speak Clearly into the Chandelier: Cultural Politics between Britain and Russia*, Curzon Press, London, 2000.

Royle, Trevor, *The Best Years of Their Lives: the National Service Experience, 1945–63*, Michael Joseph, London, 1986.

Sacks, Oliver, *Uncle Tungsten*, Picador, London, 2001.

Skillen, Hugh, *Spies of the Airwaves*, privately printed, Pinner, 1989.

Smith, Michael, and Erskine, Ralph (eds), *Action This Day*, Bantam Press, London, 2001.

Smith, Sydney Bernard, *Alexander* (chapters from an Autobiographical Novel), unpub., Portadown, n.d.

Strachan, Hew, *The First World War*, Volume 1, *The Call To Arms*, Oxford University Press, Oxford, 2001.

J. Stafford-Smith (ed.), *In the Mind's Eye, The Memoirs of Dame Elizabeth Hill*, The Book Guild, Sussex, 1999.

Thomas, Andy, 'British Signals Intelligence after the Second World War', in *Intelligence and National Security*, vol. 3, No. 4, Frank Cass, London, 1988.

Thorpe Andrew, *The British Communist Party and Moscow, 1920–43*, Manchester University Press, Manchester and New York, 2000.

Tyrkova-Williams, Ariadne, *The Cheerful Giver*, Peter Davies, London, 1938.

Urban, Mark, *The Man Who Broke Napoleon's Codes*, Faber, London, 2001.

West, Nigel, *GCHQ: the Secret Wireless War, 1900–1986*, Weidenfeld and Nicolson, London, 1986.

Wright, Peter, *Spycatcher*, Heinemann, Victoria, Australia, 1987.

Of fundamental importance, the official papers on JSSL were released into the public domain in the mid-1990s and 2001, and are to be found in the Public Record Office under the following class numbers:

ADM 116/6331–6334
ADM 1/24711
ADM 273/13
AIR 2/11994
AIR 2/11395
AIR 2/12599
AIR 2/13255
DEFE 10/137, 343, 620
DEFE 51/83
WO32/16497/19673

Select Bibliography

CSC 10/4907, 4910, 4917, 4927, 4940 (for Civil Service Exam results)

The files concerning the establishment and administration of the courses in Cambridge are to be found in the Cambridge University Library under SLAV1.

Index

Index

244

Index

Index

Index

Index

Index

Index

Index

Index

Index

Index

THE AMERICAN AGENT

Richard L. Holm

Dick Holm joined the CIA in the 1960s and rose rapidly through the ranks to become Bureau Chief in Paris, eventually receiving the Distinguished Intelligence Medal, the CIA's highest award.

The first posting in his eventful and action-packed career was to Laos, where he served in the CIA's 'Secret War' against the Communists in the lead-up to the Vietnam War. He was then sent to the Congo and suffered near fatal injuries after a plane crash in remote jungle. Healed by local tribesmen, his horrific burns treated with snake oil and tree bark, he subsequently spent two years in a United States hospital undergoing extensive surgery and skin grafts. It was a gruelling time, during which he regained his sight and the use of his hands, then fell in love with and married the widow of a close friend and fellow CIA colleague.

Dick Holm worked in Hong Kong and Brussels as well as Paris, and was instrumental in anti-terrorism operations during Carlos the Jackal's campaign of terror. Intensely patriotic, he has served under thirteen CIA directors and has firm views on policies – past and present, national and international – which, ultimately, determine how, where and why the CIA works.

In this fascinating memoir, Dick Holm not only gives an inside view of life as a CIA officer, but poignantly describes his appalling injuries after the plane crash in the Congo and his amazing fight for survival.

1 903608 10 4

THE SECRET HISTORY
OF PWE 1939–45

David Garnett

Of all Britain's secret intelligence organisations, the least known is the Political Warfare Executive, developed to conduct psychological warfare against the Nazis. Now, for the first time, PWE's history has been declassified by the Cabinet Office and released fifty years after it had been completed and consigned to Whitehall's secret archives.

David Garnett's extraordinary story tells of how such resourceful intellects as Richard Crossman, Sefton Delmer, Leonard Ingrams and Valentine Williams waged a covert campaign against the enemy, using such unorthodox and ingenious methods as black propaganda and 'false flag' radio broadcasts. It also reveals the internal conflicts with the BBC, Special Operations Executive and the Secret Intelligence Service. Once completed, PWE's history was considered too explosive to release to the public, and even the circulation within Whitehall was strictly limited because of the document's sensitivity.

At best a handbook of how to undermine an adversary, and at worst a tale of breathtaking incompetence and political infighting, *The Secret History of PWE* adds a missing dimension to recent disclosures of Britain's covert wartime operations.

1 903608 08 2

AGENTS FOR CHANGE

Harold Shukman

When senior intelligence officers from six different countries meet, among them a former director of the Central Intelligence Agency, the Deputy Chief of the British SIS, the head of the KGB's Illegals Directorate, and their counterparts from Italy, Sweden and France, sparks are bound to fly. Are there ethics in espionage? The discussions will surprise, especially as such frank exchanges hitherto have only taken place in highly classified environments. Now, for the first time, some of the world's most experienced Cold Warriors have emerged from the shadows and gathered together to debate the past and deliberate on the future. For the legendary Vadim Kirpichenko, this was a rare opportunity to meet some of his old adversaries. For Admiral Pierre Lacoste of the French DGSE, General Shlomo Gazit of Israeli military intelligence, and Admiral Fulvio Martini of Italian military intelligence, it was a welcome chance to compare notes with Sir Gerald Warner, the CIA's James Woolsey, and Ambassador Par Kettis of the Swedish signals monitoring service.

In September 1999 St Antony's College, Oxford, hosted a conference on how the intelligence services of the world should respond to the changes in world politics that have flowed from the collapse of the Soviet Union. No less important, the conference discussed the revolution in information technology that is challenging the time-honoured methods used by the intelligence community – the 'second oldest profession'. Eighty academic specialists in intelligence took part. The papers delivered at the St Antony's conference are reproduced here, together with an edited account of the discussion.

0 953615 19 7

THE PRIVATE LIFE OF KIM PHILBY

Rufina Philby

After his dramatic defection to Russia in January 1963 Kim Philby led a turbulent but unreported life in Moscow. He had hoped for a senior KGB post, but instead was kept under constant surveillance and allowed to sink into alcoholic oblivion.

Philby was rescued from his plight by Rufina – introduced to him by the MI6 traitor George Blake. Over eighteen years of marriage she was his companion on many journeys across the Eastern bloc and to Cuba, and helped persuade the KGB that he could still be useful. Inspired by her devotion, Philby began work on the second volume of his autobiography.

Now Rufina, senior KGB officer Mikhail Lyubimov and several others have broken their silence to chart this remarkable chapter in the life of the masterspy. With additional material gathered by intelligence expert Hayden Peake, this revealing memoir is an astonishing account of Philby's Moscow years.

'For devotees . . . this book is a must, for casual readers it is a good starting point'
Alan Judd, *Sunday Telegraph*

'The more of her book you read, the more convinced you become that Rufina's Kim is who Kim Philby really was'
David Hearst, *Observer*

0 95361 516 2

Now you can order superb titles directly from St Ermin's Press